Comments from Readers...

"As a minister, counselor and therapist, I have put in forty years working as a spiritual teacher. I have developed a method and written a book myself that teaches others how to work directly with spirit to monitor the accuracy and validity of information on any subject.... Korra Deaver's book is accurate to infinity and directly from spirit. It is packed with wonderful information about our universe and how it really works. Through this book anyone can learn how to enrich their life through the principles of the universe. It is delightfully factual, filled with exercises and food for thought. It would not be too bold to call this book the disciple's handbook."
—Robert Detzler, Unity minister, Spiritual Response Center

"I congratulate (the author) on a well thought out, well-written manuscript. (She) has obviously made a tremendous contribution to the psychic sciences in terms of research, time, effort, and (her) gift of words."
—P. Y.

"I was impressed with the clarity of the writing and the quality of the contents, as well as the practicality and accessibility of the techniques included."
—S. M.

"Whew! What a manuscript! I thoroughly enjoyed it and personally benefited greatly from the reading. A lot of things I had never understood before were made clear and gave me a lot of new insights to the field of parapsychology. The writing style is clear and non-pretentious. Furthermore, (the author's) personality comes through in a marvelous way so that the reader feels like he has made a personal friend just by reading the work."
—T. McK.

"...There is a lot of good wisdom in this book!"
—A. T. S.

Comments from Readers . . .

"It will help the individual find his own answers,
give the basics of psychic development, but also provide safe and
sane methods of making conscious contact with the Guiding Voice
of the Inner Self—one's own personal Soul. Because Korra Deaver is
addressing the higher self in each of us, I feel in the safe
hands of one who "knows."

"I am impressed with the author's integrated, deep and
knowledgeable presentation of the path of psychic development and
spiritual growth. She demonstrates over and over the personal
benefits of controlling one's life through attention to the inner self.
She writes with authority and sincerity and yet with
humility also. She is deeply committed to helping others walk
the path of self-knowledge, a path that, clearly, she has
walked for quite some time.

"She writes articulately in a straightforward, clear, and imaginative
manner. *Psychic Power and Soul Consciousness* presents an integrated
approach that ties in psychic development with Western occult and
spiritual traditions. A broad range of related topics are covered in
depth with especially good chapters on dreams, sex, karma, the
chakras and color.

"The main part of each chapter is followed by a series of fun-to-do
psychic development exercises which demonstrate the points
covered in the chapter, as well as a page or two of specific
meditation instruction. The chapters build on each other from the
basic to the more esoteric. The book is well suited for instructing the
individual reader as well as classroom use in group experimentation.

"Dr. Deaver's understanding of psychic and spiritual development is
deep and her presentation is well executed. Grounded in the
traditional teachings of metaphysics, this book is an updated,
modernized guide to psychic development."
—An anonymous reviewer

PSYCHIC POWER
AND SOUL CONSCIOUSNESS

PSYCHIC POWER
AND
SOUL CONSCIOUSNESS

The Metaphysics of Personal Growth

---

by Korra Deaver, Ph.D.

≈

Library of Congress Cataloging-in-Publication Data

Deaver, Korra
    Psychic power and soul consciousness / by Korra Deaver. — 1st ed.
        p. cm.
    Includes bibliographical references.
    ISBN 0-89793-077-0 : $14.95
    1. Extrasensory perception. 2. Self-actualization (Psychology)—
    Miscellanea. 3. Spiritual healing. I. Title.
    BF1321.D43   1991
    131—dc20   91–9587
                                                                    CIP

Book design by Qalagraphia
Cover design and illustration by Howard Goldstein
Text illustrations by Daniel Nyiri
Copy editing by Jackie Melvin
Production manager: Paul Frindt
Publisher: Kiran S. Rana
Set in 10 on 13 point Palatino with titles in Avant-Garde
    by 847 Communications, Claremont, CA
Printed by Patterson Printing, Benton Harbor MI
Manufactured in the United States of America

9 8 7 6 5 4 3 2   First edition
Reprinted 1994

Acknowledgments

(These acknowledgements are an extension of the copyright page)

The author is grateful for permission to reprint or adapt selections from the following works (additional information is given under the "Footnotes" on page 364):
Think and Grow Rich by Napoleon Hill, New York: E. P. Dutton, Inc., ©1979, used by permission of the publisher; "God's Heaven" from *Believe It or Not!* by Robert Ripley, New York: Simon & Schuster, ©1929, used by permission of Ripley's Believe It or Not!, a division of Jim Pattison Industries; "New Age Teachings" Issue 133, February 1979, used by permission from Illiana (see Note 3); *Awakening of Consciousness: An Interpretation of Its Process* by Carl Hulsmann, London, U.K.: Momenta Publishing, ©1982, used by permission of the publisher; *The Kundalini Experience: Psychosis or Transcendence?* by Lee Sannella, M.D., Lower Lake, CA: Integral Publishing, ©1987, used by permission of the publisher; *Spiritual Centers in Man* by Manly P. Hall, ©1978 Philosophical Research Society, used by permission; *Mark I ESP Training Manual* and *Mark I ESP Advanced Training* by Bevy Jaegers, Sappington, MO: Aries Productions, ©1972 and 1973, used by permission of the author (see Note 8); *Handbook of Psi Discoveries* by Sheila Ostrander & Lynn Schroeder, New York: Berkeley Publishing, ©1974, used by permission of the authors (see Note 10); *Hidden Secrets Revealed by the I Am That I Am* by Ann Herbstreith, 1984, published by the author, used by permission; *Biorhythms: A Personal Science* by Bernard Gittleson, ©1975, New York: Arco Publishing, used by permission of Simon & Schuster, Inc.; *The Cosmic Doctrine* by Dion Fortune, York Beach, ME: Samuel Weiser, ©1976 by The Society of Inner Light, used by permission; *The Power of Psychic Awareness* by Kingdon Brown, West Nyack, NY: Parker Publishing, ©1969, used by permission of Simon & Schuster, Inc.; *Motivation and Personality* by Abraham H. Maslow, New York: Harper & Row, Publishers, ©1954 by Harper & Row, © 1970 by Abraham H. Maslow, used by permission of the publisher; *The Extra-Sensitive Pendulum* by Bevy Jaegers, Sappington, MO: Aries Productions, ©1972, used by permission of the author; "Point-of-Power Technique" used by permission of Dr. Russ Michael; "Your Divine Self" reproduced from the poster published by The Summit Lighthouse, ©1977 by The Summit Lighthouse, all rights reserved, reproduced by permission (see Note 25); *The Human Aura* by Bevy Jaegers, Sappington, MO: Aries Productions,©1971, used by permission of the author; *Secrets of the Aura* by Bevy Jaegers, Sappington, MO: Aries Productions, ©1974, used by permission of the author; *The Dream Game* by Anne Faraday, ©1974 by AFAR Publishers, A.G., used by permssion of Harper & Row, Publishers, Inc.; *The Science of Life* by Anthony J. Fisichella, St. Paul, MN: Llewellyn Publications, ©1985, used by permission of the publisher; *Mysticism* by Evelyn Underhill, published 1961 in the United States by E. P. Dutton, used by permission of E. P. Dutton, a division of New American Library.

This book is dedicated to:

the memory of my Mother, whose nurturing built my early inner well-being and confidence in Self;

the memory of my Father, whose fiercely independent spirit set an example to be followed when I broached the frontiers of the mind;

Bill, without whose dedicated persistence I might never have found the time to write this book; and

my students, who taught me much more than I taught them.

Important Note

The material in this book is an accurate description and review of techniques used or developed by the author to enhance extended sense perception. Any of the exercises described herein should be done with care and caution, and under the overall direction of a teacher or guide.

In Appreciation

My very special thanks to:

My daughter and son-in-law, Kacey and Ron Miller, who gave me sanctuary in their home for one year during a time of great trial, where I labored with the construction of this book.

Bill Moore, co-worker and co-founder of both the parent organization, the Institute of Psychic Science, and its offspring, the Parapsychology Education Center, who taped the lectures and patiently worked the recorder while I transcribed them into the first rough draft, and who steadfastly encouraged me through my own self-doubts.

Maria Gibson, not only for her Virgoan ability to find and correct punctuation and grammatical errors, but also for her reasoning ability which pointed out undetected flaws in some of my conclusions.

All the people at the Parapsychology Education Center who worked to make the school succeed. Without their love and continuing influence, there would have been no students, hence no teacher; and a special benediction to those who came to study and stayed to teach, who helped to shape the school into what it became.

All those who loved me and boosted my self-esteem; and even those who didn't love me and fought against the work, for their opposition strengthened my backbone and taught me how to turn negative energy into positive force.

And all those who came and went through my life in the last fifty years, for each them have contributed a part of themselves to this book.

Table of Contents

List of Illustrations

How To Use This Book

≈

This textbook is especially designed to guide you through a carefully planned and effective development of the capacities already to be found within you. It is the result of more than twenty-five years of personal study and research, fifteen spent in the classrooms and at the lecterns of metaphysical centers coast to coast. It was written to take you, the independent student, beyond mere "psychism" into deeper levels of your own Being, and to set your feet on the return path of expanding consciousness through an organized and orderly program of spiritual and psychological development.

One of the problems encountered in classroom instruction in metaphysical development is the absence of good textbooks. Many, many books are finding their way into print for the neophyte who desires to grow in spiritual understanding, but who is not yet ready for the deeply *occult* works of Bailey, Blavatsky, Hall, and others. However, these books have their problems.

Before we go further, I'd like to clarify the meaning of the word "occult." In today's idiom it is beginning to take on connotations of black magic, witchcraft, and Satanism, but that is an erroneous and one-sided interpretation. Simply, it means secret, hidden, referring to deeply soul-oriented principles. This occult is "secret" because it deals with activities of the inner mind which no one else can watch, hear, or participate in. These activities are therefore "secret" to everyone but the participant.

In searching for books for the beginner in my classrooms, I have found that most are written from the viewpoint of the individual author's interpretation of spiritual law, or by gurus who uphold one form of development over another, and who sometimes are even in disagreement with each other over points of interpretation. Most authors require commitment to either a strictly scientific or a strictly mystical point of view. The few who do try to bring a balance between science and religion usually concern themselves with only one phase of life's struggles, such as: (1) how to achieve material, social, and/or business success; (2) meditation and its reflection in the inner and outer life; or (3) positive thinking with the Will as the focal point. Others espouse magical rituals of some sort to bend the elements to their command.

No book that I have found to date has developed a comprehensive, overall program of practical personal *and spiritual* development, blended with such scientific breakthroughs as have been made that can lead the practitioner to rightly use the only tool given us for personal guidance in *all* matters, both spiritual and mundane—*the "I AM" Consciousness*. In this instruction, we'll call this Consciousness the *Soul Self*, but down through the ages it has been characterized as the God of all religions, believed to be the Inner Voice which spoke only to the devout and the saintly. I believe this Soul Consciousness is inherent in all of us, but is either dormant or unrecognized in most people.

This book is a synthesis of more than twenty-five years of personal study and research, of working with a growing personal understanding of Universal Laws—what they are, how they work, and how they may be applied to the average life for enrichment, spiritual unfoldment, and mastery. The work began as a class series of ESP research and instruction at the Institute of Psychic Science, founded in 1971 in Little Rock, Arkansas. The name of the school was changed to Parapsychology Education Center in 1978, and it will be referred to under that name. An economic recession closed the center in 1984.

An independent, nonprofit organization, the Center was dedicated to education and research into the latent powers and unexplored potentials of the inner Being of each person. Unaffiliated with any one doctrine or school of thought, it was free to explore wherever conscience or Consciousness led, which brought about a synthesis of many lines of thought and a comprehensive overview that could be applied to every area of life.

The chapters of this book are reproductions of nine lectures and workshops to a class of beginners. Many students joined the group out of curiosity, but still I felt a responsibility—and an urgency—to prepare them for the deeper mysteries as rapidly as I could. The first four weeks are designed to expedite this transition period. They deal with mundane affairs and the use of the intellect, will, emotions, and imagination to create your own changes in life.

The fifth week lists thirteen of the known laws of the "Lesser Mysteries," with a brief discussion intended to spur the individual's own thinking processes into action. The philosophy behind these laws contains simple formulas for living life as you want to live it, achieving, in a sane and practical fashion, that which you most desire. It offers the ability to increase the effectiveness of communication and interaction between one human and another and, in that most intimate of communications, between you and the *Soul Self* within. It offers an opportunity to become Self-oriented, rather than Guru-oriented; to find a personal path through the growing labyrinth of metaphysical dogmas.

The last four chapters deal with developing the higher chakras and becoming more aware of the spiritual and mental aspects of your Being, which speeds up development into full spiritual and psychological Self-Realization.

≈   ≈   ≈

Here are a few pointers for using this book, an activity which will wonderfully change your life. You may do this alone or with a group of like-minded friends. By faithfully practising the eight points listed below you will put your feet on the path to healthy spiritual and personal growth.

1. Set aside two hours on one day of the week—for example, Monday morning or Tuesday evening—to read the lesson. Do this as faithfully as if you had to attend class at a public school where you knew a teacher was waiting for you. Do it no matter what else is happening in your life. Self-discipline and faithfulness will pay great dividends, not only in knowledge learned, but also in your everyday affairs, and especially in developing spiritual knowledge about yourself.

2. Keep a Spiritual Journal (see Week 2 for more information on how to do this successfully). On the day you've chosen, read the text material in *Psychic Power and Soul Consciousness* for that week. In your Spiritual Journal, write a brief outline or summary of the high points.

3. For the rest of the week, practice the exercises given, alone or with family or friends. Others can benefit from stretching their psychic faculties through the exercises, and many of them make excellent party games. The exact amount of time given to each exercise is not important. You will feel an excitement, a thrill, when the inner self is touched, and will find yourself drawn to certain exercises more than others. The delight you experience with these special exercises will keep you doing them over and over.

   Each exercise is a "gate-opener" to the inner Self. You will probably not be able to or even want to do all of the exercises, but try as many of them as you can. The thought and action required will help to awaken inner sense percep-tors of which you may have been unaware, and soon you will automatically begin to apply them to daily life situations.

4. Write down in your Journal the results you get from doing the exercises. Remember, these are not tests of your ability. You are not being graded on "positive" or "negative" results, or whether you are better or worse than someone else, so be honest with yourself in writing down your scores. Soon, you will begin to understand how your brain works, how you personally receive information, and how you react to ordi-nary circumstances in your life.

5. Once a day, if possible, or at least three times during the week, find a quiet time to do the meditation exercise for that week. Record in your Spiritual Journal the times you did the meditation and any special effects you experienced.

6. During the week, as you apply the principles given in the lesson material to your everyday living, notice any changes in your interpersonal affairs and in your own attitudes to-ward life. Report these in a brief paragraph in your Spiritual Journal.

7. Write down in your Journal any questions you have about the material covered. *Expect* them to be answered in interesting and creative ways. The information in *Psychic Power and Soul Consciousness* is directed at helping you find your own answers for any question or situation. It gives the basics of psychic development, but also provides a safe and sure foundation for making conscious contact with the guiding voice of the Soul Self.

8. Your progress will depend upon your attitude and how well you apply yourself. Just as irregular attendance at school would lower your grade, irregular application of the material and the exercises given in this book will lower the amount and quality of knowledge received and retained by you. Therefore, I urge you to keep your study days inviolate against intrusions from other activities in your life. If you faithfully follow the exercises that first prepare and then open your psychic centers, you will never be the same again. Any new experience changes the human personality to some degree, and the experiences within this book are designed to enlarge the scope of consciousness and bring into the range of your awareness those abilities and inner perceptions that are a Spark of Divinity, that vital but largely unknown part of our heritage.

≈   ≈   ≈

Many books present simplistic approaches to mystical development, but the student soon finds that spiritual growth is more than merely using "positive thought," learning to cope with a world of one's own making, or even reducing mental and physical tensions through meditation, although all of these play a part.

The effects of an undisciplined life cannot be erased simply by convincing oneself that the problem doesn't exist. The power of the old must be understood for what it is before it can be overcome. The old life must be supplanted daily—moment to moment—by continually expanding the realization and application of better action. The evolutionary process of development given in this book is one of continuous expansion in psychic and spiritual awareness—the greatest secret of a victorious and fulfilled life.

Once the mind is opened to the new, inspiring idea that there is a way in which one can, through one's own efforts, bring one's life activities under control, it will not—cannot—turn back to the old limited mode. It is as impossible for an unfolding Soul to fit into the old, once familiar, life-focus as it is for a twelve-year-old to return to the crib. There is not room enough for the Soul to fit back into the old patterns, once it has grasped its new dimensions. The Soul has grown, as the mystical Laws of the universe decree we all shall grow, to a broader vision of the plan for human evolvement.

The control of psychic phenomena, which is the conscious bringing forth into physical manifestation of such things as prophecy, clairvoyance, spiritual healings, astral travel, and similar marvels, was once thought to belong only to witches, wizards, and occult magicians. Today's spiritual pioneers recognize these activities as a natural outgrowth of inner evolutionary development. The old age of superstition and fear of psychic phenomena is disappearing along with other horse-and-buggy philosophies. The spirit of inquiry is more alive than at any other time in the recorded history of humanity.

As you learn to control and purposefully use your newfound powers, you will gain a firmer command over every aspect of your personal life. You will no longer be a chip on the stream of Consciousness, a victim of Fate, pushed to and fro by emotional storms of your own or other people's making, by circumstances, situations, or events. Instead, you will master your own destiny. You will learn how to consciously create opportunities to change life infinitely for the better, by making conscious contact with your own Inner Voice for moment-to-moment guidance.

When the experiments are finished, you may be able to speak telepathically with a friend who is miles away, be warned of dangers before they occur, or predict the future. You may realize, perhaps for the first time, that your dreams are not idle figments of a chaotic subconscious intent upon amusing itself, but valid avenues of communication with inner sources of guidance, insight, and information that often contain important data concerning the past, present, and future.

You will soon learn that hunches, though you may previously have ignored them, often contain valuable knowledge that can be used to advantage, and that your own ability to use extraordinary perceptions is limited only by your comprehension of them, or the lack of it. You may not develop all of the psychic abilities mentioned in the text, but you *will* discover the existence of dynamic new energies within. In one way or another, your personal psychic "talent" will make itself known.

This game of life is a "do-it-yourself" affair. True spiritual and psychological health and growth come only when one stands in the Light of one's own Inner Wisdom, guided and compelled by one's own Soul and the *personal plan for one's own life.*

Men and women everywhere are deeply troubled spiritually—or troubled deeply by Spirit—and seek gurus, spirit guides, or various types of mind research. They are following both the Left-Hand Path and the Right-Hand Path in an urgent universal questioning: Who are we? Where did we come from, and where are we going? Which way should we go? How do I find the right path to the future, or the right-for-me guidance for the NOW situation?

"Without a vision, the people perish . . . " (Proverbs 29:18). Our nation has been accused of being a technological giant but a spiritual midget. The inevitable result is a lack of vision among the people. From under this burden, the Soul struggles for recognition; in people from all walks of life, there is an increasing orientation towards inner spiritual and psychological probing and a desire for higher values and self-mastery.

When there rises within us this desperate urgency that will not let us Be, a feeling that "it is later than you think," then we set out upon what I call the "Path of No Return." It is when the individual has embarked upon this path—which is in reality the path of upward spiritual movement, of expanding consciousness of Self—that one finds one's way into metaphysical inquiry, alone, or in classes or groups of some sort.

One's religious affiliation is not important; neither is one's occupation or social background. The personal divinity of the Soul state of Consciousness transcends the illusion of religious and social differences, while at the same time living peacefully with them. When the principles or Laws which govern that Divine Spirit in all of us are understood, one can with self-confidence and assurance direct one's own life toward reaching the highest and best of human potentials.

I recognize that some people cannot cope with the problems they have created in life without expert therapeutic help, and that certain personality schisms may make self-probing a useless or even dangerous activity. For these people I strongly advise professional psychological attention rather than a "do-it-yourself" course. However, millions of intelligent and otherwise normal people caught in the materialistic conditioning of our society will find the path of Self-illumination presented in this book a welcome enlightenment in a dreary world, for it points the way to *Self*-mastery.

Let me clarify this point. This is not another book about developing passive "psychism." It does not encourage the individual to rely on spirit guides and teachers, Ouija boards, or any form of control by other forces, external or internal. While these "psychic experiences" are real enough, they usually do not lead to the type of *spiritual* evolution that we long for, for they are seldom under the control of the individual. Usually developed through a relaxed, receptive state of mind similar to a light trance or state of auto-hypnosis, they also leave one open to whatever entities, energies, or intelligences that may be around. Both the Will and the conscious mind are held somewhat in abeyance, leaving the person vulnerable to many forces, some of them very undesirable. If practised long enough and often enough, this approach has been known to cause the practitioner to begin to act quite irrationally.

In the course presented here the student is taken along the mystical path step-by-step, with the mind *fully alert* and capable of being directed by the Will. The student's individuality and uniqueness in the Cosmic scheme is stressed, and the program places responsibility for the control and development of that uniqueness with the individual, rather than with guides, spirits, or gurus. This way brings certain mastery of events and personal control over emotional reactions to life situations. It is a systematic process, dynamically planned to develop a co-partnership with the Soul Self, the only *true* source of spiritual knowledge and psychic awareness.

A Note About Group Work

I fervently hope that you will find this book so inspiring, uplifting, as well as *practical*, that you will want to start your own classes, using this textbook, or will simply invite some friends to your home to share progress together.

The size of the group is not important, although most groups tend to be small. Smaller groups become more intimate and relaxed, and conversation flows easily between student and teacher. Larger groups of forty-five to fifty are unwieldy if one desires personal contact with each individual, but can be effective if the students break up into partnerships, doing the exercises together and allowing time at the end of each session for sharing exciting breakthroughs with the rest of the group.

A strong leader or monitor is usually required to keep the group on track. When sharing personal experiences or revelations, individuals tend to digress easily if there is no monitor to bring them back to the issues at hand. If this happens too frequently, or if one person monopolizes the conversation, the group will tend to get restless and break up through loss of interest.

≈   ≈   ≈

Good luck on your progress. If you are regular in your application of the principles taught, by the end of nine weeks you will be a different person, with new values and a healthier, happier, more joyous way of approaching life.

A Word for the Christian-Oriented Reader

The oldest of three children, I was raised by a Christian mother and an atheist father. One of my first memories is of my mother reading the Bible to me and my two brothers when we were just able to stand by her knee while she read, but we were never allowed to mention God or any religious scripture or doctrine when our father was in the house. Strangely enough, the older brother and I grew up to be ordained ministers: my brother deeply enmeshed in traditional Christian theology, myself a New Age minister.

My father, raised in the Canadian wilds in the early 1900s, had only the opportunity for a grade-school education, but he had an inquiring mind and never ceased being aware of humankind's potential to explore the new, the untried, the unknown. He continually marveled at the plethora of new inventions that sprang into being during the first half of this century. He believed that all things should have a practical, down-to-earth application, and although he professed not to believe in a God—that didn't seem practical to him—his skill in telling tales of his own adventures in haunted houses and his sometimes bizarre experiences as a trapper alone with the elements in the north woods often left me with gooseflesh and a strange longing to experience for myself some of the extraordinary things that shared God's world with me.

My father concluded that religious principles could not be made practical, but I saw that science and religion existed side by side in the world and therefore they must, in some way not yet discovered, be compatible. For instance, "God said, Let there be light, and there was light" (Genesis 1:3). Science believes the universe began with a Big Bang, or a large explosion of tremendous energy. Can one fathom an explosion of energy as anything but an enormous burst of light? On the other hand, sound cannot exist without something solid to echo against, but the Bible doesn't say anything about sound, does it? Therefore, the Big Bang and God's creation of Light must both have been soundless.

As a child I found myself often knowing, without knowing how I knew, when company was coming to our farm home. My aunt explained to me very kindly and carefully that I shouldn't allow this sort of knowledge to be in my mind, because it was "the devil's work," so I trained myself not to know that I "knew." Still, she and others often whispered about another aunt, who was frequently stricken with epileptic seizures, that she might be "possessed" by some spirit. They didn't think it strange or ungodly that such thoughts should be in *their* heads.

I accepted wholeheartedly the theology of my church, raised my children in the church, and tried with all of my Being to live up to the moral and ethical codes prescribed by my religious beliefs. I continued my Bible study as a young adult and found myself being looked upon as a mother advisor at a very young age. However, I kept running into a strange dichotomy, an often blatant disparity between the ways that the church told me I must act and think and the plain and obvious fact that life's experiences simply did not and could not fit that pattern laid out for me.

What made humans act as they did, often not even in their own best interests? If we were born in "sin" and could only be purged of sin by accepting the vicarious atonement of the shed blood of Jesus, then what happened to babies who died before they had a chance to become old enough to take that stand for Jesus? What about the mute, the retarded? How could a loving God (if God was loving) condemn to everlasting Hell the heathen of the "dark" continents who never had a chance to make that choice simply because they never heard of Jesus? And if, as some ministers said, they were given special grace and not condemned because they were "ignorant," then why should there be such urgency to provide missionaries with enlightenment, and so provide the means for their condemnation because they were no longer ignorant? What about the millions of people who lived before Jesus came? Even in my early teens, those questions and others like them brought anguish to my heart, and the answers given by ministers in those early years only widened the gap in my understanding. Strangely, they never seemed to notice that their interpretations of some Bible statements were often at variance with their interpretations of other Bible truths.

My devotion to God and the Christian life was complete, but how could I "be in the world, and not of it?" I had no desire to be a hermit, and life's experiences often left me with alternatives that had no acceptable solution in church theology. My first experience with the inner guidance came in my young adulthood while working through some personal sexual experiences that left me horrified by the limited choices allowed me by my church. If one's very nature was sexual, then it must have been given by God, and how could that be wrong? And why? It was only my inner guidance that finally gave me information enough to come to terms with my sexuality and to live at peace with myself and my fellow man—in the male sense.

From there I experimented with trying to fit the theories of evolution into the very limited Biblical story of creation. "And the evening and the morning were the first day" (Genesis 1:5). The evening (or night) was mentioned first, because it came before the explosion of light called Day, which could have been the birth of the universe. The rest of the Biblical story of creation was accomplished in seven "days," but how could this have happened in seven twenty-four hour periods? Our twenty-four hour days relate only to the earth going around the sun, but God's Days and Nights were created before the earth and sun were created, therefore time as we know it could not apply.

We frequently speak of "day" as referring to an era or an age, such as "the day of Stone Age men," or "the day of the Viking explorers." The sequence of events chronicled as the beginning of time may equally well have been eras or ages known as days (the "day of the building of the firmament called Heaven"; the "day of the building of the land and the seas called Earth"; etc.) and the present scientific theories of evolution would fit nicely into the same sequence, in which case, science and religion would understand the same events, although using different words.

Nor could I understand how most of God's children were poor and sick and living in wretched conditions, while the "devil's adherents" lived off the riches of the land. I believed that God's plan for the world was good, therefore the world had to be good, but accepting the world as it was and reconciling that with religious theology was an insurmountable task. Nevertheless, that was the only path my inner Self would allow me to pursue. Nothing less was acceptable to my mental framework, and I lived my life under those rules until I was about thirty-five years old. At that time, I attended a Unity church worship service. I was ready for the new interpretations of old Truths that the minister gave her congregation that day, and it seemed as though my Soul could not get enough of this new kind of thinking.

A few years later, as I experimented with self-hypnosis to improve my college grades, I met my first ghost, or disembodied entity. That story is described in Week 6, but what isn't told is the horror felt by my family, who told me in no uncertain terms that I was in contact with the Devil and that I'd better leave *that* alone. Only—how could I? It was *me* the Devil had hold of—if they were right—and how did one fight something unseen? If it *was* the Devil, I felt I needed to learn as much about it as possible, so that if it came to a fight I'd have a better knowledge of how to proceed. Rather naïve thinking, perhaps, but that was the reasoning I used to find and join the educational activities of the

Spiritualist church—in a state of inner quaking, I might add, but determined, nonetheless, to be master of my own Fate.

From that point, as I studied many metaphysical and occult philosophies, my mind opened up at a dizzying rate. I found that many of the old Bible truths appeared illogical only because people were used to interpreting them in a certain way and never bothered to question these interpretations. From my new perspective I discovered new insights, new illuminations, new verbalizations that made old ideas and ideals much more practical, down-to-earth, and usable to make mundane living more joyous and free. I also discovered that some Bible stories (especially Old Testament stories) could *only* be understood from the metaphysical point of view.

The Lord's Prayer, for example, is not just something to be learned by rote, but an encoded set of instructions, a step-by-step process for meditation. This can't possibly be recognized until one has learned how to meditate, a method of communicating with God which is no longer taught in most of our churches. (See Appendix C regarding the Lord's Prayer.)

When I founded the Parapsychology Education Center in Little Rock, in an area with over 200 churches, I was kept constantly and sometimes painfully aware that I was pioneering a spiritual field that was frowned upon, even considered dangerous, by the established church. I credit that the Center thrived and grew for more than thirteen years to the fact that I never lost sight of the need to reassure the community that we were not anti-Christian simply because we espoused and explored traditionally forbidden areas of mental and spiritual research. This is one reason that my teaching and writing is liberally sprinkled with Biblical references, so that Christian-oriented students can look it up for themselves, as many do.

Being the product of both the Christian and atheist outlooks on life, I understand keenly the fear the orthodox Christian feels in dealing with the forbidden, but I also know the joy of the new illuminations that must come when one does explore the unknown. I felt obligated to those I loved to reassure them that what I was learning was only an expanded concept of what they had been trained to believe, and that it was not the "devil's work" but could actually be found in admonitions to the prophets and in the mystical words and works of Jesus. Because you, the reader, may also be forced, as I was, to defend your position to those around you who wish you well but fear for your spiritual safety, I've included many of these illuminations in this book.

Another charge leveled against metaphysicians is that we are humanists, placing our own Will-to-Good above the "Will of God." Metaphysicians do not believe that God's Will for us is ever anything but good, so we try to align our thought in the direction of the highest good for all. The spiritual instruction in this book begins with our attention focused on the external manifestations of our world (Weeks 1–4). We must first become aware of what we have created before we can exert mastery over it to effect changes (or to achieve dominion, as Genesis states it). From the fifth lecture on, however, I deal with one's relationship to one's own Soul, the Pathway through Christhood exhorted by Jesus.

I also discovered that through all the world's living religions runs a common golden thread, sometimes called the "Ageless Wisdom," the "Secret Doctrine," or "Metaphysics." This ancient teaching is at the core of all true religions. Its origins are lost in antiquity, but it has manifested in various forms down through the centuries. Under Krishna, it was known as Hinduism. Abraham's version was called Judaism, its philosophy later reformed by Moses. Under Buddha, its name was Buddhism; under Mohammed it was known as Islam; and Christ's followers dubbed it Christianity. Each of these, however, embrace this same timeless teaching which provides the foundation for character building, and the integration of mental, emotional, and spiritual faculties. From this blossoms the integration of Soul and Personality and, finally, the ultimate goal of all true religions, Unity or Oneness with God.

Thinking people find most church dogmas unfulfilling because much of this core information has been lost or carefully pruned out in the past. Jesus *was* the Way-Shower. He exemplified all the mastery occultists have ever wished for, from healing the sick to mastery over death, his own and others. His clairvoyance (the knowledge of things at a distance) and his ability to prophesy are well known to all. He said to his disciples, "All these things which I do, you can do, also, and even greater things can you do" (John 14:12), which many Christians believe was only meant as private instruction to his disciples. But do we not call ourselves disciples, too? A disciple follows the instructions and admonitions of the Teacher.

When Jesus said, "Follow me," He did not mean to do so blindly. Adoration and worship are pallid and passive. His own life was dynamic, filled with active use of His understanding of God's Laws. His ascension was the triumphant conclusion to a lifetime of Oneness with God.

"Follow me!" No words ever rang out more clearly through the centuries, but lifting one's Soul from the inertia of passive and unquestioning faith is truly a monumental task. It is this unquestioning aspect that has led humankind into our present spiritual blind alley. From the burning of the library at Alexandria to the list of forbidden books given to Catholics by the Pope during the Dark Ages, humankind has been trained not to question priestly or political edict. Fortunately, that is beginning to change in both the secular and religious world, although the burning and the banning of books still goes on. Even the right to teach evolution in the schools has recently been challenged in court.

Listed below are a few of the books by people who *did* question the common interpretation. Among them are also works that were expunged from the major faiths because of political pressures at the time they were assembled. These add knowledge that was at one time forbidden to Christians, and the loss of this information has colored our present understanding. You are invited to explore them yourself.

Addington, Jack E. *Hidden Mystery of the Bible.* New York: Dodd, Mead Publishing, 1969

Barnstone, Willis, editor. *The Other Bible.* San Francisco: Harper & Row, 1984

Cerminara, Gina. *Insights for the Age of Aquarius.* Wheaton, IL: Theosophical Publishing House, 1976

Fillmore, Charles. *Metaphysical Bible Dictionary.* Unity Village, MO: Unity School, 1931

Hall, Manly. P. *Old Testament Wisdom.* Los Angeles: Philosophical Research Society, 1987

Heline, Corinne. *The Mystery of the Christos.* Santa Monica, CA: New Age Bible, 1961

——. *New Age Bible Interpretations.* 7 vols. Santa Monica, CA: New Age Bible, 1935–1985

Hodson, Geoffrey. *Hidden Wisdom in the Holy Bible.* 4 vols. Wheaton, IL: Theosophical Publishing House, 1967

Lamsa, George, translator. *The Holy Bible From Ancient Eastern Texts.* New York: Harper & Row, 1986.

Levi. *The Aquarian Gospel of Jesus the Christ.* Marina del Rey, CA: DeVorss & Co., 1972

McCaffery, Ellen. *An Astrological Key to Biblical Symbolism,* York Beach, ME: Samuel Weiser, 1975

Platt, Rutherford H., editor. *The Forgotten Books of Eden.* New York: Bell Publishing Co, 1981

Pryse, James. *The Apocalypse Unsealed.* N. Hollywood, CA: Symbols and Signs Publishing, 1977

Pryse, James. *Reincarnation in the New Testament.* Las Vegas, NV: Health Research (Health Research does reproductions of out- of-print books)

Puech, Henri-Charles. *The Gospel According to Thomas.* New York: Harper & Row, 1948

The Lost Books of the Bible. New York: Bell Publishing Co., 1979

≈   ≈   ≈

In conclusion, within each weekly lesson are special biblical references relating to the subject matter for that week. May the study of these principles open as many new doors for you as they did for me and, more important, may they open up even greater vistas of illumination.

For the best years of your life, those which lie ahead, may your feet tread the Path of upward spiritual ascension.

A Note About the Exercises and References in This Book

In the early 1970s when I started teaching ESP classes there were very few metaphysical centers in the United States, and the few that did exist were widely scattered. Metaphysical and occult books had just begun to be popular, and most of the useful ones had been printed about the turn of the century. Teachers and lecturers traveled from center to center giving seminars and lectures, and in this seeding process information, exercises, and experiments to develop ESP were eagerly shared and incorporated by local teachers into their own classes.

In preparing this book for publication, I have tried diligently to trace the authorship of the many ESP development exercises that I found useful in my classes, but some of them have been in circulation so long I cannot locate their sources. Similarly, complete or current references for older metaphysical books, now out of print or circulated only by small, independent publishers, were not always available.

I would be most happy for any information leading to people and publishers who should be recognized, and will include those credits in future editions.

Scripture references are from the King James Version of the Bible.

WEEK 1

≈

Beginning Your ESP Breakthrough

Extended Sense Perception

ESP! What does it mean to you? The usual definition is "Extra-sensory Perception." I contend that there is nothing "extra" about it! Everyone has some capacity to experience ESP. Not everyone uses it consciously and with awareness, and that is what makes the difference. Let's give ESP a new definition: *Extended Sense Perception*. It is this definition I want you to keep in mind whenever this word is used, because this will be the awareness that you will develop in order to make ESP practical in your everyday life.

Science, with its technology and instruments of measurement, has proven that there are sounds beyond the range of the human ear, both lower and higher in octave, and that there are colors that are beyond the range of the human eye at our present state of evolution. Radio and television are obvious examples of this.

Extended Sense Perception creates within our awareness a knowledge that we *can* see a little farther, hear a little more distinctly, and feel finer vibratory rates around us in this portion of the universe that makes up our world.

Psychic Terminology

There are a number of terms used by psychics and metaphysical students which you may or may not be familiar with, which demonstrate the logic of using this definition of ESP. The most common of these is *clairvoyance*, which, literally translated, means "clear seeing." If you have a vision, if you see or sense something coming toward you in time (*precognition*), or if you can visualize anything, you are actually extending your sense of sight. Others around you need not necessarily share in this extended sensing.

Clairaudience means "clear hearing." It is the ability to hear sounds or "voices" that others cannot hear. Have you ever heard your name called, but when you looked around no one was there? Sometimes you can even identify the voice that "called." If you had checked it out, you probably would have discovered that that person was thinking or speaking about you at the time, and your name was in his or her mind. *You actually heard the thought!*

Can you hear a dog-whistle? A dog-whistle has tones beyond the range of an ordinary human ear, to which a dog responds because its sense of hearing has a higher range than a human's. With practice in intent listening, you can learn to hear a dog-whistle, though faintly. It is this practice in using our senses in a different way than we are accustomed to that gives us the ability to put these capacities under conscious control.

The extension of touching, tasting, and smelling is called *clairsentience*, which means "clear sensing." It has sometimes been demonstrated by people smelling flowers, smoke, or other odors at times when these could not naturally be accounted for, or by them "feeling" another person or presence nearby when no one else was around.

Psychic comes from the word *Psyche*, which means Soul or mind. The word *psychology* also comes from this root. *Parapsychology* literally means that which is above, or not normally known, about the psyche, or the study of that subject. Using psychology as a basis, or a beginning, the next step is to learn how we relate on a Cosmic level to other human beings, instead of just on the physical, mental, or emotional level, which is where psychology stops.

Our *extended senses* will naturally be put to work when we learn more about what our psyche, or Soul is, and what we can do to achieve harmony between body, mind, and Soul; and between ourselves and the bodies, minds, and Souls of other people.

People are sometimes confused about the difference between *psychic* and *mystic*. I like this definition: A psychic is "a person attuned to the thoughts and feelings of other persons or entities," and a mystic is "one who is attuned to the Soul Self and God." Our Soul's purpose is to do both, and practice in extending the senses will put us naturally in communication on the Soul level with both other people and God. The results, which filter down to the conscious mind, make us a "psychic."

Telepathy, the Only Sixth Sense?

Since clairvoyance, clairaudience, and clairsentience seem to be just *extensions* of our other five senses, telepathy may be the only real "sixth sense." Telepathy is a nonverbal communication from mind to mind, including: (1) from person to person; (2) from Higher Mind to lower mind; (3) from God to person; or (4) from discarnate entity to incarnate entity.

This newly acquired sense is developing in humanity so naturally and rapidly as the Aquarian Age approaches that you probably already have had experiences in telepathy. Once you become *aware* of the fact that it is a natural sense—as natural as seeing, hearing, touching, tasting, and smelling—you'll find it developing more rapidly and accurately. Your very awareness of this capacity will create an expectant, listening attitude in your mind which actually creates that which you are expecting. All of your ESP powers will grow more rapidly under an attitude of expectancy.

The First Occult Law

The first occult law to understand is: *Energy follows thought*. This is the most basic and rudimentary of all the occult laws and provides the foundation for all the "Mystery Laws" which govern the universe.

This energy comprises everything in the universe, and it can be measured in the form of vibrations. All things are composed of energy in various forms and manifestations, including our bodies, our brains, even our Spirits. Through our minds we have access to this energy, to use in any way our thought dictates, but conscious control of ESP faculties necessitates a full understanding of this energy.

The important thing to know about this energy is that it is unqualified when it comes into us. It is unmolded and undirected. It has no awareness of its own; it is totally neutral in concept, design, and desire. It simply comes in and we use it according to the pattern of our thought. We use this energy to mold our world: the environment around us, our experiences, and the material things which make up our surroundings. *All* of these things are created from the kind of thinking that we do, which changes this energy into various vibratory forms manifesting in our material world.

This energy, although very powerful, is completely neutral, neither good nor bad. For instance, electricity coming into a light switch is a totally neutral power. It can be used to kill or cure, and the electricity doesn't care which. The thought which pushes the button can use this energy in any way it desires.

Water coming down a mountainside can create very, very powerful energies. You can use it to drink or to drown in and that won't change the properties of the water. The energies of water are themselves completely neutral.

So it is with the energy which we draw into ourselves through that marvelous organ, the brain. The energy is neutral within itself. It is neither good nor bad, but you can use it for good or bad according to your motivation, your understanding of life, or your desires.

I hope that, as we go along, you will learn what constitutes good and bad use of this energy. *Energy follows thought,* and the controlling or disciplining of our thought is an important part of esoteric development. Whenever you send this energy out as thought, it circles and comes right back to you. Thoughts are things that create. Whatever we think, we send forth, or create. Love or suspicion, good will or ill will, negative or positive imagination, purposeful thought or daydreams—all of these things color our life experiences, and their reflections will be exactly as we have created them with our thought-molds.

Did you know that whatever happens to you, constructive or destructive, you deserve? Energy follows thought, and it is *your* thought which creates *your* world. No longer can you blame your mother, father, wife, husband, educators, government, or neighbors for the events, people, and circumstances which surround you. It takes a spiritually mature person to recognize and accept this fact, but once you do, you take a strong stand toward bringing all of your psychic and spiritual faculties under control. You become more spiritual, more aware, more psychic, more fully human, compassionate and loving, and more intimately responsible for personal growth, just by accepting this esoteric truth: *Energy follows thought!* You then begin to monitor your thought, so that the out-picturing is more harmonious and gracious, just as you would want your world to be.

The Law of Karma

The use of this energy results in what is known as the Law of Karma. *Karma* is a Sanskrit word meaning "action." Karma itself is a neutral concept: it is simply the idea of cause and effect. *Whatever* we send out comes back to us as our Karma, both good and bad, harmonious and inharmonious.

In our esoteric language today we've come to think of the Law of Karma as the Law of *Wrong* Action. Whenever something disastrous or inharmonious happens to us, we're inclined to say, "Well, I guess that's my karma," because we know we've sent out a thought or an action that brought back to us energies that caused some kind of inharmony or discomfort. We are then inclined to remember the negative side of karma and think of it as being the energy, or return, of something negative.

In the weeks to come we'll learn how to apply thought energy in a way that is practical and useful, so that only *good* flows out from us, creating only the possibility of good coming back to us, in whatever form our hearts can desire and our thoughts can create. Napoleon Hill says in his book *Think and Grow Rich*: "Whatever man can conceive and believe, he can ACHIEVE."[1]

We will start with some basic exercises in emotional conditioning, because emotional conditioning is part of beginning to use the ESP faculties that we have. Do you get all torn up about life? When events and people hit you in your emotional "solar plexus," is your reaction reasoned or unreasoned? Do you go off into a corner and wish you were dead? Or do you get so angry at times that murderous rage fills your heart? In each case you are using your thought energies negatively and, what is more important, you are being *used by* your emotions instead of *using them* to right what may be a wrong situation.

If your emotions are out of control, there is no way you are going to be able to use your ordinary senses effectively, much less your extended senses. It is the turmoil of our emotions that keeps us locked within our five senses, locked in with only a limited use of them.

Energy follows thought, and thoughts create emotional response. *Thought plus emotion equals manifestation.* This is the total Law of Creation (creating).

How many times have you used such phrases as: "I'm sick and tired of that! I can't see his point of view! I won't swallow that!" Examine these sentences and others like them that you use habitually in your everyday conversations. Emotional words like these have creative power, bringing their exact image into manifestation. Used in this way they effect limitations in our circumstances, our bodies, and our relationships with people, and they impose restrictions upon the manifestation of good in our lives. Careless thought-forms use our precious energy in negative ways, bringing back into our lives exact replicas of what we send out.

The first step in emotional conditioning is to learn to keep the emotional level under control and not react in an undisciplined manner. Instead of being angry, we can try to understand the person who is causing us distress. Realize that, *whatever* he is doing, he is operating at the top level of his consciousness at any given moment. How can we fault a person for not being more than he is capable of being?

Our religious concepts have led us to believe that human beings are fundamentally bad. I believe that we are fundamentally good. That doesn't mean we can't make mistakes in judgment. All of us are learning. All of us are growing spiritually. But, if we want to send out only that which we wish to have return to us, then it behooves us to be more charitable to others, and at least give them the benefit of the doubt.

Instead of reacting violently and emotionally to a situation, try to look at it objectively. Turn it around in your mind, then consciously send out a thought-form that embodies the emotion you would like to have come back into your life if the situation were reversed. Most times you will find that the person whom you were angry with did not intend to create such an upheaval in you. It was your own misunderstanding which created the emotion. Perhaps you felt threatened, or rejected, or used, and this created a storm of resentment, anger, or defiance.

Taking a good look at our emotional hang-ups is not an easy first step to psychic power, but it is a necessary one. Without emotional objectivity we cannot use psychic power constructively, much less under control, and therefore, psychologically and emotionally, it becomes an impossible achievement.

The Universal Law still applies: If we send out criticism, condemnation, anger, and sarcasm, all of these will come back into our lives in ways that create more opportunities to trigger these same emotions. So we get ever more of the same upheavals, until we learn, finally, to cope with the situation on its own emotional terms. Psychic power comes naturally and without strain in direct proportion to our ability to relate in an objective manner to others, without condemnation and without criticism.

Taking responsibility for our thoughts and emotions does not mean we should feel guilty for past mistakes in judgment or misused emotional energy. Guilt itself is a misuse of energy. Recognizing that you have made a mistake only means you are wiser than you were when the mistake was made and you will not make the same mistake again. How can you not rejoice in that?

The past can always be forgiven. We start where we are, using all we presently understand about spiritual energy. Adding what we learn each day from the teachers around us, we grow spiritually. Our mistakes are our teachers, as are those people who give us opportunities to learn.

The Spiral of Spiritual Achievement

Life evolves along a spiral of spiritual achievement. Some of us are nearer the top of this spiral, some of us are nearer the bottom, but most of us are somewhere in between. This should entail no value judgments. It doesn't mean some of us are better than others. At most it might mean some of us have learned a little bit more about coping with our emotional reactions to life. But where one is deficient in judgment, another has already learned that lesson and is working on something else. He or she may have already passed the test that is causing us distress, or may be coping with a lesson which we have already learned. It is not wise to judge others, lest we find ourselves in their shoes someday.

However, if you happen to be nearer the top of this spiral, and someone else with whom you are having difficulties seems to be nearer the bottom—relatively speaking, of course—there's going to be a problem of communication, isn't there? How can someone else possibly understand the type of problems with which you cope? And how can you understand his or her issues?

If you find yourself having emotional difficulties like this with people, perhaps you should slow your tempo a bit, or send out a thought of Love and Light to lift them up closer to your level. This is the more constructive approach to the problem. Then, instead of reacting out of control, allow them the right to *Be where they* are, fellow souls traveling along the same road you are traversing, sometimes stumbling in the dark too.

This feeling of compassion and empathy can do wonders to erase emotional stumbling blocks. If you can't in your heart forgive others for being human, as you are human, then let them *Be.* Put them in the hands of a Power higher than yourself and withdraw your emotional reaction entirely. Turn your energies away and refuse to allow any of this emotion to maintain headroom in your thoughts. Gradually, you may even find it possible to send out a little bit of Love, that Divine Agent that soothes all wounds and mends torn relationships.

Realize that there isn't anything fundamentally bad about any other person. They may simply be on a different level of spiritual aspiration than you are at this time. They are here working out a spiritual purpose, just as you are, even if your purposes do not seem to harmonize. The kindest thing you can do is to wish them well. Send Love, send energies of Light, and if you don't understand them, let it *Be,* but don't push them down farther. Don't add energies of condemnation to further complicate the situation, or create karmic backlash.

A person's sole purpose in your life may be to teach you to overcome your emotional reaction to the particular problem represented. When this is accomplished and you have achieved your new emotional stability, you may find that the person will not walk beside you very much longer, but will go and prosper elsewhere, and both of you will be blessed.

Are You a Body With a Soul?

Do you believe that you are a body with a Soul? Do you believe you have a Soul? Well, if the answer in either case is yes, you are wrong! You are not a body with a Soul—you are a Soul with a body!

The body has no volition of its own. It doesn't think, reason, or have ESP powers. It is only the vehicle which carries the Soul (psyche) around. Even that vast computer of a brain cannot use its thinking, reasoning, or deductive powers unless the Soul activates it! The body is created by the Soul for its own purposes and is composed of atoms of the material in which it manifests to give the Soul an access to that particular plane of existence. The body belongs to the Soul and is designed to accomplish the work of the Soul.

Occult Law teaches that the cells of the body have a fundamental consciousness within themselves, sufficient to nourish, sustain, and multiply themselves, but this elementary consciousness is completely dominated by the desires of the Soul which brought them together in the first place.

Scientific inquiry has found no reason why the body should ever die! It was meant originally to rejuvenate itself; it shouldn't even age. Scientists are studying the causes and effects of aging, and soon physicians will understand how our thoughts, emotions, and attitudes, acting upon the elementary consciousness of the cells, create most of the aging and illness aspects of our physical being.

You are a Soul with a body, and that Soul has a mission, a purpose. The purpose is to master or achieve dominion over the physical plane in which we live. In Genesis 1:28 we read, "And God blessed them, and said unto them, Be fruitful, and multiply, and replenish the earth and subdue it; and have dominion over the fish of the seas, and the fowl of the air, and over every living thing that moveth upon the earth . . . ."

Some highly evolved spiritual Beings, whom many people claim to contact, are called Masters because they have earned

Mastery. They have mastered the physical plane sometime in the past, as we are attempting to do now.

Jesus, the greatest Master of Occult Laws the world has ever known, said, "These works that I do, shall you do, also, and even greater works than I do shall you do...." But if we have not mastered this plane and the Universal Laws which govern it, we will return to experience the various lessons of life again and again until we have finally expressed complete dominion.

This is known as the *Law of Reincarnation*, which gives us the only possibility of climbing up the spiral of spiritual evolution, a theory taught by the majority of the world's living religions. Research shows that this theory was also taught by early Christians until purged from the texts which form our present Bible.

At the end of the fourth century, Christianity emerged as the official religion of the empire ruled by Constantine Augustus the Great. Many bitter political battles were fought over which doctrines should be accepted, and opposing sects arose, promoting Eastern or Western Rites in the Christian Church. Finally, in 553 A.D., over the protests of Pope Vigilus who refused to attend, the Byzantine Emperor Justinian, at the behest of Empress Theodora, called together the Fifth Ecumenical Council in Constantinople. There 165 bishops passed a resolution (on record in the minutes of the Council), that they would "no longer teach the doctrine of rebirth." It seems the freedom which such a doctrine gives the individual was not conducive to the absolute power desired by both church and state.

The following excerpt, originally printed in Robert Ripley's first book, *Believe It or Not!*[2] in 1929, is probably the most lucid argument ever presented for the rational plausibility of reincarnation:

> The hope is in all of us that when we die we will go to some celestial place where we rejoin the other members of our family who have passed onward. But take my advice: Make a reservation! Heaven is becoming very crowded and it is extremely doubtful whether you can get in.
>
> Let's say that you go to heaven and meet your mother and father, not to mention the rest of your kith and kin. When you meet your mother and father, they will be with their

mother and father, for they would have the same desire to be with their parents that you had to be with yours. And their parents, in turn, would be with their parents, and so on back through the countless generations of mankind.

Now if we take 25 years as a generation, we find that there have been 77 generations since the time of Christ. And if we count only your parents, their parents, and so on backward for that length of time, we find that you will meet 302,231,454,903,657,293,676,543 relatives—all different.

If that many people were on earth today, they would have to be stacked up on each other's heads! Allowing them two square feet to stand on, this would make a stack of one solid mass of folks 113,256 miles high over the earth's surface!

According to the vital statistics of all civilized countries, there are 68 deaths a minute, 97,920 daily, 35,740,800 annually, and these statistics apply only to the war-free years! According to Biblical attestments, both the pious and wicked all come to judgement.

If 68 deaths occur per minute, that means that each soul precipitated into the Divine Courtroom to be judged for all the temptations and involvements of the flesh gets less than one second of God's time to have his life's history reviewed and his eternal Fate meted out to him.

What sort of an equitable review of his life's history would that be, that had to be compressed into less than one second? And if God had to pass sentence to eternal bliss or eternal woe on 35,740,800 souls per year, when would He have time to do anything else? And this rate of new souls arriving outside the celestial portals to be judged would be year after year without surcease, we must remember.

Even taking into consideration both the metaphysical view of no time and no space, and the scientific capabilities of modern computers to process a million bits of information in a nanosecond, Ripley's thinking still presents a staggering concept! And add to that worlds without end for which God is, presumably, also simultaneously responsible.

Wouldn't it solve the problem of overcrowding the heavenly spheres if souls kept coming back into new embodiments? Let us speculate that a fixed number of souls, say about fifteen or twenty billion or so, are assigned to the earth by whatever powers make these decisions. While half of them, more or less, are on the earth, the other half are in the spiritual realms, interchanging residences as the reincarnational wheels turn. Then, consider the possibility that humans judge themselves daily, that the immutable Law of Cause and Effect, set in motion by one's own actions, creates harmonious or inharmonious circumstances through which we learn our sometimes painful lessons in our spiritual journey toward that model of perfection exemplified by Christ, the Way-Shower. Thus the process is self-perpetuating, and we learn as we live to take personal responsibility for spiritual advancement.

The First Step to Mastery

With the Soul taking on and casting off bodies, then, the first step to mastery of the Laws of this plane of existence is to recognize the point of contact the Soul has with the body it now wears. To do this, turn your thoughts inward, and say the words, "I AM." Be aware of where the "I" within you seems to be the strongest. Is it in the solar plexus, a spot somewhere under the heart? Or lower? Is it in the heart region? The throat? The brain? Outside the brain? Once located, you can shift your conscious awareness of yourself-as-a-Soul to this point of contact and know that this point is the Pilot of the bodily vehicle.

This conscious point-of-awareness is the "I AM" part of you. It is the Soul—the eternal, undying, immortal essence of your individual Spirit. This is the part that lives even after the body has gone through "death," and it is also the part that separates from the physical body during out-of-body experiences.

(I want to make it clear that although the expression "I AM" is used by several well-known organizations, my intent is not to merely adapt their expression to my use. Actually, a more accurate representation would be the simple pronoun "I" to indicate the Inner Essence that guides and directs each of us. The phrase "I AM," however, lends itself more easily to both the spoken and written word in trying to communicate what is a difficult concept to transfer from one consciousness to another. Also, using the pronoun "I" in the exercises proposed in this book would have the decided disadvantage of a suggestion to remain within the personality structure, whereas the concept of "I AM" immediately elevates one's awareness and aspirations to a higher level of consciousness.)

When we become aware of ourselves as separate from the body and can consciously function from this point, we gain the capacity to master both the emotional and the intellectual nature, and to master other Laws of Manifestation on this plane. This is the point-of-consciousness from which we draw our life and energy. It is from this point of awareness that we will take the first step in mastering the Mystery Laws of the universe. We will start by reviewing some scientifically known data about the human brain.

The Difference Between Brain and Mind

There is a difference between the brain and the mind. The brain is an organ, a highly sophisticated, specialized organ, like the heart and the liver, and it has a specific function in the body. It is *not* the mind. It can be likened to a switchboard between the mind and the body. Through the brain, the mind makes contact with the body and sends out directions for the operation of bodily activity. From our new point of awareness in the Soul, now, let's look at how the brain functions, and what we can do to control its functioning.

If you had an electroencephalogram (EEG) done, you would see wavy lines forming on a strip of paper. These represent the activity of the brain, which constantly sends out vibratory wavelengths that can be scientifically measured. Psychic researchers have discovered that different things happen when the brain is operating at different levels of brain-wave activity. When the brain is moving very quickly, you are in a certain state of consciousness, and when the brain slows down, other things happen. You might look at the "Brain Activity Levels" chart (Figure 1) to follow what I am saying.

The Conscious Level

When the brain is operating between 32 and 14 cycles per second as shown on an encephalogram, it is in what researchers have

Figure 1. Brain Activity Levels

EEG Brain Rhythm Cycles per second	Level		Category	Description
PHYSICAL WORLD Sight Touch, Smell Time, Sound Space, Taste				
32	**BETA LEVEL** Outer conscious levels, involvement with external world manifestations		ACTION	Physical activity, laughter, tears, emotional reactions, mental processes such as reasoning and logic. All external world relationships.
THE KINGDOM WITHIN The Inner or Spiritual World (or World of the Spirit)				
14	**ALPHA LEVEL** Inner conscious levels "Go into thine closet..."	HYPNOSIS, MEDITATION, AND SLEEP STATES	THOUGHT	Clairaudience, clairsentience, clairvoyance, dreams, hypnosis, meditation, memory recall, precognition, telepathy, visions, deep study or introspective states, and light sleep states.
	ESP, psychic phenomena, mental projection, psychic or spiritual healing, telekinesis, trance, etc. No time/space concepts.			
7	**THETA LEVEL** Subconscious levels Loss of sense awareness			Memory storehouse; subliminal activity; parasympathetic nervous system activities such as circulation, digestion, respiration, etc.; source of psychosomatic illnesses and compulsive behavior.
4	**DELTA LEVEL**			
	UNKNOWN Present area of intense research			
	DELTA LEVEL Coma, unconsciousness, out-of-body experiences, teleportation			Very deep sleep. Some trance mediums operate from this level.

termed *Beta* consciousness. This is full waking awareness. It is in this consciousness that we perform our everyday living, thinking, Being. One can feel, touch, think, taste, see, hear—all of one's senses are fully alert in this state.

Our active, physical life takes place when the brain is on this operational level. The Beta level is the seat of the conscious, reasoning mind; many, many people never get beyond this aspect of their Being.

But we are much more than just our conscious minds, and by becoming aware of other levels, we can develop control of our ESP faculties.

The Creative Level

If, on the encephalograph, the brain is sending out wavelengths between 14 and 7 cycles per second, it is in what researchers have termed the *Alpha* level of consciousness. Much research is now being done with the Alpha level, and much is being learned about it.

You can buy expensive biofeedback machines that will emit a signal which indicates when you have reached the Alpha awareness level. The easiest way, however, is to just shut your eyes, take a deep breath, become quiet and relaxed, and you will immediately be deep enough into Alpha on a practical basis to use the creative forces found there.

With practice you can go deeper and deeper with full conscious awareness, even into the lower Theta level, and you may want to do this later. For now, we can accomplish whatever we want in simple psychic awareness at the Alpha level.

This region or functioning of the brain has two major levels, although researchers have isolated as many as thirty-two sublevels. One of the major levels is reached in meditation, or reverie, with full conscious awareness, and the other is in the dream state. When you have been deep in unaware sleep and come up to the dream level, the brain registers at Alpha, especially when the dream is one remembered after awakening.

All ESP and other-dimensional phenomena take place when the brain is functioning in the Alpa zone. Here there are no time/space concepts. Psychic or spiritual healing can take place when the brain slows down to this rate. Memory recall, visions, hypnosis, clairvoyance, clairaudience, clairsentience, telepathy, precognition—all of these take place when the brain slows down to the Alpha state or below.

The Alpha level is the creative region of the brain. All thought-forms that go into this realm will manifest in the outer physical world of material and personal relationships. Understanding this phase of brain activity is vital to learning how to be in control of the body and the surrounding environment. In Workshop #1 you will find some basic meditation techniques which also give you some "dos and don'ts" for activating the Alpha level of consciousness. Using the proper techniques of meditation, we can create anything in our lives that we desire.

The Subconscious Level

The third level of brain activity, called the *Theta* level, is when the brain is registering between 7 and 4 cycles per second. This is the storehouse of the brain, known as the *subconscious* area, and it lies below the normal waking awareness of the *conscious* mind. Everything you've ever been, done, said, heard, or seen— in other words, all the accumulated data of the five senses—is stored in the memory cells of this area. There are even prenatal memories stored here, which can often be stirred to life under hypnosis or triggered by emotional impact.

In an untrained brain there is little or no conscious contact with this portion, but it can be reached by hypnosis. This portion of the brain never sleeps; it records whatever is going on around it day and night. It is inactive only if brain activity drops below 4 cycles per second. Some people who have been under anesthesia have later, under hypnosis, been able to recall things that went on in the operating room—what the occupants of the room said and did while they were under, with the conscious mind blanked out.

The parasympathetic nervous system works from the Theta level. All the automatic workings of the body, such as heartbeat, digestion, breathing, the circulatory system, and involuntary muscle operations are functions of the subconscious or Theta level. Every habit you have, every learned action, such as driving a car, typing, reading, writing—things you do without thinking about how to do them—is programmed into this area of the brain.

Compulsive actions which stem from traumatic events in our early years are buried deep in this region. The source of these compulsive actions cannot be reached or discovered by the Beta consciousness in the untrained brain, but the conditioned reflexes and emotional reactions burned into the Theta level can continually cause distress, because they keep coming up to be reflected out in subconscious action, like bubbles rising from beneath the water. Finding the buried source of present emotional problems is a valid reason for learning to reach the subconscious levels of the brain.

This area of the brain works like a gigantic computer. Whenever you ask yourself a question, the first thing the brain does is go scurrying through all the information that is stored in its memory. If the answer is not found there, then the information must come from the levels of the *mind*, rather than the brain. This is where controlled and knowledgeable psychic awareness comes in.

It is my desire in these lessons to help you forge a bridge between the Beta, Alpha, and Theta levels so that you will have a greater use of the brain, and so that its functioning may be enhanced through conscious control. This will make you more aware of yourself as a living Being.

The Unconscious Level

If your brain is operating between 4 and 0 cycles on the encephalograph, you are in the *Delta* level. This happens during total unconsciousness, in coma, in very deep sleep, and in some recorded cases of trance mediumship.

The evidence indicates that the brain itself nearly stops operating. The only things still functioning in the body are the heart and breathing. Digestion stops. The respiratory and circulatory systems are activated just enough to sustain life.

Unlike the Theta level, one does not ordinarily bring back conscious awareness of brain functioning from this point. Recent experiments seem to indicate, however, that under certain controlled conditions awareness of *mind* activity may be brought through when the brain is in Delta, such as through trance mediumship.

Zero cycles activity of the brain would indicate total stoppage of all life, yet some instances of clinical death have been recorded in which the memory of awareness of physical world activities (as well as certain mystical experiences) was retained when the person returned to normal life processes.

This would lead one to speculate that astral travel or out-of-the-body experiences may begin somewhere near this level of brain activity, and that the astral body returns to the physical body when the brain activity speeds up and draws the Soul, or astral essence, back to it.

"Go Into Thine Closet and Shut the Door"

Jesus said, "I go to the Father within. . ." (John 14:12). That Creative Source within all of us can be used to "do even greater works" that He told us we could do.

The slower the brain operates, the less awareness you have of outside noises or other influences, and you can go so deep into meditation or reverie that you are even unaware of the body, the room you are in, or anyone in the room.

As you go into the lower brain levels, you first lose the sense of sight, then the senses of smell and taste, then the sense of touch, and last of all the sense of hearing. As you go deeper and deeper into the inner world, the brain functions more and more slowly. This is truly going into the "closet and shutting the door" to all the things of the senses.

I think this is what Jesus meant when He talked about going into the inner closet and leaving behind the "world of the senses." Our present distorted interpretation is that He was talking about the sensual, meaning indulging in sexuality. It has more to do with being *sensuous*—related to the senses—and the input of data from the objective world through the senses. In deep meditation, this awareness of the input of data from the senses disappears, although awareness of *oneself* as a conscious, living Being remains, and even becomes enhanced.

This loss of sense awareness is necessary to relax tensions and open the doorway to communication with the Soul Self that functions outside the brain. Here you become aware of another dimension of Being, the transcendent world of the "I AM."

The Superconscious Level

There is a portion of the mind which cannot be recorded on instruments, and this we call the *Superconscious*. This is essentially an electromagnetic energy field, rather than a brain level. It is the area that is the "sense perceptor" for the Soul, forming the link between Soul activity and the physical/mental/emotional activity of the body and personality.

Everything within the brain is learned. We had to learn to eat, to walk, to talk; we even had to learn to breathe. We had to learn everything that we do, because when we were born all that we had in our brains were a few prenatal memories impressed there. Everything that we now have in our brains came after we were born.

This is not true of the superconscious, the true Mind. This mind can make contact with people and places and situations in time and space that the brain has no contact with. Information brought in through this contact then becomes a part of the subconscious levels of the brain and can be brought up again at will for future use. We store information from accumulated data from the outside senses, and we also store data from the superconscious that comes into our awareness through inspiration, intuition, dreams, and other psychic impressions.

This part of the mind has access to all the information we will ever need, but only the trained student can tap this information at will. We're trapped, most of us, within the brain, within the sense world, within our awareness of the senses as we now know them. If we can learn to think outside the brain and become aware of this extension of our senses, we can transcend time and space. Then we can know what is going to happen in the future, what has happened in the past (even when we weren't there), and we can know many other things without empirical data, as we presently understand it.

Universal Mind

The superconscious has access to information not normally available to us. Let us call this information source the *Universal Mind*. To call it God is to release from our conditioned memory storehouse stereotyped images of what we have called God. If we are to become psychically aware and build a conscious bridge from the brain to the mind, it is helpful to first expand our concept of God.

One philosopher said, "God made man in His image, and then man returned the compliment!" Too often we think of the "Will of God," for instance, as delighting in our suffering, because in some mysterious way this is supposed to chasten us, make us obedient, and help us, somehow, to become more pure. It is incongruous that we should suppose God to be a God of Love, and blithely talk about "free will," and still believe that God is someone up in the Invisible, who is pulling strings to make us walk and talk as though we were puppets. This is truly "in man's image," not God's.

Let us look at ourselves as the Divine Image of God, as God imaged or imagined us. Whatever your present religious concepts may be, or even if you think you are an atheist, I'm sure you will agree that every religion claims, "God is all." Let us ponder this statement. If God is *all*—there can't be anything else! All is *All*—everything!

All right, if God is *all*, then what did He use to create the universe, the earth, the rocks, the trees, you and me? Logic deduces that He must have used His own Substance. If there had been other substance from which He built His Creation, then He couldn't have been *All*—there would have been something else besides Him. It follows then, if God is Divine, His Creation, created from Himself, must also have that Divineness within it. Jesus said, "Did I not say, Ye are gods?" (John 10:34)

The Apostle Paul spoke of "one God and Father of all, who is above all, and through all, and *in* you all" (Ephesians 4:6). We need not go far to seek God. Paul adds in Acts 17:27–28, "for in Him we live and move and have our Being," so that we understand that God is not only the Father of all things, having created all things out of His own Substance, but He also ensouls or permeates all that He has created—living, experiencing, evolving in a pantheon of eternal exploration. God is Life itself, the living vital breath as well as the essence of every cell, of every atom that has ever been created, as well as all forces and forms visible and invisible. He is the intelligence and power that moves the Cosmos as well as our own puny affairs. We are part of God and God is all of us. The Essence of God may be spoken of as Energy, Force, Power, and Substance. It is all these and more, going beyond form, definition, and description. God functions in you, through you, and *as* you. Everything is endowed with infinite potential for expansion and expression.

If we took a bucket of water out of the ocean, would that bucket of water be any less ocean water because it is no longer within the ocean? It still has the same properties, the same potential. It couldn't contain a whale but it has the *potential* of holding a whale, if it were put back into the ocean.

Expanding our awareness of God's potential within us is a major step in crossing the bridge from the prison of our brain and body to the freedom of the superconscious, which knows it is part of the vast substance of God and has access to all the information stored in the *Universal Mind*—our new expanded concept of God.

The movement within the Universal Mind (or God) is in a constant state of creating, forever expressing in new, different, eternally expanding ways. God is infinitely creative. He has never created two things the same way. There are no two snowflakes alike, no two fingerprints alike, no two hairs on your head alike. There aren't even two grains of sand on a beach alike. So why should you consider that you should be like your neighbor, or that your neighbor should be like you? Neither of you is better than anyone else. Nor are you worse than anyone else. You are different. Each of you is unique!

It is that uniqueness that we want to become aware of, to enhance, to bring out in all its splendid Glory. You are a unique Creation of God, one of a kind, a unique Being, a totalness of God-expression (or Creation) in your particular way, a way that no other Being on this planet or anywhere else in the universe can duplicate.

Look at your neighbors with this new insight. Think of them as you are now thinking of yourself—unique creations of God. Do you dare to not love this aspect of God expressing and experiencing the Divine in this unique way? Do you dare to not love yourself?

Awareness is the key! Open up your mind. Think in new terms, new concepts. Begin to realize that there are potentials within you that you have never before remotely tapped, or even considered. Potentials so great that you will be astonished at what will come through you.

Uri Geller made headlines a few years back with his ability to bend forks, keys, and other metals by mind power alone. Since then, some of my students have said to me, "My son can bend spoons!" or, "My husband bent a spoon!" Do you know why they never did it before? Because they hadn't tried it! I want to open up such a whole new world of the potentials in you that you will be utterly flabbergasted. Don't be afraid to try something new. Think of yourself as a modern-day explorer. There are frontiers of the mind that have never been touched.

It is said that the greater part of the mind is like an iceberg. Only about one-tenth of an iceberg is visible. Psychologists say we only use about one-tenth of our minds. Your brain can be trained to make conscious contact with the superconscious, and you will have tuned into the extended portions that make up this invisible nine-tenths of your mind. Unless you shut out the outer world, and its clamorous demands on the senses, you cannot hear that inner voice within. It is heard only when you are using the slower, calmer levels of the brain.

If you have ever had psychic experiences—such as precognition, visions, telepathy—you may have discovered they come at a moment when the mind is still, quiet, functioning in slower vibratory rhythms. It stands to reason that if you learn to live like this most of the time, or learn to tune into these levels at will, you will have more awareness, not only of yourself, but of the activities around you. And this is truly a greater extension of your senses.

Workshop #1
Putting the Brain Under Control

≈

Some people have extreme difficulty visualizing. This could be because as children they were scolded or made fun of by their elders and told to stop "imagining things," so the faculty of visualization was turned off or repressed. Some basic practice in visualizing may be necessary to reopen this doorway to creative ability.

The following exercises can be done either as a group or in individual study.

Exercise #1: Visualization Enhancement

Study the pictures on the following pages one at a time (cover the others with a blank paper so that they do not distract you). All are simple pictures, such as might be found in a child's coloring book, but they become progressively more complicated, with more lines and more detail. Look at one picture and absorb as much detail as you possibly can. Then shut your eyes and try to see the same picture in your mind's eye. This is called visualizing.

When you have as much detail as you can remember, open your eyes and compare what you saw in your mind with the picture in front of you. Part of this will be retina retention—the image that remains very briefly on the retina of your eye after you've looked away—and some of it will be simple memory recall. Both will be valuable in reprogramming your mind for creative visualization. The mental pictures may be fuzzy at first, but the fuzziness will soon be replaced by clear, sharp images as you progress and practice.

Figure 2. Visualization Aid

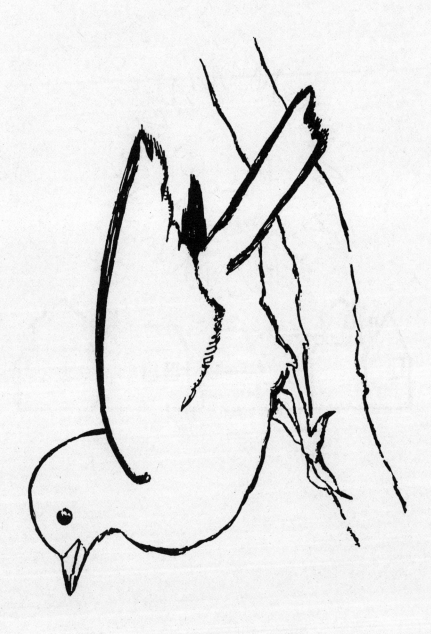

Figure 3. Visualization Aid

Figure 4. Visualization Aid

Figure 5. Visualization Aid

Figure 6. Visualization Aid

Figure 7. Visualization Aid

Research indicates that there may be two types of brain action; there are visualizers and non-visualizers. Some people simply are not "visualizers." If, in spite of practice, you find it impossible to master the art of visualizing, try this: Think of an umbrella. Whatever happens in your brain when you "think" of an umbrella—or a dog, or a mountain, or an alligator—this is your equivalent of "visualizing." This is how *your* brain functions, and you have to learn how to work with it. When other people say, "I see," meaning that they "see" with their mind's eye, you may substitute the words, "I think," in your own mind, if that feels more right for you, and you will achieve the same thing.

People who cannot visualize often express their ability simply by saying, "I know." Their intellectual activity exemplifies the same psychic awareness. Some people may "feel" or "sense" information, instead of "seeing" it. Visualization is the most common form of receiving information on the psychic level but it is by no means the only way. You *are* psychic! The *method* of receiving information is irrelevant—you need only determine how you personally receive inner knowledge.

The following exercises will increase your visualizing ability if it is latent, but feel free to "sense" or "feel" or "know" if you cannot visualize. Developing all of the inner senses will increase your psychic ability.

Exercise #2: Creative Visualization

Picture in your mind a table (any size, shape, or color). On the table, place a lovely tall blue vase. From the right side of your visualization field pluck a perfect red rose and place this rose in the blue vase.

Now from the left field of your mind pick a gorgeous, prize-winning yellow rose and place this in the blue vase beside the red rose. Now, directly in front of you, you will see a breathtaking pure white rose. Place this rose in the vase also. For just a minute, hold the entire picture in your mind, and then lean over and *smell* the roses!

Exercise #3: Really Extend Your Senses!

These exercises can add more of the senses to your extended visualizing.

We've built a camp site beside a gently flowing river in a quiet wooded valley. Gather sticks and wood and build a warm, crackling campfire. See the flames leaping against the night, smell the smoke from the burning wood. Feel the warmth of the fire.

Now place a coffeepot on the flames to boil, and smell the coffee aroma. Listen to the quiet evening sounds.

Suddenly a truck roars by on the adjacent roadway. Listen as it fades away and the night becomes quiet again. Listen to the sound of the water murmuring against the river bank.

Somewhere a frog croaks, and you hear the answering cry of a nearby night bird. A soft, refreshing breeze springs up. Reach down and touch the moist, cool earth.

Exercise #4: Add Movement

A. You've built a bird feeder outside your window. See the birds hopping around and chirping to each other. It is time to feed the birds, and you pick up the birdseed box. Hear the birdseed rattle against the box as you shake some onto the platform. Watch the birds feeding. Suddenly one bird bursts into song.
B. Sit down and take a warm, furry puppy onto your lap (in your mind, of course!). Stroke its warm, wiggly body and ruffle its ears. It licks you with a smooth, friendly tongue. Let the puppy go, and hold a soft, cuddly kitten in your lap. What color is the kitten? The kitten curls up and goes to sleep as you stroke its fur. Hear its purr of contentment.

Exercise #5: Add Taste

We've been invited by a good friend to a backyard picnic. Let us sit comfortably in pleasant company and enjoy the good smells from the grill. Is our host using hickory or charcoal? Listen to the hiss of melting fat on the flames.

(If you are a vegetarian, by all means substitute a vegetarian hotdog or hamburger for this one. Likewise you can substitute honey for sugar, or simply eliminate sugar or salt if these are not on your diet and you do not want to visualize these items.)

Check out the picnic table. What kind of wood is it made of? What kind of material is used to cover it? What kind of dishes and cutlery are being used?

Now our host serves a steaming hotdog on a bun. Savor the taste of the meat and the bread. It needs some mustard. Taste the mustard.

Pick up a glass of lemonade near your plate. Taste how sour it is. Put some sugar in your hand. Taste the sugar.

Now you are served a dish of corn. Taste the delicious, separate kernels. It needs some salt. Put some salt in the palm of your hand and taste it with your tongue.

From a plate of hors d'oeuvres, take a pickle and eat it. Taste the sour tartness and feel the crisp crunchiness of the pickle between your teeth.

Exercise #6: Add Emotion

Think of someone you love very much. It may be a child or an adult. Visualize his or her face. Hold your loved one's hand, and feel the shape and warmth of that hand. Now embrace your loved one. Savor the good feeling of love and companionship.

Kiss your loved one goodbye. Still holding this feeling of love and friendliness, project this feeling out to everyone in the room. Feel it come back to you enhanced and multiplied in power by the number of people in the room. (If you are practicing this exercise while alone, send the feeling of love and goodwill out to the world at large. Include all peoples and all nations in your imaging.)

Now store this feeling in your heart and mind, and never again approach any entity, either embodied or discarnate, with any feeling but this feeling of love and happiness that you are now expressing.

Do this exercise frequently to build your feeling of warm human comradeship for all people.

Exercise #7: Find Yourself A Parking Space!

This exercise is a preview of what your mind can do for you. Use it to enhance the pleasure of your driving activities. This simple use of mind energy is very, very effective and has been used by even the most skeptical of beginners with excellent results.

In most large cities the downtown area is heavily congested, and finding a parking space is a motorist's biggest headache. By consciously directing your mind energy, you can *always* park right in front of the building where you want to go! (That is, unless there are "No Parking" signs there!)

The secret lies in visualization. In your mind's eye, "see" or visualize an empty parking space nearest to the door you wish to enter. When you get there, simply drive into the empty parking place that will be waiting! Sometimes a driver will pull out of the space just as you get there, reserving it for you!

This visualization can be done in two ways. You can force or create a picture in your mind of the parking space exactly as you want it, or you can think of the building and simply allow an empty parking place to form in your mind's eye. The first way uses Will and the second uses Expectation. You *know* the parking space is going to be there, so you wait expectantly until the picture forms, telling you where to find it.

Try both ways to see which you are most comfortable with. Both of them work, but for you one uses more energy. Use the easiest and most comfortable way.

BASIC MEDITATION TECHNIQUES

Keeping in mind that the Alpha level is the creative level of the brain, we realize that conscious control and positive use of this level is possible. Here are a few dos and don'ts of meditation.

Under no circumstances should you take your problems, heartbreaks, or negative emotional reactions into this creative level of the mind. Since that which we visualize during this state of Being will always manifest outwardly into our lives, we must be aware that squirrel-cage thinking (the mind's tendency to go around and around a situation unproductively, especially a negative or emotionally charged one) will succeed in reproducing—reprogramming as it were—more of the same action in our lives. We remain in the same situations year after year because we continue to give mind energy to the *problem* rather than to creatively look for a *solution*, thereby regrooving into our lives the very situations we *do not want*.

A visualization of what you *do* want is one secret of using your extended senses to make your life different. You are using creative force on the God-Substance to channel mind energies into a more productive way of living.

Pay attention to the action of your brain when you are thinking. Vibrant, energized activity takes place on the Beta level and is the manifestation of previous thought-forms from the passive level.

Quiet, introspective thoughts are creative thoughts, and reflect your emotional reaction—inner turmoil or inner peace—according to the quality of your present spiritual makeup. Introspective thoughts, whether calm or turbulent, are always found on the creative level, the Alpha level, and serve to bring into focus in your life that which you have visualized or imagined. Mental discipline is a necessary step in learning to consciously control your creative power.

It has been said that prayer is talking to God and meditation is listening to God. Using this very practical definition, we can preface meditation with a brief prayer in our own fashion to the God we know, outlining the situation that troubles us as objectively as we can and asking for help. Then, allowing the mind to become quiet, we *listen* for a new approach, a new understanding, refusing to allow ourselves to think about the situation as it *now exists*, but just being quiet, open, and receptive to whatever idea of proposed positive action comes through.

Another way to use this meditation time is to *visualize* the situation as you *want* it to be, giving it positive emotions of joyous acceptance, loving every moment of the new picture, and gratefully acknowledging the power of this Creative Presence to change the outflow of manifestation in your life. If you can hold this new visualization for one minute (60 seconds) without the picture wavering or fading, it *will* manifest. Interpersonal relationships can be smoothed over, healing in your body can take place, material things can come to you, direction for your life can be given to you, if you use the energy waves of the brain to tune into the Higher Forces of your own Being that are at this moment struggling to make themselves known.

Disciplining the brain may seem to be an insurmountable problem at this point in your progress. Your mind races in its accustomed fashion, visualization becomes fuzzy, attention wanders and you drift into some preconceived morass of negative recollections.

One technique to hold the mind at the desired level is the use of a *mantra*. This is a prescribed sound to which the mind can cling without reflection. The use of a mantra will allow the body to relax from the unremitting tensions of daily life and will prevent negative thoughts from intruding upon your quiet time, allowing healing of both body and mind to take place. Many types of mantras may be used for different purposes. A good all-purpose mantra is an ancient word for God, "OM" (pronounced as in "home"), said aloud on a long, exhaled breath.

Your assignment for this week is to practice this basic meditation method, which will begin your journey into the *Inner You*.

1. Seat yourself in a quiet room free from distractions or interruptions. It's a good idea, if possible, to disconnect the telephone before beginning to meditate, so that a loud ring will not jar you in this very sensitive state.

2. *Keep your spine straight at all times when doing meditative or occult exercises.* Place your feet flat on the floor to align yourself with earth energies. Clothing should be loose, and shoes may be removed. Let your muscles relax. Palms may be upturned, or thumb and forefinger may be placed together in a closed circle.

   You may sit crosslegged if you prefer, spine straight, hands or wrists on knees. In this position, spine, arms, and legs form a triangle, and it is said that triangles have more power.

   (These are "ideal" setups for meditation. Once the practice of meditation becomes familiar, you will find that you can drop into a meditative state at any time, in any place, without ritual, whenever there is a need to tune into a source of information or find the wellspring of inner quietude and strength. The only important thing to remember is to keep your spine straight. Meditation uses energies that flow up and down your back, and it is important that these forces are not impeded.)

3. Focus your attention inward, allowing your mind to become quiet, relaxed. Still all emotional reaction. Deliberately turn your thoughts away from any negative situation in your life. Instead, focus your attention on something pleasant—a quiet, tranquil scene, someone you love, or an occasion you are looking forward to.

4. When your body is as relaxed as you can get it, take a deep breath and exhale with a long "O-O-M-MM," until all the breath is gone. Repeat three times.

5. Now gently allow the silent "OM" to hang in your mind. Do not attempt to make your mind blank of all thoughts. Just let your thoughts *Be*, whatever they are, and observe them with detachment, being neither happy nor sad, nor in any way emotionally involved with them. The "OM" sound will keep them from returning to the negative. If the sound drifts away, gently bring it back. Remain passive and detached. Simply observe.

6. After a few moments, conclude with a prayer of thanksgiving. Since thoughts are creative, being grateful for the good that is now in your life will magnify and increase that good, leaving less room for negative situations.

7. Come out of the meditative state slowly. The mind and body have been functioning at a slower vibratory rate, and the nervous system needs at least one or possibly two minutes to readjust to the more active condition.

8. If you have not been in the habit of meditating, *do not* meditate for longer than 15 or 20 minutes at a time. To do so may create a tendency towards a sense of disassociation or disorientation. When you have been meditating for at least six months, preferably a year, and you find you desire to meditate for longer periods, you may then do so without undesirable side effects.

≈   ≈   ≈

The purpose of the material and exercises in this book is to help you find your *own* path to Self-Realization among the many that are being offered throughout the world today. There is *one* right way for you, and it is my desire to help you find that *one* right way.

The techniques and directions presented here have been tested and found effective for all those drawn to them. However, be alert to modifications that may be right for *you*. Remember, you are *unique*, and I want to help you find and develop your own uniqueness, not become a carbon copy of someone else.

To achieve the full potential of that uniqueness, a discipline of some sort is necessary. The discipline, far from being an onerous task, should be an *active awareness* of your own process of Be-ing, and actively—deliberately—directing that Be-ingness into channels of God-Realization, or Soul Self development. (See Week 6 for more on the meaning of Soul development.)

Many questions have been raised about the process and practice of meditation. Paul, in his message to the Thessalonians (I Thess. 5:17), exhorted them to "pray without ceasing." One New Age channel calls this "Action-Devotion." The following excerpt from "New Age Teachings" is worth quoting. This message from Higher Consciousness comes through the channel, Illiana.[3] (Capitalization, emphasis, and punctuation are taken from "New Age Teachings." The messages are strongly Christian-oriented, with definite spiritual aims and language.)

> The Realm of Light speaks: "To all Beloved Suns of Light, I speak precisely about this Inner Communion: MEDITATION . . . Be aware that diversity in ALL things is part of the Pure Realm of LIGHT and it is never ordained that 'fixed' patterns be the order of things for everyone! Meditation is no exception. There are as many ways to contemplate on God as there are to perform your daily tasks. There is no 'rule' in Cosmic Law which states only *one* method is correct!
>
> "Those who find difficulty in 'silent' contemplation . . . (sometimes) suffer physical and emotional ills when they attempt a silent technique. They may also be taken over by

alien (or outer) forces. This must NEVER be allowed!! Instead of the silent Inner Meditation, let these practice an AC-TIVE MEDITATION.

"By active meditation we mean this: Begin the day by offering prayers and affirmations upon arising. Become God-centered in this way. Perform some physical exercises (such as Hatha Yoga asanas) to bring the body and mind into balance. Then take time to read some inspirational literature which will help in centering your heart and mind on Divine Concepts. The remainder of your activities can then be performed AS ACTS OF DEVOTION. This is . . . a form of meditation . . . known as ACTION-DEVOTION (Karma-Bhakti) MEDITATION . . . . For some of you it is even more practical and aids in 'working out' some needed Karma.

"You who practice Inner Contemplation would receive added blessings by ALSO incorporating ACTION-DEVOTION in your daily activities. We tell you . . . how important it is to devote every moment of time to God-Realization . . . . Many think (this) is impractical—and indeed it would be literally futile if what we suggested was sitting in seclusion, performing no action, just being in SILENCE! But that is NOT what we advocate. The point we emphasize is that EVERY ACT can be an ACT OF SERVICE and DEVOTION, thus keeping the Mind always on God and His Divine Attributes . . . .

"The Divine Parent is flexible and understands the needs of His/Her children. Therefore, there is no 'dogmatic rule' in the Divine Plan. Many methods—many avenues are open to all of you in *every* aspect of Spiritual Growth. Let NO one dogmatize TRUTH and the DIVINE WAY by stating that 'such and such' is the only correct method—or 'this and that' is the only correct interpretation of Divine Law! Let the understanding come from your own Heart Center! Never become enticed or pressured into a 'belief' by another's interpretation—Let YOUR mind sort out Truth for Itself. Let your Spirit be open and flexible. Seek by testing, which method is best for You in achieving God-Centeredness.

"The important thing is to be sincere; loyal to the Knowledge you do have; open to MORE understanding; compassionate in your affairs with others; virtuous in all your activities; always an example of Divine Love; and FREE to enjoy the Gifts of Universal Spirit! Thus you will be a perfectly balanced physico-spirito Being . . . .

"At various times . . . reference is made to 'pure meditation.' It is constantly stressed by the Realm of LIGHT that . . . PURE meditation must be the ultimate goal of all Suns of LIGHT who embark upon the Royal Path . . . .

"Countless systems of meditation are used by as many teachers—and all have their valid place since each method used serves to benefit those drawn to it. The goal of one form may be 'concentration'—the goal of another may be 'knowledge.' The fact is that EACH METHOD is a stepping stone to PURE MEDITATION! . . . . Earth embodied entities become attached in so many ways: attached to physical objects, to people, to ideas, yes, even to the mind! These attachments must be released before one can find freedom and satisfaction in PURE MEDITATION, so these other methods are productive for many, many people. But you must be on guard that you do not BECOME ATTACHED TO A METHOD—TO A MANTRA—OR TO A TEACHER.

"PURE MEDITATION is that state of Mind-Soul awareness wherein you are totally free from any system, any 'tool,' as it were! In PURE MEDITATION your mind releases itself from pre-conceived ideas as it allows Itself to be filled with noble notions of Love, Compassion, and Understanding. It no longer EXPECTS anything—It is simply receptive to the Holy Vibrations as pure Wisdom flows in, like a river flows into the ocean! Such a pure Mind is no longer attached to anything, either physical or spiritual! IT IS FREE . . IT IS LOVING . . I T IS ALL-ENCOMPASSING . . . .

"The great mystics and saints of ages past often described their ecstasies—they experienced a CONSTANT at-one-ment with the Beloved: God. It was not a 'technique' which they observed once or twice each day—it was not a 'practice' which they felt obligated to perform . . . . Those God-Realized Saints were in a CONSTANT STATE OF PURE BLISS even when performing the most mundane task. THIS IS PURE MEDITATION!

"This, then, must be your aim, Suns of Light. Of course,

it is good to begin and end your day in a secluded area where you can 'tune in' and 'tune out,' as it were, and where you can serve others through health meditations and channeling session . . . . BUT between the beginning and end of each day REMAIN IN THAT PURE STATE (of) MEDITATION wherein all activities are noble gifts presented as acts of Devotion to the ONE, the COSMIC-BELOVED, Father-Mother of the Universe. Thus will you obtain BLISS—thus will you . . . ascend in HOLY CONSCIOUSNESS—thus will you experience GOD!!! I . . A M . . T HAT . . I . . A M . ., THE ONE IN ALL."

≈   ≈   ≈

For the beginning student, some type of mental discipline—consistent, persistent inner cognitive reflection—is required in order to make conscious contact with the Higher Self. This type of discipline is achieved only by an inner desire, or spiritual aspiration, which will not allow you peace until your whole Being yields to its demands.

At that stage of aspiration, I advise you to test various methods and use the one that brings results for you. As these sessions proceed, many other types of meditation will be presented for your experimentation and many suggestions given for the uses of meditation. As you become more familiar with the promptings from the Soul Self, you'll recognize when you've "found" the method or technique that fills you with a feeling of contentment and satisfaction. Keep an open mind and heart, and *expect* good results.

WEEK 2

≈

ESP: Extended Sense Perception

Our scientists and academics spend millions of hours and trillions of dollars exploring what we call the "real world." As individuals, we have each dedicated an entire lifetime to the assimilation of the input of data from the sense world, thinking that this is all there is to Life.

As long as our perspective remains at this level, we will continue to make faulty judgments and react in an emotional manner to situations which appear to be not of our making. We will continue to believe that we are victims of Fate, that we have no control over what happens to us.

But now you know there is another perspective, the "I AM" awareness within yourself. From this perspective we recognize that "sense data" can be colored by our emotional conditioning and imperfect perception. The old adage, "Don't believe anything you hear, and only half of what you see," is never truer than when attempting to evaluate the "real" world that we see around us.

Let's take an example. In your home, let's say you have a beautiful large vase. On one side is an engraved figure, a painted picture, or some other special effect. The other side is plain, with no adornment whatever.

In our imagination, let's hold this vase up for a friend to look at. Now, he is on one side of this vase, and we are on the other side. If we asked him to describe the vase from his point of view, it certainly would be different from ours, wouldn't it? He might see the figured side, while we would only see the plain side. We would need to turn the vase around and look at it from all angles before we would know the "real" vase.

It's the same with the "real" world. Everyone perceives it from a personal point of view, and each viewpoint is perfectly valid for the perceiver. Extending our senses will be an attempt to perceive the world from our friend's point of view as well as our own, and in so doing, extend our own perception and understanding of this vast Creation. That understanding will automatically eliminate many of the roadblocks to our spiritual growth.

Now, let's do another mental exercise. Close your eyes, and pretend you are way up in the air looking down at the roof of your house. What do you see? Describe the roof, the backyard, and the surrounding environment from the perspective of being up in the air looking down. Does it look different from this point of view? It does, doesn't it?

Suddenly, you are struck with another thought! You have never been up in the air over your house before, yet somehow in your imagination, you are perfectly aware of what it looks like from that angle!

This is an excellent example of an extension of the input of data from your senses. You have put together in your mind the picture of the roof as you have seen it from many angles at ground level, and have added a recall pattern of looking down on things that have been below you in other situations. The two mental pictures of previously experienced dimensions have fused to present to you an accurate mental image from a heretofore unknown dimension.

Something similar takes place when we "psychically" pick up impressions, flashes, or hunches from data that we feel we could not have known in an empirical way. The more we know about the objective world that appears to be around us, the more we can know about the inner subjective world that appears to be "just our imagination."

And what is imagination, anyway? It is the creative process at work. It flows ceaselessly through us. Its flow cannot be stopped without the application of tremendous effort and purpose. It can be allowed to daydream the hours away, amusing itself with harmless fantasies, or it can be put to work to solve every problem and baffling situation in your life!

How often were you told as a child: "Oh, that's just your imagination! Forget it!" As a result, many of us reached adulthood ignoring the only thing that makes us different from the animals—the ability to use our imagination in constructive and profitable ways!

"The Kingdom of Heaven Is Within You"

Jesus taught, "Seek ye first the Kingdom of God, and His righteousness; and all these things shall be added unto you" (Matt. 6:33). He even told us where to look when he said, "The Kingdom of God is within you." That's a far cry from the doctrine preached so often that Heaven is somewhere up above, and that one cannot hope to reach it until after death—if, indeed, even then.

Let us analyze this human body, with its sense perceptors and its faculty of imagination, from a different viewpoint—the perspective of our new "I AM" awareness. Let us pretend we *are* the "I AM" looking down on this body which is the earthly vehicle that carries us around. The preceding sentence contains Truth, but to achieve the full realization of the Truth, we need to start with the imagination, just as we had to pretend to be above the house looking down on it. Mentally experiencing the following statements in imagination, or pretending, will begin to bring into inner realization insights and understandings that cannot be conveyed by spoken or written words. So in your imagination, now, try to see the body as I will describe it.

The physical body, the emotions, the brain, and the ego-drives are tools that the Soul uses to experience this dimension in which we are incarnated. Objectively, in the same manner that we might examine any other thing not attached to us, let us consider what these tools really are, so that we might use them more effectively.

The physical body is one of seven fields of energy employed by the Soul for the exploration, evaluation, storing, and use of information brought to it by the sensory equipment, the five senses. The other six energy fields are the Etheric Body, the Causal Body, the Astral Body, the Emotional Body, the Mental Body, and the Spiritual Body. (I'll talk about these in more detail in Week 6.)

The physical body is a conglomerate of specialized atoms made up of Earth substances functioning under the supervision of a vital magnetic force which directs the health and harmony of the cells. This magnetic energy is the Etheric Body to which we owe our physical well-being. Within the Etheric Body is a series of centers to which the other bodies are attached. They are called by the Eastern term *Chakras*, and they act as powerful transformers for the great Universal Energy field.

Each chakra represents a different level of consciousness and produces a special kind of energy which we can consciously appropriate for various purposes. All centers must be understood for the perfect functioning of the complete Spiritual Being and the mastery of both the physical body and physical plane of existence.

It is interesting to note that the colors of the chakras, ranging from red to violet, have the same ascending values arranged in the same order as the rainbow. This is referred to as the "Rainbow Bridge" in occult terminology, each chakra being the lower terminal of a connection between the dense physical body and a finer body of higher vibratory rate. It is also part of a much larger concept of "bridging between Heaven and Earth." The reader is invited to search for more information, both in personal meditation and through other reading.

The Crown Center

This is the highest chakra, located at the top of the head. Occultists down through the ages have believed the pineal gland in the center of the brain to be its physical counterpart, the place from which the crown center operates.

This center is considered to be the seat of the Soul, the place from which we may make contact with the Superconsciousness, an entranceway to making full use of the energies from the Spiritual Body.

Its Eastern name is *Sahasrara*. Its color is violet, and it is an instrument for the highest spiritual attainment. It is activated when the third eye center is opened.

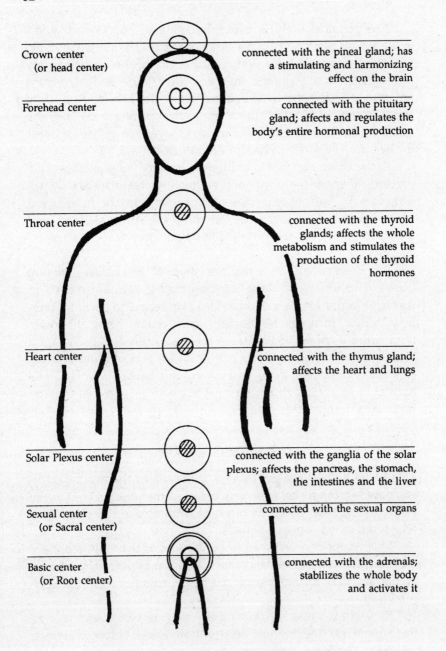

Crown center
(or head center) — connected with the pineal gland; has a stimulating and harmonizing effect on the brain

Forehead center — connected with the pituitary gland; affects and regulates the body's entire hormonal production

Throat center — connected with the thyroid glands; affects the whole metabolism and stimulates the production of the thyroid hormones

Heart center — connected with the thymus gland; affects the heart and lungs

Solar Plexus center — connected with the ganglia of the solar plexus; affects the pancreas, the stomach, the intestines and the liver

Sexual center
(or Sacral center) — connected with the sexual organs

Basic center
(or Root center) — connected with the adrenals; stabilizes the whole body and activates it

*Figure 8. The Chakras (Energy Centers)
of the Human Body*[4]

The Third Eye Center

This chakra is located near the pituitary gland in the brain, just behind and slightly above the eyes, and is the doorway through which the crown chakra is aroused.

The activation of this center gives one the powers of higher clairvoyance, and control of the Mental Body. It is the seat of all psychic ability. It is aroused through the conscious use of the Alpha level of the brain coupled with the desire to employ its powers for spiritual unfoldment.

Its Eastern name is *Ajna*. Its color is indigo.

A spiritual healer who learns to use the Ajna or third eye chakra in healing will be directing the healing energies straight from the Universal Healing Consciousness directly into the patient, instead of through the lower heart center, which while filled with empathy for the patient might also drain some of the healer's own energy, a situation not to be desired.

There are two paths to the attainment of the powers given through the opening of the third eye center. Both are achieved by desire, and we are judged by the motivation of our hearts. The lesser path is the seeking of psychic powers for the sake of the powers alone, which invariably leads to misuse of the energies attained and the downfall and degradation of the individual. This is the path trod by some in the past, which led to the old super-stition that psychic powers were the "instrument of the devil," for psychic power in the control of an untrained or unspiritual person can whiplash back on its operator, causing much havoc.

The higher, more desirable path is the seeking of conscious attunement with the Soul and the desire to be led in all activities by instruction from this superconscious seat of Mind. This desire will lead through the Ajna center straight to the arousal of the crown chakra, giving you—almost as a by-product—the perfect unfolding of the psychic powers you desire. That is why, through-out this instruction, we will seek to purify the desires and to help you understand the consequences of various possible choices to be made in your daily relationships.

The Throat Center

Located in the thyroid gland, this is the center of highest creative energy, symbolized by the spoken word. The energies released are enthusiasm, authority, zeal. It represents Intelligence-in-action and Power energized into manifestation, and it is the point of contact for the Causal Body. It is especially active in lecturers and orators in any field.

Its highest use is the spoken word of devotion and mystical evolvement, with the individual speaking creative words of power from the "I AM" point of detached mental control.

Its Eastern name is *Visuddha*. Its color is blue. Its corresponding element is ether.

The Heart Center

Located in the area of the physical heart, it is the middle chakra, and its positive energies of love, compassion, and empathy act as the perfect balance between the passionate heat of the lower physical drives and the intellectual cold of the higher mental centers. It is the doorway through which we emerge evolutionally from indulgence in the self-serving nature and first direct our aspirations toward spiritual attainment.

Some healers use the magnetic and radiating energies of the heart as the principal energy of healing. It is the most frequent point of attachment for the Astral Body. Its highest use is outwardly directed love, compassion, and desire to help.

Its Eastern name is *Anahata*. Its color is green, its element is air.

The Solar Plexus Center

This is located in the navel, or physical solar plexus, and is the most active center in the average person at this time. Our volatile human emotions center here. It is a sensitive receiving station for the tumultuous emotions of other people. All negative emotions such as anxiety, despair, envy, fear, greed, hate, jealousy, and lust hit us in this center, and we feel the physical effects of these stormy emotions in the form of butterflies, indigestion, knots, ulcers, and other stomach upsets.

The solar plexus is also called the desire center, and sometimes the emotional center, so it should not surprise you that it is the heart of the Emotional Body. At first it produces ambition and progress, then evolves into aspiration for enlightenment which prepares the way for the opening of the heart center.

Trance mediums who now work unconsciously through the solar plexus center may later, given sufficient understanding, arouse and use the Ajna center in full consciousness. Fully conscious mediumship represents a higher state of spiritual attainment than trance, since conscious control is the full state of mastery.

Its highest use is peace and goodwill towards all of humanity. The mental control of the emotional center, by directing its energies into and through the heart center for purification by love and compassion, is a necessary step towards Mastery.

The color of the solar plexus center is golden yellow, and its element is fire. Its Eastern name is *Manipura.*

The Spleen Center

Some authors lump the base of spine and sacral centers together as one and add the spleen as the sixth center. Other authors say that the spleen center, like the appendix, is in evolutionary atrophy because it has no higher counterpart through which its energies may be transmuted.

Some who give powers to the spleen center claim that its awakening allows one to travel at will upon the astral plane while away from the physical body. People who have experienced astral travel differ in their apperception of the point from which they leave the physical body. Each of the centers, from the sacral center to the crown, has been noted as the point of detachment. I believe each astral traveler leaves the body at the point of the highest awakened chakra. Later, we will discuss the astral plane in connection with the sacral center energies.

It may be that the spleen center is given attention in some programs as a way of avoiding the dangers of the sacral center. It seems to me that this is only trading one danger for another, and ultimately leads to a dead end. There are many minor centers throughout the body. It is possible that the spleen may be one of the more important minor centers, brought to our attention by early writers who wanted to create Western definitions for Eastern concepts, and in the process gave unwarranted importance to the spleen center. Without a higher center to transmute its energies it cannot be activated as a spiritual springboard, as the other centers can, so in my program I ignore it. I have listed it simply for your information and further reading. It has been listed in Egyptian books but not Indian ones, so it has no Eastern name.

Its color is rose, and its purpose is to draw Life vitality from the sun.

The Sacral Center

Located in the gonads, the sacral center is associated with physical creativity of all kinds and controls the sex life. It provides most of the energy that drives people to work and produce. Of all the energies, it is the most easily converted into unproductive, violent, even destructive channels, or it can be used for constructive, ennobling programs. It is the drive center of the physical body and produces sheer animal energy for physical activity.

Its highest use is to create and maintain vitality and health for the physical body. In the disciple of the spiritual life, this energy is transmuted to the throat center, and results in power, self-control and authority-in-manifestation by the Spoken Word.

Its Eastern name is *Svadhisthana*. Its color is orange. Its element is water.

The Base of Spine Center

Sometimes called the root chakra, this center is located at the base of the spine and is the center of the Etheric Body. It works automatically as an energy purifier, transforming low vibration energy into higher. The opposite pole to the crown chakra, it is the last center that should be consciously aroused. It energizes in natural order as one's spiritual aspirations increase, but when once aroused, one must be prepared to have conscious and intellectual control of the energies created by its force.

Its Eastern name is *Muladhara*. Its color ranges from wine to a bright, scintillating red-rose, depending on the spiritual evolvement of the subject. Its element is earth.

The highest use of the base of spine center is the energy of transmutation, creation, and regeneration. Its arousal creates a sparking together with the crown center and the raising of an energy known as the Kundalini or Serpent Fire. Incomplete or premature rousing of the Kundalini can ignite lower center emotional energies, driving them out of control, leaving their hapless owner overwhelmed.

When the lower emotions have been brought under mental dominion and the heart desires purified and cleansed, when the Ajna energies are being used as a positive, constructive force and the crown center has been opened to release full guidance into the whole Being in all daily activities, then the energy of the root center can be safely released to transform the total physical, mental, and emotional Being into a dynamo of spiritual energy.

Kundalini energy is a sleeping force in the average individual. In the spiritual aspirant whose motives are inspired by love and compassion, the Kundalini has already begun to be aroused. It can then be consciously directed to further purify desires, cleanse and spiritualize emotions, and send healing energies into any body part that is not functioning properly.

The Energy Generator

Some spiritual leaders insist upon subjugation of the body and its ego-drives, but without a healthy body, we cannot function properly on this plane. We are a Trinity—Mind, Body, and Soul—and we must bring our whole Being along on a program of well-balanced development. The following exercise is designed to promote an equalized increase in your overall psychic/physical/spiritual activity. Do this exercise daily, if possible, but at least three times a week.

This is not a process to project concentrated force with the idea of "opening" any designated center. One does not develop a center by working directly upon it through visualization, breathing exercises, etc. These things are not only useless, but may even be dangerous if a center is overstimulated through the accumulation of too much energy. This can lead to the eruption of uncontrollable emotional and physical devastation.

One develops each center as a result of *doing* that which enhances its particular virtue and by consciously using the highest energies associated with it. For example, any act of unselfish loving or giving expands the influence of the heart center. Working, teaching, or writing in any creative field vivifies the throat center. It is by intelligent, determined, external action in conjunction with aspiration that the Inner Self grows.

This exercise can be used for great benefit if the purpose and meaning of the meditation preceding the exercise is understood and followed. You may substitute your own words in this meditation, but the desires of the heart must be of the highest order and directed towards merging with the Divine Will-to-Good.

Consider and ponder deeply the meaning of this meditation:

"I will to will the Will of God! Father/Mother/Creator, help me to be humble, willingly abiding by Thy Law. Help me to make attunement with my Soul Self, which is always attuned to Thee, and to be guided by Wisdom, Good Will, and Love."

The purpose of this meditation is to direct the desires of the heart towards communication with the Soul and to help release and harmoniously discharge any subconscious negative attitudes or resistances which may be blocking guidance from that point. It will also help to build the "Body of Light" that increases the vibratory level of the physical body and that must ultimately uplift and integrate all aspects of the whole Spiritual Entity that is *you*.

Choose a place where you will not be disturbed, and sit or stretch out comfortably. Relax your body and quiet your mind as much as possible. Remember to keep your spine straight whether sitting or lying down. Now concentrate your attention on the base of spine center. Try to imagine that all of your consciousness exists at that one spot, that all of your thought, feeling, and sensation is centered there. In a short time, you will feel a warm, energizing sensation begin to grow.

At this response to your thought, begin to imagine a whirling circle of golden Light ever growing and increasing its speed in a clockwise rotation as it steps up the power of the center that is being energized.

Now direct this energy to the solar plexus center, causing an excitement and creating a vortex of whirling Light. Transfer the focus of your attention to this center, and imagine the Light growing and rotating faster and faster. Feel the increased energy flowing through this center!

Now direct this energy to the heart center, and repeat the whole process. Intensify the Light and lift it, repeating the steps in turn to the throat, third eye center, and crown center. When you feel your Crown Center tingling with all the energy you can bring to it, make the following prayer request:

"Spirit within, I offer my whole Being, emotional, mental, physical, and spiritual, to become a purified, perfected channel for Thy Will. Silently, now, I listen for the voice of my Soul Self."

Quietly listen for a few moments, objectively observing the thoughts, images, and ideas that flow through your brain. You may receive nothing at first, or you may be amazed at immediate results. As you raise this living Light through your centers, you can help increase the flow of health through any malfunctioning part of your body by using the flow from your own energy generators. As you consciously bring each center to its maximum vibratory rate, mentally direct its healing force to any portion of your body that is afflicted, before transferring your attention to the next highest center. See the ailing organ or body part engulfed in a clockwise whirl of Light, and visualize that body part in a state of complete health and rejuvenation. In so doing, you are treating the limb or organ with Healing Energy brought through your own energy transformers from the unlimited universal healing field. It will definitely be improved, and often it will be entirely healed.

You may end this exercise with a visualization of violet Light flowing upward and permeating the entire body. Violet is the color used to cleanse and dissipate residual karmic vibrations in the Etheric Body.

You may note that I left out the sacral center in our upward spiral. This is because this center is already quite developed in most people today, and undisciplined use of these energies creates most of the problems that beset our troubled society! If, however, you have physical problems of health involving the sex glands or lower organs, by all means direct the healing power of the Light to these areas. Sexual health is important, too.

A word of caution is appropriate here. When once you start this Living Energy rising along your spine, *do not stop* its upward spiral. This is not harmful if an unexpected interruption happens occasionally, but habitual incomplete use of this exercise will energize the lower centers more fully than the higher spiritual centers. This would lead to an imbalanced stimulation and/or overemphasis of the sex drive and other strictly material urges. *Psychic power enhances what you ARE.* The lower centers open first and, like Pandora's box, they spill out whatever violent emotions are still uncontrolled.

All parts of Life are equally important and none should be neglected, so we seek to live our lives in balance. When the lower centers with their physical and material drives are brought under the dominion and guidance of the spiritual centers, the values of life change. We lose our self-centeredness and can achieve happiness, peace, and contentment beyond anything the lower self can imagine.

The Path of the Kundalini

If you employ a consistent or structured type of meditation, sooner or later you will spark the spontaneous raising of the Kundalini Fire. This is a natural spiritual and evolutionary development, and most people go through this experience with little or no trouble, but without preconditioning or being told what to expect it can be a nightmarish experience for others.

Pseudo-convulsions, muscular spasms, sexual orgasms, searing heat or icy cold, sharp pains, sounds, inner lights, and visions, temporary paralysis, and many indescribable but intense sensations can accompany the Kundalini energy. Its onset can begin within a few weeks after beginning meditation practice, or it may come some years later. It may last from a few weeks or months to several years, coming and going in sporadic fashion. Each symptom is experienced only briefly and is usually more alarming to the emotional system than to the physical since, for the unprepared, it can be accompanied by intense fear, doubts, and the feeling that one is going insane.

Although its early stages are sometimes marked by stress, confusion, disorientation, and even schizophrenia-like symptoms, it does not impair one's capacity to function normally at every-day tasks, as true psychosis does. Shock treatment or drug therapy will only compound the problem, rather than relieve it, and may halt the process entirely for the balance of this lifetime. This is a great loss, not only to the individual, but also to society, which could benefit so enormously from the creative potential that is released by the Kundalini. The only medical therapy recommended by the author would be a good chiropractor or osteopath to keep the spinal column in proper alignment, so that the Kundalini need not be additionally hampered by physical blocks.

The end-product of the raising of the Kundalini is a feeling of intense bliss often accompanied by a tremendous explosion of light within the body, usually the skull area. If allowed to progress to completion, no matter how many weeks or years it may take, this process will usually culminate in deep psychological balance, strength, and maturity. There is a dramatic strengthening of the whole personality structure, character, and way of dealing with both the inner and outer worlds.

The pathway taken by the Kundalini Energy, or bodily sensations, as it travels through the body varies from person to person. The classical Yogic description is that it rises from the base of the spine and culminates in a burst of light within the skull. Many people of the Western tradition, however, find that it begins with a burst of heat and warmth in the bottom of the feet, travels up the back, the hands and arms sometimes become fiery hot, it goes on up the back of the skull, down the front of the nose, through the throat, culminating in the navel. Some writers find it begins in the forehead, going down the face and throat, through the abdomen to the base of the spine, and then back up into the skull cavity.

Whichever route it takes, it must pass through the chakras or energy centers, which connect the physical body to the other six energy fields that make up the total human Being. These chakras contain impurities in the energy flow which the Kundalini must remove before it can continue its course. Different people have different areas of blockage, therefore the Kundalini experience is different with each one.

In its rise, the Kundalini is a violent force which causes the nervous system to throw off stress and clear away karmic and psychological blocks to spiritual growth and emotional stability. It is postulated that the convulsions and pain that sometimes accompany this arousal may actually be part of the cleansing process. When Kundalini encounters these stress points or blocks, it begins to act on its own volition, engaging in a self-directed process of spreading through the entire physical/psychological system to remove these blocks.

Once a block is removed, Kundalini flows freely through that point and continues its upward journey until the next stress area is encountered. It passes through every part of the system, removing blocks and awakening consciousness. Pain, tension, and imbalance may be intensified if fear or doubt result in resistance or interference with it, whether conscious or unconscious. It may be hazardous to engage the Kundalini prematurely through special invoking exercises, but it is also detrimental to willfully stop the process once it begins. If the symptoms become too severe, simply stop meditation practices until you regain equilibrium.

Usually the process, left to itself, will find its own natural pace and balance, and the symptoms will disappear spontaneously in time. Because it is essentially a purifying and balancing process, and each person has only a finite amount of impurities to be removed, its action is self-limited. Instead of considering this process pathological, we need to remember that it is therapeutic, constituting removal of potentially pathological elements.

This is "being born again," the rebirth process that Jesus said was required to reach the Kingdom of Heaven. The Kundalini is an impersonal, self-directing force, part of the evolutionary process of the total Entity known as the Human Race. It arises spontaneously when the individual joins forces with the forward evolutionary push of humanity.

The Kundalini Experience, by Lee Sannella, M.D.,[5] is the best and maybe at present the only book written on clinical research of the Kundalini and its symptoms and after-effects. It is clear and easily read, and most heartily recommended for supplemental reading. Much of the foregoing has been gleaned from this work, although I've added from my own experience.

The Path of Action

Having ESP is a useless gift unless it can be made a part of our daily lives, unless we can use it to create harmony in relationships, progress in spiritual growth, and the ability, power, and authority to choose whatever we wish to experience on the material plane. That is, we should be free of limitations that make us believe we are not psychic, that we are not prosperous, that we are not physically whole and well.

Changing your perspective to Soul Consciousness, or to the "I AM" point of awareness, will change your beliefs about yourself and your relationship with this plane of existence. It will change your entire way of experiencing Life.

Psychic abilities should be under your own control; they should not rule you, nor should they exist in your life in a haphazard or random fashion. If they exist at all, they have to follow some sort of Universal Law. To put these abilities under our control, we need to learn how this Law operates and then tune into it, or direct our actions by it, every moment of our day, waking or sleeping.

The remainder of this chapter explains my basic program for psychic development. I call this the Path of Action. These seven steps are the core of any disciplined spiritual work.

The Most Important Word
You'll Read In This Book Is "Listen"

The Path of Action starts with conscious determination to simply *be aware*, to *listen* to inner direction in *all* of our daily activities. Psychic energy comes in from the universe without any qualifications or strings inhibiting or directing its use. Our thoughts and motivations create the limits to which it can be used. Developing a psychic awareness means becoming totally aware of how this energy is used by us every moment of our lives.

The basic purpose is to maintain a well-balanced life, one in which you are in control of the thoughts, images, and impulses coming from various parts of the brain as well as the mind. At the same time, you want to participate wholly in the daily world of conscious activity. You must eat, sleep, live and love, work and play, laugh, and cry sometimes, and be very much a part of the normal, healthy activities that make up your life. If there is an outward sign of your inward progress, it should be one of loving amazement from your family and friends in recognition of the powerfully loving, forgiving serenity of the inner you that will develop as you begin your spiritual journey.

The *new* you will be confident, loving, relaxed, and at peace with the world, accepting yourself for what you are and allowing others to be whatever they are, recognizing that all people are on their own "trip," their own journey through this plane of expression.

To open up the pathway between the brain and the Superconscious we must first become still and listen. Listen, and then evaluate what comes through. When we first open up our centers in an attitude of receptivity, we will find ourselves barraged by subliminal images and emotional impulses from every direction. For instance, just watching television becomes a jungle of emotional bombardment, not only from the dramas portrayed, but also from the levels of emotional appeal projected by the commercials.

A more exciting prospect is the ability to comprehend mental and emotional messages from other persons. Unknowingly, we have been using telepathy in communicating with friends and relatives all our lives, but as our centers develop we begin to consciously differentiate between our thoughts and those of others. As the excitement rises, we may also feel threatened or overwhelmed by all the outpouring of emotional appeal that clutters up our psychic atmosphere. Our purpose is to learn to walk the fine balance between emotion and thought, strengthening our own inner shields that keep us from being bowled over by too much psychic input. This is a process of first sensitizing ourselves to finer octaves of knowledge and then desensitizing ourselves so that we can control our own thoughts and emotions. In other words, allowing the information to enter and then taking command of it, rather than being swayed by it.

There are many "how-to" plans for psychic development, and most of them are good. The daily plan given here is one which has been proven successful by many, many students in my classes. It is a program of daily living, as well as daily psychic development. You will actually use those latent talents within you.

1. Listen to What Your Dreams Are Telling You

Begin your day by recording whatever dreams or dream fragments you had during the night. In Week 7 I will devote an entire session to dream analysis and interpretation, but begin now to become aware of your dreams. Keep paper and a pen or pencil by your bedside, and in the morning, as soon as you awake, write down as much of your dreams as you can remember.

Because dreams deal with the subconscious, they are fleeting, and immediate recording is necessary for proper interpretation. As you develop communication with the superconscious, dream interpretation will give way to more immediate direction for your life's problems and situations. A beginning step towards that end is to become aware of and to understand your dream life.

If you do not remember your dreams, use the Alpha state just as you drop off to sleep to request that your subconscious help you to remember your dreams. Writing down whatever fragments you can remember will help to convince your subconscious that you are serious about this and really do want to remember and be guided by this part of your intuitive faculties. In just a night or two, sometimes the very first night, you will begin to remember.

Writing down your dreams also helps you become aware of the pattern of symbols that your subconscious uses to communicate with you. Since each person is different, each subconscious has its own shorthand dream symbols, and you must learn to interpret yours. By the time we have reached the lesson where we deal with interpretation you will have a good backlog of dreams recorded, and will have begun to formulate some opinions about what *your* dreams mean.

2. Meditation—Listening to God (Your Soul Self)

Spend a few moments morning and/or late afternoon in meditation or in quiet introspective reflection. As I've said before, a quiet time for yourself is essential for inner growth.

In general, a morning meditation should have as its purpose: a review of what you expect the day to bring, being receptive to changes that might be projected along the time belt; a brief visualization of your goal, either for the day or a long-range projection; and at least ten minutes of quiet *listening.* This last step is just being aware of thoughts, ideas, and images that float through your mind, without in any way trying to direct them or to anticipate what the thoughts or images should contain. You will receive many insights at this time into your personal situations, relationships, and goals. (Strengthening the centers with the Energy Generator exercise is a good beginning for a morning meditation. If you find this generates too much energy to allow for quiet meditation, then do it afterwards.)

An afternoon meditation can be a ten to twenty minute mantra meditation with the mantra of your choice. "OM" is good. This will create new energies throughout your body, refresh your mind, and increase your physical and mental health. (Caution: Do not use mantra meditations after 4 P.M. Using a mantra in meditation feeds energy into your brain, and you will spend long sleepless hours until the energy wears off.)

An evening or bedtime meditation should be tranquil. Reviewing the day's activities is useful during meditation if you do not allow interfering thoughts of blame for yourself or others, personal pressures or deadlines, or anxiety over how a project or a relationship may develop. Keep in mind that you have come to the end of the day's activities and that the most important thing you can do for yourself—and others—is to prepare for a refreshing night's sleep. Indulging in anxieties of any kind at bedtime will be detrimental to your physical and psychic well-being. Remind yourself, if necessary, that there is presently nothing more that can be done about any negative situation, and that it is an unprofitable and useless waste to spend mental and emotional energies on it at this time of day.

Let your bedtime meditation be a reaching into the Superconsciousness, reaching to the Soul Self, becoming One with Universal Mind, and asking to be led in ways that are spiritually uplifting and spiritually evolving. Let your attitude be one of gratitude for the good things in your life and for the past day or week. Since one's thoughts are creative energy, allowing the mind to dwell on one's blessings will increase the number of blessings. Gratitude increases the things you'll have to be grateful for.

With these as your nighttime thoughts, you can calmly drift off to sleep. The Astral Body travels during the time your physical body sleeps, and it will be drawn to the level in the astral realm where your thoughts were at the moment of sleep. This, you will find, is often the cause of nightmares, which are merely astral contact with horrible thought-forms of the lower astral levels. So take special care to elevate your thoughts and desires at the moment of drifting off to sleep, for your own protection and your spiritual growth.

Your preparations for bed might include an inspirational reading from the Bible or some other source. This isn't a good time to cram for studies, watch a TV horror drama, or read an emotionally stimulating story.

As you develop your sensitivity to internal responses, you'll find it is as important to your spiritual and psychic well-being to program good sleep time as it is to program good daytime living. Soul Consciousness is an entire way of life that reaches into every hour of your day. It begins the moment you wake up and goes through the entire twenty-four hours, through the night as well.

3. Listen To Your Intuitive Perception of Others

Your most important development of daily psychic activity will be an inner understanding of others that surpasses that which you are now consciously using. You will know when you can trust another or not and will have a clear perception of the psychological state of those you meet.

Your conscious *listening* to this inner voice of guidance where others are concerned is a major step in the development of your telepathic faculties. You will soon recognize that many of your thoughts are not yours at all, but a telepathic recording of what another person is thinking. This faculty then allows you to direct your own actions according to the reality of the situation instead of just its appearances.

Telepathy can be consciously developed and placed under our control only when certain conditions within ourselves are met. A selfish or manipulative use of any of these gifts will destroy their delicate balance and create schisms within ourselves. Besides— according to the Law of Cycles—all that we send out (and that includes ill will or manipulative thoughts and actions) will be returned to us.

Intuitive perception of others, which includes telepathic reception, operates best when we are relaxed and totally accepting of the other person. This means that, although we might recognize that the person we are relating to is on another wavelength, there is no value judgment within as to the relative "goodness" or "badness" about the other's actions or relationship to the world. We simply accept this person for what he or she is.

You, of course, have the right (and the obligation) to decide whether this "wavelength" is compatible with your course of action, but if you decide that it is not, you do not place any blame or condemnation on *another's* course of action. You recognize and accept that others are learning their own lessons in their own place, and allow them to Be wherever they have decided they should Be. Your decisions and obligations, then, are to either move away from their orbits, or into them, whichever seems good to you, but not to force, coerce, or manipulate in any way, or to pass judgment on what seems good to them at the moment.

This attitude toward others, even those within your own family and circle of friends, will relieve you of any feeling of obligation about their spiritual pathway, placing that obligation where it belongs—on the individual person.

Your Path of Action leads to service in all forms, including teaching, guiding, inspiring, and all forms of encouragement, but never to insisting that the other person follow the directives you give. Allow each person freedom of choice, as you insist upon your own freedom of choice in your Path. The Law will bring its own returns in its own way.

Children, of course, are our legal and moral responsibility until they reach age eighteen, but the people of India call them "old souls in little bodies." Our responsibility is to guide and train them in the use of the unfamiliar vehicle of the new body they have incarnated into; to teach them how to listen to their own inner guidance and to accept responsibility for their own decisions and judgments, so that they might live harmoniously within the society in which they have chosen to incarnate. Esoteric philosophy teaches that the Soul takes responsibility for the actions of the child beginning at puberty, so our most important training must take place before that time.

An attitude of totally accepting the other person will create within you a desire to be of service to him or her, to help in any way that is given you, and this will automatically open the pathway of perception and communication within you. Your attitudes flow first *from* you, then back *to* you, with their measure of intuitive, personal understanding.

This open pathway of communication also brings back sure knowledge when someone else wishes you harm, along with the instinctive perception of how to handle the situation, should it develop further. When your impulse towards others is "How can I help you?" very few persons whose attitudes and actions are detrimental will cross your path, since you have done nothing to attract them through your own actions. If it should happen, you'll find every word and movement within the drama serving to protect you from harm. You may even be moved to discover and minister to the need within the individual that caused him or her to act in such a way in the first place, and you will go your respective ways, a little better spiritually for the experience.

Persons working in law enforcement and social services may, at first, have some difficulty with this concept, and there may be times within our present society when the "hands off" policy cannot apply, such as when it is necessary to keep an individual from injuring others. However, I believe that a deeper study of the Laws of Karma applied to spiritualized methods of re-education and rehabilitation could turn more than 90 percent of those presently in jails and mental institutions into useful, contributing citizens. (This is a more troublesome area than most of us are required to deal with and could be the subject of an entire book in itself. So, for the present, I'll leave that thought for the spiritual insights it may bring to those whose lifework designs them to fill this role in our culture. It can be done, and the present influx of mystical revelation will eventually permeate even the most hardened individuals.)

Part of your intuitive perception is an extension of clairvoyance called *claircognizance*, a term coined by Manly P. Hall in his book *Spiritual Centers in Man*,[6] to define that peculiar mental relationship to "knowing the unknown" that any person expert in a field often credits to "inspiration."

This particular sense of mental acuity or awareness comes in a purely intellectual form, rather than an extension of the senses as we usually think of them. The mind suddenly becomes aware of something not previously known, like an occult truth or philosophical insight, without any involvement of the lesser senses. The information most often comes as words imprinted upon the mind—yet the mind itself registers no awareness of words spoken either physically or spiritually.

Like most psychic abilities, claircognizance usually operates on a need-to-know basis. I experienced this sense of mental awareness for several years before coming upon a term to define it. Often, during a classroom discussion, a student would ask a question in an area to which I had not given previous thought. My instinctive reaction was to say, "I don't know," but before the words could come out of my mouth, I found to my amazement that I *did* know! From some vast storehouse of knowledge beyond my own previous contact, the answer would come in an instantaneous flash!

Hall says, "If the lay instructor is actually in contact with higher worlds he will learn far more while he is teaching than will those to whom he is explaining the subjects under discussion, the claircognizance revealing spontaneously that which the faculties of the mind under normal conditions could not reason out in months."

Although Mr. Hall claims this ability as the particular reward of the teacher, I have seen it at work among people who were not especially occult-minded or even spiritually minded. During a recent sojourn in Hawaii, our lanai (veranda) was in danger of being flooded during exceptionally heavy rains. The local Samoan maintenance men were called, and they attempted to put an additional layer of protective sandbags over some that had been placed there during a previous downpour. I pointed out that as the first sandbags were already saturated, with the water coming through onto the floor, another layer on top wouldn't do any good.

"Then I don't know how to fix that," he said. "What you really need is a trench to carry the water off, but the rain hasn't let up enough to allow us to dig one." Then, in the next movement, he was placing the sandbags parallel to the previous row, which effectively caught and held the water. I recognized the familiar "tuning in," which brings the right answer and the right action at the same time that the conscious mind is saying, "But I don't know the answer to that."

Claircognizance seems to function best in the area of thought or action with which one is most familiar. You have put your whole effort into solving a problem or learning a skill, or into any act of creation. Then, at the moment of letting go of your own effort, often subconsciously voiced by the words, "I don't know," at that moment, the Higher Sense activates and in a flash of inspiration you *do* know. You have the answer to the problem; you know the next step towards perfecting your skill; or, at that moment, the act of creating becomes a completed product!

In this book I call this faculty "Inner Guidance," and it is this kind of thinking that will ultimately solve even the toughest kind of social problems. The teachers struggling with unruly students in classrooms and hallways; the law enforcement official handicapped by outdated, unenforceable laws and overcrowded detention centers; the social worker stricken to the heart by human degradation and hopelessness; these people will find the Inner Light, the sudden flash of inspiration, that will bring about new approaches, reforms, methods, inventions—whatever is required—to solve the immediate problem or even turn the tide of human destiny. All psychic gifts, including claircognizance, are activated most frequently in the area in which you have given your best attention, whether it is a day-to-day struggle for survival or the handling of ideas and plans too immense for the average mind to follow.

4. Your Spiritual Journal

Buy yourself a blank book or a notebook which you will label "My Spiritual Journal." This book is to be yours privately and is not to be shared with anyone else.

Record in your Spiritual Journal, as you would in a diary, everything that pertains to your personal psychic development. Record all insights and inspirations that come to you through meditation. Use it to write down your dreams or to record the results of any series of ESP tests. Writing down activities, or the results of activities, serves to impress upon your Inner Mind that you really mean business, and it will help to increase the response from both subconscious and superconscious levels.

The most effective use you can make of your Spiritual Journal is to record everything that happens to you as a result of your personal desire for psychic mastery. When you have a hunch or an intuition that turns out to be accurate, write it down. If you correctly foresee a future happening, write it down. If you effected spiritual healing for yourself or another, write it down.

Use it to write down your goals for the future and to record the attaining of those goals. Write down whenever you have successfully and harmoniously moved through a series of challenging events by using your Inner Guidance. Every time you succeed in overcoming a personal trait that hinders your mastery of the qualities you desire, joyously record it. (I have developed a Spiritual Journal workbook based on the exercises and meditations in this text. For more information about it, see the order forms at the end of this book.)

As you go through the upcoming weeks, you will find more and more uses for this book. This is your own psychological "pat on the back" for a job well done, and it will have a more positive effect in your life than a whole train of other people telling you how wonderful you are. Of course, that is nice, too, but other people's plaudits affect only our emotional nature, and that part of our nature is never appeased. It never gets enough applause. It is always hungry.

We desire to find and to identify with that Something Else, the Objective Watcher who, when placed in charge of our life, uses both the mental *and* the emotional nature to bring about balance and harmony and to put you in the right place, doing the right thing, always.

Here is an affirmation that you might write on the very first page of your book. If you keep it always in your mind as well, it will serve as a beacon to pull that Inner Force ever more strongly into activity, and you'll move automatically into right action.

Whatever I need to know—I know.

Whatever I need to do—I do.

Wherever I need to be—I am.

5. The Shield of Protection

"In the beginning was the Word, and the Word was with God and the Word was God . . . " (John 1:1). ". . . . and the *Word* was God . . . ." The spoken word *is* the Creative Force. We were made as God imaged us ("in His image"), and *our* spoken word is *our* creative Force.

The first words spoken were, "Let there be light" (Gen. 1:3). Therefore Light became the Primal Substance, forming the building blocks of the universe. Scientists now say that every atom and every cell has a nucleus of Light. "Ye are the Light of the World," Jesus said (Matt. 5:14). So we can know that within the cells of our own bodies is this Creative Substance, this Light that we can use to create a White Light circle of protection or to use as the basic substance of anything else we choose to create.

The energy of Light has tremendous building power. We can use it to build a shield of protection around us that is 100 percent effective against any negative thought-form that does not belong to us—that is, one that does not have either its origin or any response mechanism within us.

In my personal use of the protective Light shield, I have verified its trustworthiness daily. In today's perilous times, I can (and have) walked unscathed through many potentially dangerous situations. Sometimes I have not even been aware of the danger that threatened, but was told about it later by someone more observant than I.

Part of the shield's protective ability, of course, lies in the user's belief in this invulnerability, but there's more to it than that. I have faced both robbery and rape, so secure in my inner belief in the protection of this shield of Light, that there was no answering fear in my heart when the situation presented itself, and both incidents dissolved into the nothingness of which they were made—the other person's fantasy.

Let me tell you how to build your own protective Light shield, and then I'll share some of my adventures with you.

This is the easiest of all visualizations. Simply see (or feel) yourself surrounded by a field of White Light. Make it as brilliant as you can. If you are scientifically oriented, think of every cell in your body glowing, and enhance this Light until it fills the space around you. (While this is not exactly the same kind of Light Energy as used in the meditation exercise, it has similarity of action, inasmuch as it is directed by your intent.)

If you are religiously inclined, think of this Light as the Christ Light, the Christ Consciousness that all people aspire to. Feel it hovering protectively around you, like a blanket of security. You could consider it the Christ Presence.

As the Tibetan teacher, D. K., says, "What the scientist calls energy, the religious man calls God, and yet the two are one, being but the manifested purpose, in physical matter, of a great extra-systemic Identity." You may call it Energy, Light, God, or Christ Spirit, no matter, the end result will be the same—protection.

Now, because we are in troubled times, you might feel you need an extra ounce of protection. Then, in your mind's eye, add a clear, hard, impenetrable plastic shell, as another force field around the aura of Light. This is thought control of energy, as what you see in your mind's eye becomes actuality.

You can test it, also, with your visualization. In your imagination, see something flying towards you, and watch it bounce off the hard plastic shell around your protective Light shield. If you can do that, if it bounces off, you have your protection complete, and you can walk into the day's activity without fear of anything. (Remember that non-visualizers can simply think this shield into action and know that its effect is just as powerful as the shield created by the visualizer.)

Lobsang Rampa reported that this shield, or energy field, has been known to flatten bullets among the Lamas in Tibet. Each time you use this technique the protection becomes stronger and more concrete, and soon clairvoyants will be able to see it.

Do this every morning and every night for the rest of your life, and before and after each meditation. It should be the first thing you do when you wake in the morning and the last thing when you go to bed at night. Also, renew it after any near-accident or fear thought that may have drained off the energy through alarm or shock. Consider this a vital part of your survival mechanism.

This shield has proven itself hundreds of times. One day I went visiting. When I got in my car to come home, I had an intuitive flash of an accident. I accepted the warning for what it was, a revealed result of a present course of action, and set about to change that course of action.

My car was not in the best condition: the tires were getting smooth, the brakes needed some adjustment, and to top it off, it had just started to rain, making the streets slick with oil.

I quickly put the White Light protective shield around myself and the car, visualized myself pulling into the driveway at home with both myself and the car intact, and then drove with much more caution than usual.

Just as I moved into a left-hand turn lane, a woman came barreling out of a service station across the street and stuck the nose of her car into the traffic lane in front of me. She was so close I couldn't have missed her if I *had* had good tires and good brakes.

Naturally, in an emergency, one steps on the brake, but on the rainy pavement, I started to skid. There were two lanes of five o'clock traffic to the right of me, and as the rear of my car slid to the right, I felt a "bump." Then as I squeezed through a very small space between the cars, I felt a "bump" on the left.

I did make it through, and I had not touched metal to metal with either car. I am convinced that only my protective shield could have made that psychic "bump" in my mind as I went by. The important thing is that *I did not have an accident*, even though the possibility had been projected. My protective shield kept me safe. Naturally, I was a little shaken, but I breathed a prayer of thanksgiving, re-energized my White Light shield, and continued on home safely.

At another time, four of us, all metaphysical students, were driving along a country road that was just being graded. Lots of loose gravel lay on the roadway, and the tires of a truck in front of us threw bits of gravel onto the windshield and fenders of our car. Almost with one breath, all four of us automatically threw a protective shield around the car. That shield was so strong from the mental thrust of the four of us that the loose gravel flying towards the windshield continued up and over the car roof, as though it were being propelled by an invisible energy field, as indeed it was.

You can use this White Light shield to protect your family and loved ones too; but remember that we cannot do for others what they will not do for themselves. This mental energy that forms a protective force around your loved ones, however, will be energy that they, themselves, can use in time of emergency and it may be just enough extra power to lift them above a dangerous situation, or at least mitigate its effects.

The only negative effect that can come back through your protective shield is a return of your own resentments, angers, fears, and hostilities. So dwell on the positive; look for solutions, not at the problem; and know that all things are working together for good. When there is a negative reaction in your world, look for the good that comes out of it. Live in the NOW moment, and see what blessings there are around you.

As you consciously employ your protective shield there will be a relaxing of fear, which will bring about a recognizable enhancement of the positive virtues of attractiveness, courage, decisiveness, energy, love, radiant health, respect, self-confidence, and strength. These come from the dynamic, powerfully positive intensification of your own Soul's force field, created by your spiritually aware use of the White Light. As you go about your routine activities these qualities radiate out from you, and as you daily grow in joy, love, and spiritual strength, you also know that whatever you radiate out comes back!

6. Sharpening the Senses

Sharpening and refining all the senses provides a foundation for mastery in learning to use and control your inner senses. If your input from the external environment is distorted, hazy, or incomplete, your judgments concerning the events in your life will be faulty, based on faulty information.

It may seem like a paradox that in our journey to find the inner world, I ask you first to become aware of the outer world, but training the powers of observation is an important point. The keener your external sensing, the more accurate your inner ESP will be.

Gautama Buddha used and recommended this method as an initial step in training the mind. While instructing his students, he would walk among them, then suddenly stop and ask, "Where was I standing when I spoke the word, Love?" At other times he would pause in his lecture and say, "What movement did I make with my hands when I spoke of Harmony?" In this way he trained the students' powers of observation, while he taught attentiveness. Your daily routine need not be interrupted, but instead will be greatly enhanced by becoming more aware of the input of data from the senses.

The subconscious mind records in detail everything that happens around you. Everything you see, hear, touch, taste, and smell is recorded in the Theta level of the brain. Most of us make instantaneous, but subliminal, judgments about what we deem to be relevant and what seems, at the moment at least, to be irrelevant. With these judgments, much that the senses record is never noticed by the conscious Beta mind.

If James C. walks by a department store window, he may be partially or completely consciously unaware of what was in that window. If later he should be asked to tell what he saw, he would have extreme difficulty remembering what was there. However, research shows that if he were put under deep hypnosis, he would be able to recall in almost exact detail every item in the window.

Experiences in childhood can be remembered in such exquisite detail under hypnosis that the smells, sounds, and sights as well as emotional involvement can be remembered with complete revivification, as though the person were reliving the actual moment in time.

We're not asking our senses to do something more than they are already doing. We are only learning to be more alert with the Beta level of our minds to what is going on around us.

In the morning, the senses are fresh and undulled by an overload of activity, such as might happen later in the day. As we often stretch our physical body early in the morning to tone and awaken the muscles from their inactive position during the night, we might consider stretching our senses in the same way. Try sharpening them, one at a time: sight, hearing, smell, feeling, and taste.

When you eat breakfast, and indeed, all your meals throughout the day, savor each mouthful completely, chewing slowly and enjoying fully all the sense flavors of your food. This will have other benefits as well. If you chew more slowly, and savor each mouthful longer, you will eat less and be full sooner.

Most of us eat far too much, and the physical activity that we do cannot burn up the energy units we take in. This might not seem important to the person whose metabolism burns up energy so fast he is constantly underweight, but every person will enjoy food more if eaten with full awareness.

A slow, pleasant meal will break the cycle of hurry, rush, rush that is often a self-perpetuating cause of tension. If you take five or even ten minutes more to eat and savor a pleasant meal, will the world stop? Will your own personal world be irreparably damaged? On the contrary, it will probably be much improved.

Speak to your senses with such affirmations as, "I hear exceptionally well today; I see with great clarity of vision today; my senses of smell and taste are very acute today." Such declarations, frequently repeated, will serve to alert your subconscious mind that you want to be reminded to see, taste, smell, touch, and hear better than you have done before.

Listen to sounds that you might otherwise disregard. When you hear a fire siren or an ambulance going down the street, try to project ahead to where it will stop. See in your mind's eye where the accident or the fire is. You can check this out in the newspaper later, and you will be amazed at how close you can come to knowing, simply by extending your sense of hearing "ahead of time."

Cultivate a wide sweep of listening after you go to bed at night, when daytime sounds are muted. Pinpoint individual sounds, such as night birds calling, crickets chirping; locate the house where a dog may be barking. Listen to sounds in the house that you normally ignore, such as the sound of the refrigerator, the air conditioner, or the night sounds of children or pets.

Sharpen each of your other senses in the same way. Be more alert to sights, smells, and touch. Enjoy your senses. Treat each experience as though it were the very first time such an experience had ever happened to you. Get everything you can out of it. Take a moment to prolong the enjoyment of the perfume from a woman who passes by. Enhance your tactile sense by being thoroughly alert to sensations from your fingertips: from fabrics, wood, metals; or textures—soft, rough, embossed, etc.

Then begin to blend your senses, using each one in an unusual fashion. Try to literally hear with your eyes, see with your sense of touch, etc. Persons who are blind often find other senses are enhanced in a compensatory fashion. It is recorded that some blind people can see with various parts of the body, such as an elbow, or some part of the hand or the fingertips. Light and dark can be distinguished with these body parts. One Russian woman, Rosa Kuleshova, can successfully distinguish colors, words, shapes, and fabrics using her toes and elbows.[7]

This phenomenon is known as derma-optics, or skin-vision, but the point I am trying to make is that if it can happen at all it must follow some Universal Law, and researchers can find and identify the process.

Try this experiment. Place a copper penny in the palm of your left hand (use the right hand if you are left-handed). Close your hand and turn full attention on the penny. Feel it, rub it with the fingers of that hand (don't use the other hand), see it in your mind's eye, become very attentive to the qualities of that penny. Then—without taking the penny out of your closed fist—*taste it!* Suddenly into your mouth will come a strong, acrid, coppery taste, even though the penny is nowhere near your mouth. You are now using all of your senses to know and understand that penny.

Now rove your eyes around the room you are in. Choose various objects in turn, and as you look at them closely, try to imagine what they would feel like, smell like, how they would taste. Remember the sound of a cuckoo clock, or some other periodic noisemaker, if there is one in the room. Do all of this in your mind. You are now using your eyes to see, taste, feel, and hear. Of course, most of this is recall, but there is something else at work, also. Some other ability deep in the inner mind is stirring awake as you practice sharpening and clearing your senses.

Now extend your senses to remember in detail something that happened yesterday, or last week, or last year. In your mind, not only "see" the event take place, but also use all of your senses to hear, smell, touch, and taste what happened. Recall the event with all of your senses.

While you are doing all of these things, be *aware* of that point of focus within you that is doing the doing, that is thinking the thoughts, that is receiving the input of data from the senses. Be aware that that "point of focus," which we have called the "I

AM," is not the thoughts, is not the feeling nature, nor the physical body which obediently moves around to its command. This detached "point of focus" is the *real* activator behind all of these things. It is from this detached perspective that you can take charge of the doing, the thinking, and the feeling, and be the master of your own life.

7. Project Yourself Into Future Action

This last step in our program for daily psychic development is the most fun of all and is immediately practical. It is the use of your extended senses to "see" into the future: to know what is going to happen on your next birthday; which of several job opportunities you should apply for; whether your trip is going to be harmonious and uneventful or filled with obstacles and trouble; and any other thing you might wish to know about.

This step covers not only events coming towards you in time that you might not now be aware of, but also the ability to make the future bring to you events, situations, and people according to your desires.

To tell you about this activity in your life will take the next two sessions, so your assignment for now is to practice the first six steps of the Path of Action. We'll cover the control of future events in Weeks 3 and 4.

Workshop #2
Keys to Your Own Expanded Senses

≈

Under no circumstances should these or any other exercises in this book be considered "tests" of your ability, because your present ability, no matter how remarkable, is still in a latent stage and can always be developed much further. Nor should you enter into these games with others in any spirit of competition, trying to outdo someone else or feeling unworthy if someone else outdoes you.

We are not trying to decide who is better. All of these exercises are "gate-openers" only, designed to open pathways into your mind, to suggest to your subconscious that it has a great future ahead, if it will just wake up and take notice. Regardless of instant results, or lack of them, when doing any of these exercises be aware that you have only touched the surface of the potential that lies untapped deep within your mind.

So do not be elated or downcast about the results of any experiment. Simply remain detached, an observer of what happens inside of you during the experiment. Analyze objectively how you feel, what activity is taking place inside your brain, heart, and emotions during these experiments. This objective evaluation is the only observation that will be of value to you as you explore your own potential. *You* are what you need to be concerned about.

Exercise #1: What Do You Feel?

Brightly colored pictures of scenes depicting intense emotions, such as anger, ecstasy, fear, hurt, love, pleasure, terror, etc., may be glued on identical 8"x11" sheets of thin cardboard or stiff paper. Place each picture in separate identical 9" x 12" envelopes, and number these envelopes consecutively.

Hold one envelope either against your solar plexus—the emotional center—or in your left hand (or right, if you are left-handed), and try to feel what emotion is depicted by the picture within. Write the number on the envelope and what you feel on a separate sheet of paper.

When all of the envelopes have been examined, open them and check your answers against the pictures inside. People may differ in their reactions to a particular picture. These responses may be determined by their backgrounds and/or feelings toward the event depicted.

There are no "rights" or "wrongs" in this exercise. Each experiment will tell you something about how you relate to emotional stimuli in your environment and thereby help you get in touch with your own psychic responses.

Exercise #2: Let's Meet Your Friend!

This is a good party game. Choose a partner, if possible someone you do not know very well. Sit facing each other, and place the palms of your hands together—both hands. Try to "sense" something that has happened to that person in the recent past, either today or in the past week, if you can.

To do this, let your mind become quiet and just allow thoughts, images, colors, and feelings to come into your mind. See that person in some activity or action or in some association with an animal or person. Your partner will tell you if you are accurate, and probably even elaborate on the simple picture in your mind by telling you the full story behind it. You'll be amazed at your own accuracy.

Take turns telling each other what you see, feel, or sense. When you are finished, change partners and do it again.

Exercise #3: You and The World Are One!

Gather a number of articles made of similar appearing metals, such as steel, nickel, lead, and silver; or gold, brass, copper, and bronze. Explore these metals with all of your senses: touch, smell, taste, sight, etc. Then close your eyes and try to explore them with your mind senses. Try to imagine what the inside of these metals might be like.

Explore with your mind how the elements are put together. Imagine that you are microscopically tiny, small enough to fit inside an atom in the metal, or that the atoms grow large enough that you can walk inside. See how the particles are shaped; how the sunlight filters down through the spaces; how it smells, being inside the metal.

Gemstones may be explored in the same way. For instance, a crystal ball that gazers use might be made of acrylic, glass, or genuine gemstone crystal. Exploring balls made of each of these materials is an enlightening experience. They all "look" alike to the eye, and they all can provide the same function for the gazer ("scryer"), but there is a vast difference in how they "feel."

Exercise #3-A:

Place similar substances, such as salt, sand, and sugar, or milk, water, and strained fruit juice, in small plastic envelopes or dishes. With eyes closed, run your fingers through the substances, absorbing information through the sense of touch and determining by feel alone which is which.

Exercise #3-B:

Prepare a bowl or basin of lukewarm water. With your eyes shut, dip your fingers into the water. At first you may have difficulty knowing exactly when your fingers make contact with the water, but as you practice, your fingers will become more and more sensitized.

Exercise #4: Derma-Optics

Bevy Jaegers, a pioneer psychic researcher living near St. Louis, Missouri, developed the following exercises.[8]

She has discovered, she says, that one hand receives, or perceives, certain kinds of energies from the environment, while the other hand projects energies out from us into the environment. In right-handed people the left hand is the receiving hand. In left-handed people the right hand receives.

Let's accept this bit of information as fact while trying the following experiments. Use the left hand to receive extended sense perceptions if you are right-handed, and vice versa if you are left-handed.

Obtain samples of paint colors—red, blue, yellow, and green —in bright, vivid, primary colors from the local paint store. Glue them to the middle of plain white file cards. Start with no more than three or four, and add more colors as you become more proficient.

Select one card, holding it in your receiving hand, color side down, and let yourself become sensitive to the color. Allow some air space between the card and your skin, as the tighter you hold the color, the less it will react. Close your eyes and try to see the color in your mind's eye, or feel a temperature radiating from the color. Push your fingers across the color and feel the resistance of the color to your skin. Do this with all the fingertips across the colors, trying to differentiate among them. Some colors will feel rough, some smooth, some sticky, some cool, and some hot, when the fingers are pushed across their surfaces.

Now place the cards face down on the table, and mix them until you are not sure which is which. Take one and try to determine which color it is from the mental picture you get, the temperature difference you feel, or the texture you encounter when you push your fingertips across its underside. Decide what it is and jot it down. Go on to the next card. Evaluate your hits and misses. Don't be discouraged. Practice will increase the number of hits.

Exercise #4-A:

Place all the color cards face down on the table. Try to locate a red one by holding your receiving hand about a half-inch above the cards and slowly moving it from one card to another. Try for a sense of difference in "feel," perhaps of temperature, vibration, or something else that "clicks" in your mind that says, "This is the one I want."

Exercise #4-B:

Have someone else look at the colors, one at a time. Close your eyes, and try to visualize the color your partner is thinking about. Keep a record of your hits and misses. This is also an exercise in clairvoyance and telepathy.

Exercise #4-C:

When you are more adept with the colors, fill a bag with solid-colored marbles, game tokens, jelly beans, or poker chips that come in a variety of different colors. Choose one color at a time to experiment with and follow the same procedure as with the cards. When you have tested the colors, first with your eyes open and then closed, take one item out of the bag without looking at the color. Hold it tightly in your receiving hand and feel what the color is. Write it down, and go on to the next one. Keep score and evaluate yourself.

Exercise #4-D:

Try the above experiment using bits of brightly colored yarn or ribbon all cut the same length. Make sure the fabric and texture of the different colors is the same, such as all rayon, wool, cotton, etc.

Exercise #4-E:

Use the 8s, 9s, and 10s from a deck of ordinary playing cards. These have the most color in them. Place four red cards and one black card face down on the table after shuffling. Try to locate the black card. Reverse the procedure to find a single red card among four black ones. Then try two red cards and four black. Continue adding cards until you are able to identify five red cards or five black cards out of a set of five red and five black.

Finally, try to separate the entire deck of fifty-two cards into red and black piles, face down.

MEDITATION PRACTICE

Meditation is never passive. It is a dynamic awareness of the "I AM" point of focus, and the "I AM's" ability to know itself as something apart from thoughts and emotions.

For this week, during your meditation time allow your mind to be aware of body sensations only. After you've reached the Alpha level, turn your attention to what your body is doing. Think about the heart beat, the digestive cycles, and the flow of breath through your lungs.

Be aware of energy patterns created by the impact of sense impressions on your body which focus the soul's interest or attention, such as the warmth or coolness of the air, the yowling of cats or the screaming of children at play, or traffic noises outside. An itch is an energy pattern. Be aware of what it is like to feel these energy patterns without doing anything about them.

The purpose here is to not allow your body to distract from your meditation time. If you become aware of an itch, a pain, or any sensation of discomfort, don't do anything about it. Just let your mind be aware, without any corresponding action. By regarding these sensations as just energy patterns you develop the freedom to watch them dissolve and re-form in other ways, while you remain aware of yourself as separate from all that is happening in the body.

If the itching or discomfort becomes more than you can control or release with your mind, and you have to break the meditative state to move or scratch, then make it *your* decision to stop the meditation for this time. Don't try to regain the meditative state. You must maintain psychological control over the body, and if *you* decide to break meditation, the body hasn't won its fight for your attention.

It is beneficial to begin and end all meditation times with an infilling of the cleansing, purifying, protective White Light. After meditation this infilling time can be the bridge back to Beta consciousness, as you slowly change mind levels, so as not to jar the sensitive realignment of the nervous system.

WEEK 3

≈

Where Are You in Time and Space?

Time does not exist! As startling as this concept may be, it is true. There is neither past nor future, there is only the *Eternal NOW*. Time is a measurement we have devised to record Life's changing existence in the NOW.

The earth goes around the sun. Time is relevant *only* in the chronological recording of events in relation to where the sun was when the event took place, and that measurement is relevant *only* to the physical plane on Earth. For any of the finer or denser dimensions of matter on Earth (or on any other planet or body in space), Time as we know it does not apply. There may be other ways to record the passing of events on those planes, which are not readily available to the searching mind, but we need not trouble ourselves with those now.

How, then, can we transcend the artificial Laws of Time which affect our bodies, our minds, and our fortunes? To overcome the time/space syndrome, we must return to our point of "I AM" awareness, the point of contact where we are aware of ourselves as the "I," the thinker, the observer, and recognize that this "I" within us is not involved with the passage of time or events, is not touched by outer manifestations at all.

In its nature, the "I AM" consciousness is calm, objective, peaceful. It watches and evaluates, neither accepting nor reject-ing the turbulent manifestations which flow around us. It is that part of us which can think about thinking, aware that it is the

Thinker, not the thought. This Spark of Identity can be identified as the "Objective Watcher," the Soul. This Watcher lives only in the NOW moment, unmoved by the ceaseless illusions created by time and space.

Living in the NOW Moment

NOW, right this moment, *is* Eternity. The NOW moment never passes. Yesterday never was, tomorrow never will be. NOW is all the time in Eternity you'll ever have to work with. You cannot go back and relive the past, except in memory or in the recording of those events that once transpired. When I speak, that action of speaking and the words themselves are already in the past at the instant of delivery and cannot be changed.

Nor can you take your next breath NOW. Every inhalation of your lungs is the NOW breath. No matter how you try, you cannot live in the future, even though present planning may bring future events to become the NOW. How you acted in the past cannot be changed. How you will act in the future is of no relevance until the future becomes the NOW. *How you are responding to the NOW moment is the key to transcending time and space.*

What are you doing with the NOW moment? Are you holding grudges, resentments, ill feelings about the past? The past does not exist in the NOW and therefore cannot be changed. Mind energy used in guilt or condemnation about things that no longer *are* is wasted energy, and energy misused in this manner creates conflicting beliefs about oneself. These beliefs will result in NOW manifestations of psychosomatic illness in our bodies, or actions which result in accidents and other forms of self-punishment.

Are you frightened or apprehensive about the future? Most things we worry about in the future never transpire. The mind energy used in needless worry and anxiety is also wasted and is useless in effecting change. Any mind energy that we use in negative emotional responses to either past or future time is being used in the NOW, is creating our world in the NOW, and is affecting our present enjoyment and fulfilled living in the NOW!

The "I" responds only to whatever emotion or reaction we are transmitting in the NOW—it does not respond to either past or future events. Psychologically speaking, present responses are often subconsciously influenced by past events, but even accepting that, the present response is the only thing we can change. As masters of the situation, and of ourselves, we certainly can do that!

So the NOW moment is all we have to work with. The NOW is changeless. Time and space are eternally changing. How you think and how you act in the NOW changes time and space. Realizing this releases us from terrible burdens of anxiety, regret, frustration. If we can release the negative emotional burdens we carry, our ESP will unfold naturally and harmoniously.

Energy follows thought. Thought directs energy. All directed thought comes back like a boomerang to its creator. Negative impulses sent out gather to themselves alike energies from similar minds and return a thousandfold into our lives, our bodies, and our circumstances. Releasing our mental and emotional holds on negative responses allows the natural, normal impulses of love, joy, and harmony to flow like a mighty river of positive, creative energy through our Being, which, utilizing the same boomerang effect, returns a thousandfold into our lives, our bodies, and our circumstances. Make the NOW quality time. Use the best of your ability to make the NOW a happy, relaxed place to *Be*. Our NOW responses create our future. When the tensions created by negative responses are relaxed, we can transcend both time and space.

The Secret to the Mastery of Time and Space

In one sense, all events in time are simultaneous. All things that are, have been, and will be exist in the NOW. This doesn't mean that our experiences in life are predestined, or that we are limited in any way by Fate. It means that all things that *can* be already *are* in potential, and have been and will be experienced by countless souls throughout Eternity. Our *free will* decides which of these events we will experience NOW, and which of them we will create in the future. We can choose the *order* in which we will experience these events, or we can choose not to experience them at all.

We might liken time to a conveyor belt. It brings people, situations, and events to us according to the blueprint we are projecting in the NOW. The characteristic of a conveyor belt is that the things it carries come *through* our lives, not into them.

Any situation predominant in my life in the present is passing in review to record my experiences and my responses. It is designed to draw my mind energy into some form from which future events can be molded. People, situations, and events fade into the past, and the experience forms the basis for NOW action in respect to the possible future events my conveyor belt of time might bring me.

The emotional response we give to our present circumstances creates our future circumstances accordingly. My present event will remain on my conveyor belt of time only as long as I continue to give it mind energy. Nothing in time or space is permanent. No relationship is permanent. All relationships of any kind (mate, child, parent, boss, or friend) are dissolved in time by separation or death. It doesn't matter if the relationship is harmonious or inharmonious, the attention and energy I give it will keep it suspended in time and space for my experiencing. *When I turn my attention away from it, it will dissolve for lack of sustenance. This is the secret of Mastery.*

Living in the NOW Space

As it is with time, so it is with space. Space might be called "solidified time." We are constantly building our world by our responses in the NOW. The objectified NOW world of our senses is the result of past thinking and decisions. Time will bring into the outer manifestation what appears to be a solidified creation for our experience.

Even in space, the NOW is the only place that exists for you. If you live in New York, as far as your NOW experience is concerned there is no such place as Los Angeles. Why are you living in New York? You are living there because your past decisions have placed you or are keeping you there.

If you had made a decision to go to Los Angeles, your conveyor belt of time would have manifested a *space* known as Los Angeles for your experiencing. The inner Soul awareness would have been as objective about the experience of location in space as it is about the experience of location in time. Only the NOW exists to the inner Soul awareness; your conscious and subconscious reactions to the NOW experience create further experiences in both time and space.

Release from your consciousness all concern about anything except the NOW moment and the NOW space, and you automatically transcend the time/space barrier. You are no longer bound by either of these non-entities. Release all anxiety about past and future, and you can see all events in both past and future. You are no longer trapped within the physical body but become one with Universal Mind. You have access to, or contact with, All-Knowledge.

This awareness of being in the All-Knowledge lets you receive information that seemingly does not come from any empirical source. The technique is so simple it is difficult. We have to practice and practice to recondition our relationship to Soul Consciousness in order to do that which should come naturally and easily.

I have already discussed the principle of exploring external senses in order to become more acutely aware of internal sensing. This is the same technique used to understand time and space. When you can truly focus attention on the NOW moment and fully understand its concept, then expanding into non-time and non-space is both subjectively and objectively possible.

Space, like time, is fluid. That which seems to be solid today will, a hundred years from now (or even tomorrow), no longer exist. *Both time and space are subject to the laws (or influence) of the Mind.*

Awareness is one key, objectivity is another. The secret of using your six senses is simply being aware that this source of knowledge exists, and that we have shut ourselves off from it by having uptight emotions, apprehension, and anxiety, so that we have not been able to relate to life in a relaxed (objective) manner.

As it is with you, so it is with others, whether they are aware of it or not. All people build their own world according to their beliefs about themselves, and their thoughts and reactions to the NOW time and space.

If another's world happens to coincide with yours, it is because you have a similar creative consciousness. There is a "sameness" about you and your reactions to life. You can live in the same town as or even next door to another person for years and years and never meet, because the only sameness about your two consciousnesses is that you have chosen a close location in space for your physical bodies to reside.

"Sameness" of consciousness can create a harmonious or inharmonious relationship, or even one of indifference. Nothing can come back to us that we have not projected, as hard as that may be to accept. Changing your NOW response to any negative relationship will either cause the relationship to change to one of harmony or to dissolve. Dissimilar consciousnesses cannot reside together.

In our particular place in time and space—i.e., physical plane, planet Earth, twentieth century—we are subject to physical, mental, and emotional laws which constitute the Creative Laws of this region of God's great creation. We have chosen to experience this level of creation in order to understand and master the laws of this plane.

When we have accomplished this purpose, then in our long journey through eternity we will similarly experience other planes or levels of awareness. "In my Father's house are many mansions," Jesus said (John 14:2). Our present purpose is to understand and rule over the level (mansion) where we are.

Prophecy

My definition of *prophecy* is a foreseen or revealed result of a present course of action. Change the present course of action and you change the prophecy. When you have learned to transcend time and can see events taking shape in the future, your understanding of the conveyor belt effect can help you rechannel the causes of that event.

Our NOW attitude towards NOW events creates future action which eventually becomes NOW experience. Changing our NOW attitude will change future events. This can be done in the Alpha level of the brain, by replacing inharmonious thoughts with loving, releasing thoughts. A NOW attitude of loving harmony toward any situation will re-create that situation into one of loving harmony, *or* the situation will dissolve to be replaced by one that will conform to the mold presented.

A Technique for Seeing into the Future

Here is an exercise that allows you to bring the future into focus in the NOW moment, so that your conscious mind can make a proper evaluation to either anticipate or prepare for that which you see coming to pass.

Allow your body to become relaxed, keeping the spine straight. Focus your attention in the "I AM" part of you. When you feel completely relaxed, direct your attention to the chosen point-in-time in the future. Review what you know or expect to happen on that day. Allow your mind to be receptive to any image or thought that arises in response to that time. Record in your journal what you "see," "feel," or "sense." Practicing will encourage results to come to you, and soon they will be very reliable.

Use this technique to scan the day ahead before rising in the morning. This is an exceptionally good time for this, while your brain is quiet from sleep and you are still in the Alpha state. You are more open and receptive, and important insights can come to you, giving you guidelines to direct your workday. You can scan the whole week or month ahead in the same way, moving along one day at a time until you have covered the entire time desired.

You can use this technique to project ahead on a planned trip to see if the journey will be enjoyable and without incident, or if there might arise some problem for which you should be prepared; or you can just let your thoughts roam, picking up whatever seems to be happening anywhere. Always record what you receive. Writing it down impresses on the subconscious that you are serious in your desire to know.

One word of caution: Don't *expect* problems, dangers, or disasters. Expectation will create that which you expect. You are simply looking ahead for the outcome of a present course of action. If that action seems to be heading toward trouble, then, as master of the situation, you can take proper steps to change or alleviate it.

Go on your mental excursions in the same way you would check the weather outside. If it is sunny, you dress accordingly; if it is stormy, you don't dress for warm weather. But in checking the weather, you neither *expect* sunshine or storm, you merely accept what is.

A psychic reader must be responsible and take care how a precognition is worded to a client. One psychic, reading from the emanations of a client, saw an accident in the immediate future. He could have said, "I see an accident about to happen," thereby making it seem foreordained, leaving the client apprehensive and worried. By adding his client's fears to his own vision, his very words may have solidified Substance so that the accident would, in fact, have been unavoidable. Instead, he said, "On your way home, watch out for a driver who may not be watching out for you."

When the client got home, she telephoned back immediately and reported that just as she was entering the freeway an on-coming vehicle unexpectedly changed lanes, and if his advice had not alerted her there would indeed have been an accident. Being aware ahead of time, she changed her course of action and averted a tragedy.

A Technique for Overcoming Space Barriers

You can use a similar technique to *know*, without empirical data, what is happening at any other place in space. Being one with the Universal Mind, you can project into any place that Mind is, as long as your need or right to know does not violate another's privacy. You can even overcome the privacy barrier if you *will* it strongly enough, but to do so sets up reverberations in your own environment that cause inharmonious reactions. (Remember the boomerang effect!)

Relax your body, keeping the spine straight. Center on the "I AM" part of you. When completely relaxed, direct your atten-tion to any other person or place. At first choose only persons or places with which you are familiar. Later you may find you are successful even with unfamiliar persons and places.

In a passive state, allow a setting to create itself around the person or place you are considering. Make a mental note of what you see—actions, colors, events, impressions, thoughts, whatever comes. Later, write down what you receive. With prac-tice you can truly be "one in Spirit" with any loved one any-where.

You can practice "seeing around corners." When the telephone or doorbell rings, try to decide before answering who is calling. If someone unseen is approaching, try to determine who it may be. Use all of your extended senses whenever possible. Known odors, sounds, movements can be used to good advantage in extending the pickup value of your present senses.

These exercises will develop your clairvoyant abilities and will be fun besides. Enjoy your newfound senses, but rule them, don't let them rule you. You are the master of your life, and that means you are also master of the tools you use to enjoy life. To keep yourself well-balanced, participate joyously in the physical world around you, so that the trinity of Mind, Body, and Soul will grow in proper perspective. Keep in mind, however, that the "I AM" part of you is the ruling agent.

Following Your Hunches

As our consciousness learns to transcend time and space, we begin to become aware of a larger *knowingness*, which reflects itself in insights, intuition, impressions, dreams, or even visions. At first this *knowingness* is very nebulous, a hunch, a fleeting impression. If we are not alert we may pass it by and not recognize it as a bonafide awareness until it is too late to act. Gradually, however, as we *listen* to the thoughts that pass through our mind we learn to act upon these fleeting awarenesses and they become stronger, more sure, more reliable.

Sometimes, when acting on a hunch, it seems that nothing happens. Perhaps, however, you averted something that might have happened if you hadn't followed your hunch. I have two ways I can come to my home from a nearby shopping center. Out of habit, I usually follow Route A. One day I had a strong hunch to take Route B but ignored it and took my usual route. I soon ran into a congested traffic situation which I would have avoided if I had followed my hunch. However, I would never have known *why* I had been sent in the other direction.

You may get some startling results. One day I followed a hunch to stop at a different service station than the one I normally use. The station manager was going out of business and gave me a complete dinnerware service to get rid of his stock, when his usual practice was to give one piece of dinnerware for each purchase of gasoline. (This, of course, was before the energy crisis, when service stations were still giving premiums to attract customers.)

You can train your subconscious mind and convince it that you really want to be guided by your extended sense perception by following your hunches every time you get such a flash. You should continue to do this even if nothing seems to happen. Every time you follow a hunch, whether or not it brings visible results, you strengthen the response mechanism from the Theta level of the brain, so that it will bring back more and more reliable data to you.

Symbology vs. Conscious Contact

In training you to be conscious of this inner-mind awareness, some metaphysical schools teach you to look for symbols arising from the subconscious, in much the same manner as dreams. Then you have to learn to interpret the symbols. (For instance, a tree might always represent money to one person's subconscious mind, or a car might represent a trip.)

I am inclined to believe this is the hard way to do it. You may, at the beginning, get symbols. I did, but I think that is because my teacher taught me to expect them. Consequently, it took me many years of hard, determined work to overcome the "symbol syndrome." There is always the possibility of misinterpreting the symbols, thereby getting or giving false information.

So I tell my students to demand straightforward answers or directions from their inner mind. These should come as clearly imaged or spoken concepts or ideas, something to relate to, not just symbols. If you do get symbols, then ask for an immediate translation and don't be content without it. If none is forthcoming, reject the symbol as inconsequential. After all, the meaning of the symbol must come from the same source that provided it, the inner mind. Why not go directly to the meaning and bypass the symbol? You can and should get direct messages from both the subconscious and superconscious levels of the mind.

For the sake of argument, the idea of "symbol" can be expanded to include words themselves as being "symbols" of the concepts they portray. And, as we broaden those concepts, we'll also recognize that people, events, and circumstances are "symbols" of the creative processes going on in the inner mind.

One could debate the philosophical concept of symbols and their value interminably. The point I'm trying to make is that mental translation of internal messages should come so simultaneously with the concept projected that the intent of the message is immediately clear. It should not be necessary to struggle for clarification. All that said, there will still be enough information coming through that is ambiguous and subject to different types of interpretation to keep you pondering for a long, long time.

Don't be afraid to explore old concepts, as well as being open and receptive to new ones. Old beliefs about yourself and your environment are creating your present situations. A new affirmation, more in keeping with what you want your life to be like, can bring up for your attention the old conflicting memories, concepts, and beliefs to be reevaluated.

It is a mistake to repress an unwanted thought. Instead, examine it. See where it came from, where it leads. What has it done for you? Against you? Is it your own, or one that someone else has forced upon you which up to this time you have accepted without question? Many of our most cherished beliefs were the beliefs of our parents, trusted teachers, or other authority figures. Now we need to know if they measure up to the new, expanded ideas about life that we are exploring.

Only after you have thoroughly examined an old belief can you safely say, "I no longer find you a valid concept in my life, because I no longer need to play that role." Then you can dismiss the thought and its effect in your life, and allow it to dissolve. Repressing or ignoring an unwanted negative attitude only buries it deeper in the subconscious, where it remains an active, creative force.

Relax the rigidity of present concepts, even those that you feel are still positive and useful to you. It isn't necessarily the last word because your minister, your professor, or a scientist says it is so. Revealed truth is always changing, expanding, evolving, growing. What was thought true yesterday may have a whole new face tomorrow. *Expect* the new, the unexpected.

Remember, you are unique, different from every other expression of Life anywhere in the Universe. What is Truth for another may not necessarily be Truth for you. What is Truth for you may not be Truth for another.

We are all working out our own destiny through life, and we must learn to tune into the Soul Self, which has our own personal plan for God-Expression on our own unique path. Understanding this, you release those you love to find and accept their Higher Beingness, and you also release yourself to accept exciting new things that will flow in more freely on your own conveyor belt of time.

The Universal Mind

Everything, manifest as well as unmanifest, is contained within itself. This is expressed in the Law of Cycles. Everything that goes out must come back to its starting point. This applies to the seasons of the year, the circulatory and respiratory systems of the human body, the solar system—the action and reaction of any part of the macrocosm and the microcosm. Even the rhythms of our lives ebb and flow.

In its journey through Eternity, the Soul leaves its emanating point from God, begins its long *in*-volution into matter, and after aeons of time in which it experiences and experiments with everything in all levels of creation, gradually starts its long *e*-volution back to oneness with God again, bringing with it all the individual experiences that it has known, reacted to, and interacted with. The cyclic Law of Cause and Effect acts as an umbilical cord to keep us attached to our Creator, just as the same Law brings our own creations back to us.

Our Free Will is the right to use the Creative Force in any way we choose. Our personal experiences are the result of trial and error in using that free will, for, as we have learned, everything we send out from our creative minds forms the world around us, including the people, situations, and events in which our lives are focused.

Our thoughts give us the ways and means. What we send out comes back in the cycles of life. If we send out hatred, or any injurious thought to or about another, we will get the same formula back, perhaps at a time when we have forgotten completely about the originating thought.

If we send out love, can we get back hate? No, because if you don't send out hate, it can't come back to you. It can be sent your way, but it can't enter into your world unless there is a corresponding thought to open the door and let it in.

People who don't understand what you are doing, or are envious or threatened by your responses to your world, can hate you for what they think you are doing. That is their problem, to be solved by them in their own world. You can't be touched or harmed by it if there has been no answering thought from your own creative mind.

Every thought we think is a prayer. In essence we are asking God to return to us whatever emotion or thought-form we are entertaining, and that is exactly what happens. The thought-form and/or emotional reaction that occupies the NOW moment in our mind creates future events to correspond with its essence. When we have convinced the subconscious mind that we really want to be guided by inner perception, we find ourselves making automatic actions that put us in the right place at the right time.

Leonard D. had a very rare and painful fungus on his foot. He had been to the best doctors and clinics in the country and none of them had been able to find a cure. He had an understanding of Universal Mind, so he said to himself, "A problem cannot exist without its corresponding solution, therefore the Universal Mind can find the answer for me." He asked for help from the Universal Source and left the solution completely in God's hands, knowing that the right person or persons would come into his life to bring him the perfect health he asked for.

More than six months went by with no change in the status of his disease, except that the doctors found a substance that would hold the spread of the fungus in check. One day, Leonard stopped into a small café for a meal and slid onto a stool at the counter beside another customer. He began, in a companionable way, to talk to the stranger, and soon found himself telling about his problem, although he hadn't mentioned it to anyone for several months.

It so happened that the stranger had just returned from several years in Africa where the disease was more commonly known, and he also knew the cure! Coincidence? Not at all! It took our friend more than six months to discover the solution to his problem because the man who knew the answer was more than halfway around the world, and it took that long to bring him to Leonard's space-in-time. But when he was near, Leonard's superconscious so directed the movements of the two men that a meeting was arranged in a manner that, on the surface, would appear to be completely coincidental. In such a situation, anyone who is consciously working with Universal Mind can always retrace the steps that led up to any outward manifestation.

The Alpha and Theta levels of the mind and brain can be reached through discipline of the thinking processes, but learning to reach at will into the superconsciousness requires changes in our mental and emotional concepts of living and understanding, and even, sometimes, expansions in the religious and philosophical concepts by which we govern our lives.

We have heard our elders and church leaders saying, "Vengeance is Mine, saith the Lord" (Romans 12:19). Yet most of the time we try to take on this responsibility ourselves, even though there is a strict admonition in the same chapter of Romans to return good for evil to our enemies.

The original Hebrew word which has been translated "Lord" was also used interchangeably for the word "Law." Now, remembering that whatever we send out comes back to us in full measure, let's reconsider this passage, substituting the word Law for Lord. Does this not give us a new concept to consider? The Lord *(Law)* of His Own Being will repay your enemy, or anyone who treats you unjustly. You don't need to even be concerned about it.

We might read other passages from the Bible, exchanging the word Law for the word Lord, and find many different and expanded concepts of the old truths taught by Jesus and the prophets opening up for further reflection.

The Law of Cycles

The Law of Cycles relates to the Law of Karma, or the Law of Cause and Effect. Whatever you send out comes back. "Whatsoever a man soweth, that shall he also reap" (Gal. 6:7). Don't be concerned with your neighbors' lack of understanding. Their experiences will change that in their own journeys through Eternity. We need to be concerned about our *own* understanding and progress.

Return good for evil, send out love instead of hate. *Don't* even think, triumphantly: "Boy! Is he going to get his just desserts!" This is still using the Law of Return adversely, and this, too, will come back to you.

The easiest way to handle a negative situation brought about by someone else's action is to leave him to the results of his action. Let him *Be* whatever he is. His reactions, responses, frustrations, or creations—either external or internal—are *his* problem, not yours, or mine. The only part of the situation that is ours to deal with is our own reaction or response. Beyond that we have no spiritual responsibility.

Our reactions may be negative or positive, joyful or sorrowful, sympathetic or distant, understanding or distrustful—it matters not. We, and we alone, must deal with the results of *how* we react.

A cause creates an effect, which in turn becomes a cause which creates a new effect, which in turn becomes a new cause, ad infinitum. The only way to break the cause and effect chain is to monitor the causes which go out from us and to break the reaction effects within ourselves. If you refuse to fight with someone, there is no way the fight can continue. The cycle has been broken. If that person's desire is still to fight, they must find someone else who will be accommodating.

This attitude will free you from negative emotional involvement with other people and their pettinesses. Nothing is to be gained by perpetuating a negative cycle. Dominion over our personal world is rightfully ours, but no master can rule without taking up the scepter—the discipline—and the responsibility that goes with it.

Let us trace the action of a negative thought-form as it goes out into the world we have created and brings its manifestation back into our lives.

Consider three hypothetical people, all part of the Universal Mind Substance and all linked together by a common level of evolvement (or involvement, as the case may be). We'll call our trio John, Al, and Betsy.

John woke up one morning feeling at odds with his world. The paper wasn't delivered, the milk for his cereal was sour, his wife was grumpy and preoccupied, the kids made too much noise, and in general nothing went right for him.

John's reaction to the whole miserable situation was one of frustration and resentment. He left the house in a bitter, angry mood. Who wanted to go to work, anyway? Maybe he just wouldn't come back to such a bunch of lousy ingrates. They probably wouldn't even miss him. No one appreciated him; even his boss was tyrannical!

At this point, John is radiating negative thought-forms out into his environment in an impassioned way. These thought-forms, which are emotionally charged prayer-forms, are just asking for trouble. Subconsciously John feels he would really like to lick his weight in wildcats, if he could just find someone to oblige him.

At the service station, John meets Al and just grunts in response to Al's cheery, "Good morning!"

Now Al has run up against John's thought-forms, and he has a choice. He can let John's grumpy mood ruin his whole day by reacting to the surliness in a hurt or angry manner. If he does, he then takes on and becomes a part of John's problem. Or he can shrug off John's black thought-forms and refuse to allow them any headroom, so that they can find no lodging in his life.

Al decides to ignore John's pettiness and continues on his way, allowing only happy, positive thoughts to charge his day. Nothing John has done or said or thought will have any influence in Al's life because of his choice not to accept John's dubious psychic gifts.

The script now flashes to Betsy. Neither John nor Al have previously met Betsy. John's negative, emotionally charged thought-forms go out into Universal Mind and search for and congregate with other similar thoughts to add substance to the projected manifestation. The person who brings to pass the manifested thought-form is just as likely to be a stranger as not.

Betsy, too, arose rather out of sorts, but tries to put a good face on the circumstances of her life. She still hasn't made up with her friend Jim after the bitter quarrel they had last week, and Betsy decides they probably won't. There are plenty of other fish in the sea, she tells herself; nevertheless, she's feeling lonely, hurt, and rejected.

It's been a black week for Betsy, but today she feels resigned to the situation, although she's still not in control of her world. She leaves her apartment for work and, a few blocks later, she and John meet—in a head-on automobile collision.

Now, it doesn't matter who the law decides is the guilty party in this accident. Neither could have been there, in that place at that time, if there hadn't been corresponding thought-forms of anger, resentment, and frustration which drew the two of them together. Either one might have prevented the accident had he or she been more alert and less preoccupied with hurt and angry feelings.

≈   ≈   ≈

This illustration is, of course, very general. Many of life's little tragedies are much less obvious. Sometimes we need to really search our hearts and minds for the cause, but if we look with an honest will and a concerned desire, we can always find it.

≈   ≈   ≈

Now, let's take these same people and place them in another situation. This time the circumstances are happier ones, but they still present a problem, and John's mind is seeking a solution.

His wife, Pat, has just told him that their son, Fred, wants a bicycle for his birthday. John's income doesn't stretch far enough to cover many extras, but like other loving fathers, he wants his children to have the things they desire. So, using a better understanding of his contact with Universal Mind, he sends out a prayer-form to help him get a bicycle for Fred. He asks for help, then confidently leaves it in charge of his Superconscious Mind.

Betsy, in this little saga, is the friend of a coworker to whom John confides his problem. The friend knows that Betsy's son bought himself a new motorcycle a few months ago and might still have his old bicycle. She checks, and sure enough, the bicycle is gathering dust in the garage. Betsy is willing to sell it at a reduced price to get it out of the way. This time when John meets Betsy, the meeting is friendlier and both are benefited by the contact.

The Law, you see, is exactly the same in both stories. It works like a giant and efficient computer to search out persons with corresponding thought-forms and bring them together to manifest an outpicturing of whatever use has been made of it.

Tune to Your Own Superconscious Mind

It is this universal interpenetration of all Life that allows us to be in control of our own world, the master of our own creations. The Superconscious Mind, which has been called the "Christ Self" by some teachers, is our own particular link in this meshing together of thought-form with like thought-form, which allows us the possibility of extending our psychic awareness through such gifts as clairvoyance, precognition, psychometry, and other psychic talents.

That is why, again and again, I'll refer to your own personal attunement with the Superconscious. This is the ultimate goal towards which we all strive. When this attunement is made, the phenomena which you now consider supernatural, or supernormal, will manifest as a natural ability over which you will have much greater control.

So-called occult power, which I term psychic awareness, is not an end in itself. This ability comes from conscious attempts to use present capacities to their fullest extent. Everything you now do with the brain, such as walking, talking, seeing, listening, thinking, even abstract cogitation, is learned. All of these are Divine Gifts, but none of them came into this incarnation fully developed. You, as an individual, had to put your capacity-to-learn to use, and all that you are and do is a result of your efforts to use your capacity-to-learn.

Every occult or psychic "power" that you develop is a natural capacity of the brain and body. Practice, understanding, and conscious application are the tools you must use to develop these powers, in the same way you would develop any other skill of mind and body. A baby just learning to toddle couldn't break the world's broad-jump record, but the ability is inherent in its body; what is needed is practice, determination, and maturation.

As your understanding and discernment develop, you'll find something beyond the "power" itself. That something is the Soul: the Source of the power, the end toward which we struggle, the Superconscious Mind, the Soul Self. Finding shortcuts to the attainment of psychic awareness depends upon how well we fasten our thoughts on the attainment of the ultimate goal: attunement with our own Soul. It is the only source of guidance that will never steer you wrong.

Some teachers train their students to seek for guidance from spirit guides, Ouija boards, or other types of "outer forces." It would take a book in itself to chronicle the misinformation that I personally have witnessed from these kinds of channels. I will touch upon some of this in the lecture on Spirit Evolution (Week 6).

One cannot necessarily trust contacts with so-called spirit masters. Even a quick look around in the metaphysical world will turn up a large number of spirit-guided organizations. The head of one claims to be Jesus Christ reincarnated, several claim to be world messiahs, and two claim to be the same disciple reincarnated. Obviously they can't all be right!

Jesus said, "By their fruits ye shall know them" (Matt. 7:20), and wherever the orientation is toward self-aggrandizement or the gathering of "disciples," you may confidently expect to find other misinformation. When teachers become bigger or more important than their teachings, then beware of delusion and fantasy in their instruction.

Even Jesus felt that His teachings were greater than He was— "It is . . . the Father that dwelleth in me, He doeth the works . . . ." (John 14:10)—and he lived simply and unpretentiously, even though He had access to all the wealth and prestige He could wish for.

The channelling of "Masters" or spirit guides has become very popular among metaphysical students, but I think it should be brought to your attention that a large percentage of "channels" eventually develop erratic or irrational behavior, some ending up in mental institutions. The energies of discarnates are very different from the energies of physical bodies, and many physical and mental bodies cannot tolerate the interchange for extended periods of time.

It is also true that much information that is really needed is being received through some of these lines of communication, and those who give their bodies and minds to these entities could be considered "sacrificial souls," sacrificing their own rights for the sake of the greater good. But, unless you are very sure you were destined to be a "sacrificial soul," it is better not to become an unconscious channel.

Instead, study to become attuned to the "still, small voice within," the guidance of your own Soul. Follow your own hunches, flashes, and inner revelation. You will maintain control over your own consciousness, and the "still, small voice" will soon become your partner in living, accurately leading you through the labyrinth of propaganda, misconceptions, and misinformation which the conveyor belt of time carries through your world. You may walk beside these unenlightened mischief-makers, but you will not be touched or harmed by them in any way. You will be able to separate the wheat from the chaff, and those who proffer their knaveries will be known for what they are.

Workshop #3
Clairvoyance and Precognition:
Perception Beyond Time and Space

≈

Exercises which help to detect, define, or train clairvoyant or precognitive talents within you are excellent tools with which to develop your latent abilities to transcend time and space. Here are some easy, fairly well-known exercises you can try, or you might think up your own. Some of these are useful in a group study situation, some are good party games, and some can best be used in solitary practice sessions.

Don't be afraid to be wrong. The score, although important, should not be the focus of attention. What you are looking for are the inner signals from which you draw your conclusions. Sometimes a wrong score is simply a misinterpretation of a signal. Learning why you were wrong, or how the inner signal was misread, can be more productive and at least as important as correctly reading an inner signal which leads to a better "score."

In all these exercises, unemotional objectivity is essential. It is *not* important whether you win or lose. It is *not* important whether someone else has a higher or lower score. You are learning to use your mind powers, and competition, criticism, fear of failure, or even desire for reward or recognition will damage and distort the inner sensitivity. You are different from everyone else, and you will develop at our own pace, in your own way. You are pioneering new territory. Explore how you feel and what happens in your mind as you do these exercises. That is their only purpose.

Exercise #1: What's in the Box?[9]

Here is an example of clairvoyance, often used by Bevy Jaegers in public lectures as well as in group training.

Have someone fill a small cardboard box with several small objects of different kinds, sizes, shapes, and colors. The objects should be as different in composition as possible, e.g., rubber, plastic, metal, paper, cloth, etc. They should also differ in shape, such as round, long, flat, square, etc. Seal the box with tape or a rubber band.

When you are ready, close your eyes, take a deep breath, and let your mind quiet down to the Alpha level. Visualize or think about a blank screen somewhere in the frontal part of your head or in front of your eyes. Then ask yourself what items are in the box. Let sense impressions come to you. Try for the color, size, texture, shape, and "feel" of the objects. Usually, the first mind-clue that comes to you is the one to take, no matter how nearly imperceptible it is.

At first, you need not try for actual identification of the items. This will come later. Don't try to be too logical, or "guess" what might be in the box from what you know of the person who filled it or what you think might be easily available.

Write down any impression that might relate to the five senses. If you want to try for smell and taste, that's all right, too. After you have practiced and increased your accuracy with sense impressions, then try for identification of the objects. You might want to hold the box in your receiving hand.

Exercise #2: The Old Shell Game!

Use three coins or other small objects, such as marbles or poker chips, and twelve paper or plastic cups. Make three rows of four cups each. Have someone hide an object under one cup in each row. Use your extended senses to determine which cup covers the object, allowing one guess for each row. Repeat as many times as you wish. Each correct call is worth one point.

This is an excellent party game for small children, using pieces of candy or small toys. When the child chooses the right cup, he or she gets to keep the prize.

Exercise #3: Get That Number!

For this exercise use fifty bingo chips, slips of paper with the numbers 1 to 50 printed on them, or fifty chips from a Scrabble game, using letters instead of numbers. Place the slips (or chips) in a large jar or other container.

Write the numbers 1 to 15 in a column on a blank sheet of paper. Ask someone to pull fifteen numbers or letters at random from the jar. You are going to try to perceive in advance what those fifteen numbers are, so let your mind become as relaxed as possible, express the wish or desire to know what they will be, and then write down each number that comes to mind, in the order in which you perceive it. As the slips are pulled and read, check your accuracy.

Exercise #4: ESP Cards

ESP testing cards originated at the Parapsychology Laboratory of Duke University, in Durham, North Carolina. A special deck of twenty-five ESP cards was developed by Dr. J. B. Rhine, made up of pictures of geometric patterns in distinct shapes. There are five circles, five squares, five crosses (or plus signs), five with a wavy line pattern (of three lines), and five stars. These can be found at most metaphysical bookstores, but you can also make your own using small cards and a felt-tip marker. Make certain that the card material is heavy enough that no visible impression comes through to the reverse side. Since the oils used in many felt-tip markers have a penetrating quality, try crayon, charcoal or different varieties of paints instead.

(The Foundation for Research on the Nature of Man which now holds the copyright on these ESP cards refused to grant permission to reproduce illustrations of them, stating, "There is no good evidence that psychic ability can be trained, and we regard the tone of the text as misleading." Since I became much more aware of, and more in control of, my own psychic ability through conscious training, it is my personal opinion that this statement is debatable.)

ESP cards can be used to develop latent clairvoyance, precognition, and telepathic talents. Have someone "send" you the mental image, or turn the cards yourself, mentally recognizing ahead of time what the card will be.

Jot down the first image that appears in your mind, then later write down beside the recorded symbol what the actual card was. In this way you can also tell if you are receiving a large number of images ahead of time, i.e., writing them down just one turn before the card actually comes up. This is a good indication of prophetic ability.

Five correct readings out of twenty-five cards can be attributed to the laws of chance. Between eight and twelve correctly called cards indicates a better than average clairvoyance with good possibilities for easy training.

Gifted psychics fall into the category of fifteen or more correctly called cards. If you score within this range, you already have strong clairvoyant abilities and should pay close attention to impressions that you've only considered passing thoughts before. You could also proceed to more difficult self-tests, such as predicting the scores of ball games before they are played, or predicting when a future event might take place and its outcome.

≈   ≈   ≈

Bevy Jaegers reported some difficulty in using the Rhine ESP cards because of repeated right-hand angles between the cross and the square, which tended to confuse her students. So she invented her own. Bevy's cards use a wishbone, a six-pointed star, an oval, a square, and one jagged line, as illustrated:

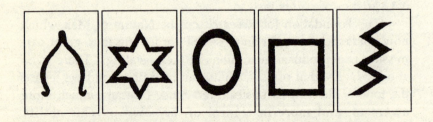

Figure 9. ESP Card Designs by Bevy Jaegers

These cards may be purchased directly from Aries Productions. (See Note 8.)

≈ ≈ ≈

Sheila Ostrander and Lynn Schroeder, in their *Handbook of Psi Discoveries*,[10] having tried out a great number of different combinations, came up with four other combinations of five symbols, which they called "tele-sets." In their experience, these worked best, with a minimum amount of psychic confusion.

Tele-set #1: Use the numbers 4, 5, 6, 7, 8.

Tele-set #2: Use the letters B, A, Z, O, W.

Tele-set #3: Use the colors red, yellow, blue, green, and purple.

Tele-set #4: Use the symbols Rain, Clover, Fish, Tree, and Crescent Moon.

Figure 10. ESP Card Designs by Sheila Ostrander and Lynn Schroeder

Ostrander and Schroeder suggest that you may want to cut the images out of black construction paper and place them in a "teleflasher," a box with a flashing light inside. They found that the rhythm of the flashing light around the symbol gave strength to the sender's thoughts and allowed the receiver to pick them up with greater accuracy. Dark symbols placed on the teleflasher screen will be highlighted by the light pulsing around them. Or you can draw the silhouette of the image on a piece of white paper and blacken the rest of the sheet, so that a light symbol flashes against a dark background.

A portable teleflasher can be made by using a battery-operated flasher lantern, a flashlight with a flasher switch, or an auto safety flasher unit, available at most automotive stores. Remove the red cover over the flasher unit and place the unit inside an opaque plastic box. Holes should be punched through the underside of the box to permit heat to escape.

Color cards can also be made, or you can put colored paper or tissue paper, or pieces of colored cloth, on the teleflasher lens. Colored plastic, colored celluloid, or colored glass may be cut into circles or squares and put in the center of the flasher so that the light pulses around them.

Exercise #5: Ace in the Hole[11]

Dr. Rhine also devised the use of playing cards to test for ESP abilities, but Bevy Jaegers expanded the concept into ideas for the training and development of ESP. At a time when few people believed that ESP existed, let alone that it could be developed, Bevy was busy training herself and others to recognize and enhance their own native abilities. Her mind was sharp and analytical, with the ability to make unconventional concepts easy to understand. With her permission, I have included in these workshops a large number of the exercises that she developed and which I found extraordinarily effective.

Shuffle a pack of cards, place it face down in front of you, and cut it into two reasonably equal piles. Now, think of a certain card, usually an ace since they are the most sharply defined, and try to decide which pile it is in.

Shuffle through the pile you did *not* choose. If the ace is *not* there, take the remaining pile and divide it again. Decide which pile you think the ace is in now. Look through the other pile. If it is not there, divide the remaining pile. Keep choosing and eliminating the pile the ace is *not* in, until you are down to two cards, one of which has to be the ace.

If you pick the right card, you have correctly and clairvoyantly chosen the right set of cards all the way. If you lose, anywhere along the way, start over, as you would in any game of solitaire. Practice enhances your clairvoyant abilities.

Exercise #6: Aces High

Remove the four aces from a deck of cards and lay them face up in front of you on a flat surface, about six inches apart. Shuffle the remaining forty-eight cards and place them one by one face down in front of the ace you believe matches the suit of the card in your hand. When all forty-eight cards have been placed, turn the piles up and record the number of hits.

This is not a guessing game. Do not be passive, but be dynamically involved with each card as it is taken from the pile. Wait each time for the inner signal, impulse, or intuitive feeling that will come before placing the card. Remember to follow the first thought that comes to mind. It is usually the best one.

Exercise #7: Tune Ahead!

While in the waiting area of an unfamiliar office, such as a doctor or lawyer, try to clairvoyantly visualize what his or her office will look like. When you enter, mentally verify what you perceived. Take advantage of any waiting moment to practice your mental skills.

Exercise #8: Practice Your Recall

To increase your mental acuity, practice your recall whenever you have a spare moment or lapse of activity during the day. In your mind, remember—as acutely as you can—taste and smell sensations or impressions, such as flowers, perfume, mints, vinegar, ammonia, sweet, sour, baking aromas, etc. Also remember sounds, such as music, the clock on the wall, crickets chirping, your pet's meow or bark, your loved one's voice. Practice, practice, practice constantly.

MEDITATION PRACTICE

Meditation is the art of remaining consciously, vividly self-aware from the objective "I AM" point-of-focus, with thoughts and emotions being separate or outside this Awareness.

Start your meditation with an infilling of the White Light to cleanse and purify. Remember to keep your spine straight in all meditation practices. Relax your mind to the Alpha level. For the next week, during your meditation time, observe your thoughts only, and see how they function. See how emotion rises in response to certain kinds of thoughts.

Quietly contemplate thought and emotion. Separate them in your consideration, and then allow both emotions and thoughts to float away without any mental response to either. Observe your thoughts objectively, without letting them make any demands on you.

Be aware that as your thoughts flow easily and freely, new ideas for a course of action and new solutions to old problems will arise. These will give you an emotional surge to get busy and put your new insights into action.

The purpose of this meditation is to discipline all mental, physical, and emotional activity so that you can complete fifteen to twenty minutes of *observation of the mental function*, like a supervisor taking time out to watch how well the employees are doing. This observation will give you the key to "problem solving" through meditation.

Finish with an infilling of the White Light for protection as you go forth into physical activity. Return slowly to Beta consciousness.

WEEK 4

≈

Life Is a Do-It-Yourself Project

The goals of the metaphysician are to transcend time and space and to be able to control events, instead of being controlled by them. When this has been accomplished, then we have truly mastered the material plane on which we live. In order to control events we need a firm understanding of the causes behind situations, people, and material manifestation.

Why are we tied to people who continually create inharmony around us? Why do we always seem to come out at the bottom of the heap in the situations in our lives? Why must we always drive secondhand cars instead of brand-new ones? Why do we remain in occupations that are never really fulfilling?

This isn't another monologue on "Think and Grow Rich." Thousands of words have been written on that subject. Our aim is to deal with the invisible, primal *Substance* behind the manifestations we experience in the world.

Our Personal World

When we consider time and space, we realize that our world, our space-in-time, is an illusion, created through a conglomerate of atoms drawn together into various manifested forms by our own desires—overt or subliminal—either consciously programmed or energized by deeply hidden motivations.

Our world (our *NOW* space) consists of that part of creation that we have awareness of through our six senses. We know intellectually that other aspects of this world exist, and that other embodied entities like ourselves create, re-create, shape, manipulate, and respond to similar or dissimilar aspects of manifested substance in their own individual space-in-time.

Although we know this because other people tell us about their experiences in their world, and we can relate to these because they are similar to our own, we cannot actually experience their experiences. We cannot feel their pain, nor thrill to their personal ecstasies.

We can have the experience of listening to the story of their activities and the experience of our own emotional reaction to that which is told us, but that is as far as we can go. Each person's experience is distinct. Our experiences are our own and can never be felt or known by another.

Even if two or more people share the same house and are part of the same family, still their worlds (or conglomerate experiences) are distinct, unique, and personal.

No matter how *much* other persons experience, if their experience does not touch us through one of the six senses—taste, touch, sight, hearing, smell, or telepathy—it *doesn't exist in our space-in-time*. Therefore the only thing that makes up our individual world of experience is that which can be perceived through the input of data from one or more of the six senses.

Now, if our inner beliefs corroborated that definition of reality, we would have no incentive to go beyond our own garden gate in search of other, newer sensations of experience. But the human Soul is innately aware that additional knowledge, other sensations, other experiences, lie just beyond its present limited perception and it continually seeks to expand its perceptional experience.

Therein lies the key. It is the *desire* to expand that brings about expansion. Before you can move out of your chair, or set foot out of your doorway, the wish to do so must precede the action. The constantly creating, ever evolving Mind activity is the guiding agent that brings about whatever experiences make up your world. Mind makes the decision to move the body with its sense perceptors into a new arena of action-response coordinates and—presto!—a new world of experience is created.

The Beta level of the brain, with its concentration of attention on the input of data from outside influences, is seldom aware of the chain of events and decisions that precede the manifestation of activity. People whose state of consciousness is concentrated only on what they see, hear, feel, etc., are very prone to blame circumstances, people, and events for the situations in their lives, unaware that a guiding portion of their self created the condition just for its own experiencing, whether the outcome is pleasant or unpleasant.

The Law of Manifestation

All that is in the outwardly externalized world, be it relationship, event, object, activity, or situation, is an *end-product*. It is a finished, completed product of Mind activity. As an end-product it is already on its way out of your world, and it will remain in your sphere of experience only as long as you feed it, nourish it, and give it sustenance by giving it your attention.

It is energized by your mind, held in place by your mind, and as long as your mind concentrates on it or thinks about it, it will continue to belong to your realm of experience. As soon as you turn your attention away from it and no longer give it the energy of your thought, it will die, or fade out of your space-in-time for lack of sustenance.

You can apply this Law to any activity in your life. Suppose you make the decision to move from Chicago to New Orleans. Your mind would then concentrate on ways to move your body with its sense perceptors to a space-in-time known as New Orleans, and if you kept your attention on the thought of moving, you would ultimately arrive in New Orleans.

Or, you may have activated a sequence of events which brought about the move seemingly against your Will, in which case you need to probe further back in your consciousness to find the motivating force which triggered the sequence of events. In either case, you'll find the original instigation was your own Will, which brought about the end-product—New Orleans—for your NOW experiencing.

Chicago NOW is no longer a part of your experiencing world, except perhaps in emotional ties to loved ones and companions, or in memories or reflections of past events. Chicago does not exist in the present to you. New Orleans does. And New Orleans will continue to exist for you as long as you find interest in exploring the experiences to be had in the space known as New Orleans. When there is no further interest in New Orleans, or there is greater interest someplace else, you will move your body to a new space.

The word "interest," of course, implies both negative and positive applications of its effects. Frustration, hurt, impatience toward one's space-in-time is attention centered with negative application. Love, excitement, enthusiasm for a person, place, or event is a positive application. Both will hold your attention on the manifested end-product.

Relationships and situations in your life are also end-products and will remain in your world only as long as there is interest and attention centered on that person or circumstance. Change the focus of your attention, and the person or condition will also change.

You can move out of a situation or relationship by the simple expedient of moving your body to another space, or you can change the relationship or situation by instigating a new mental and emotional response to it. Either one is within your power to achieve through understanding how the Soul creates experiences for you. Changing your emotional response to a situation is one of the steps of creating a new kind of experience out of an old one. Your new emotional response is a new experience, bringing new sensations, and the external manifestation changes accordingly.

Every person is brought into your life through your desire and for your benefit. Of course, the same Law applies to the other person, so that you are in their life for their benefit, too. The Universal Mind brought you together for your mutual benefit and mutual experience, because your attitudes and beliefs about life complement each other. This may be harmonious or inharmonious, but you interact with each other as long as both minds remain within the same framework of attention.

With each person in your life, you must learn something, receive something, or give something. When that something is satisfied, then attention changes, and that person or circumstance moves out of your experience.

The Law of Substance

To understand the Law of Manifestation, we must understand what Substance is. "Substance" comes from the Latin word *sub-stare*, which literally means to "stand under." Substance is *not* material manifestation; it is what stands behind the aggregation of atoms which form the manifestation.

Manifestations may range in quality from the invisible, such as certain gases, ether, air, color, and sound vibrations, to the densest metal or mineral component. Manifestation may be natural (God-created) or synthetic (man-made) but these are end-products. They are not the originating cause.

All manifestations are in a state of flux, constantly changing, dissolving, dissipating, and realigning into new forms according to the strength of force of whatever causal elements are focused upon them.

Substance is an element that is influenced by the mental and emotional vibrations of the individual. Substance is, literally, the *Idea* behind the manifestation, a kind of prototype from which can come an unending number of actualities for your experience.

Let's consider a chair. What kind of substance stands behind a chair? Within the Universal Mind is a prototype of something we might call "chairness," which can result in an infinite variety of chairs.

To find out what kind of Substance generates chairs, we'll have to first seek the Idea behind a chair. What is it used for? What is its purpose and what is its ultimate destiny? We can say that the basic idea of "chairness" is functional, something for comfort and utility, something to sit on, which can also be made ornamental.

There are, however, big chairs, little chairs, high chairs, low chairs, wooden chairs, metal chairs, folding chairs, overstuffed chairs, rocking chairs, swivel chairs, benches, footstools, and thrones —in fact, as many different kinds of chairs as there are people who use them. An endless diversity of materials can be used or combined to create a functional object, such as a chair, from Universal Substance (the Idea, or "chairness" behind the end-product).

The final manifested product, the chair, has served many minds. The original creator, or inventor, used Substance to *dream up* the design of that particular chair. The manufacturer used Substance to *find* the right kind of materials, and *locate* the person, or persons, who would sell it. The supplier of the materials and the seller of the chair used Substance to *find* a buyer for their products. You, the buyer of the chair, used Substance to *find* and *purchase* exactly the right kind of chair for your needs.

The Idea of "chair" is part of the Universal Mind Stream, and it moves from mind to mind to touch and benefit all who come in contact with it. As long as the atoms of the chair remain in that form, the chair will continue to serve all who use it, regardless of how many "owners" it may have.

Atoms, once solidified into a manifestation such as a chair, can rarely be changed very much. They may be modified, decorated, and sometimes re-shaped, but the solid form appears to remain static for awhile.

However, appearances are deceptive. In actuality, at the moment of coalescing, atoms immediately start to disintegrate. A metal chair may seem to last for perhaps a dozen years, or maybe longer, but rust, use, and abuse ultimately cause the atoms to dissolve back into the Substance from which they came, so that eventually there is no trace of the original form.

Have you noticed that a house that is deserted will fall into decay in just a very short time, while one that is lived in will maintain its livability for many, many more years, even without much attention to repair? That's because the energizing attention given by those who believe and visualize that this is their home maintains the flow of Substance into that structure, and the atoms remain in place, creating for the inhabitants the experience of a home.

And so it is with all manifestations on this level of existence. Even mountains eventually erode down into the plains. It is important to comprehend this so that we may have a proper perspective on the solidified objects around us.

The Soul aspect of ourselves, which views these things objectively, knows that no solidified object is permanent. It should remain in our lives only so long as it is useful or gives us pleasure. If and when it is removed from our lives, either through disintegration (wearing out) or by physical removal, it should be allowed to go without regret. Substance can create an unlimited number of other objects for our enjoyment and utilization. All we need is to know how to master the use of Substance to either replace a lost object or bring into our experience a new or different one.

Situations and relationships are also created out of Substance. The Substance of a relationship can be determined by seeking the Idea behind it. What do you get out of this relationship? What have you to learn, give, or receive? What emotional attachments, pleasant or unpleasant, are found in this experience? What would you like to change? What *new* experience would you prefer in place of it?

Substance is fluid. It is held in place by the power of your attention until or unless you create a new manifestation. Your thought process is the mold into which Substance pours physical or emotional atoms to create a solidified object or a relationship. Keep your mind on the problem—an old car about to break down, a state of poverty, or an unhappy relationship—and the power of your attention will continue to pour Substance into the manifestation you are contemplating.

The Illusion of External Manifestation

The ancient Mystery religions state that the external world is an illusion, and we are bound to that illusion by the concentration or focus of our attention. In other words, the average person can't see beyond his nose! He's hypnotized by that which is happening around him and believes he is the victim of circumstances.

We who are achieving dominion, however, have another story to tell! Recognizing that all manifestation is an end-product, all we have to do is to turn our mental and emotional attention away from that which is finished and with mind and heart begin to create a new product out of the eternal Substance which flows freely to fulfill our desires!

Another way to state this is that the Idea behind an object, situation, or relationship is whatever our personal experience with it is. We may be able to control the external manifestation only to a limited degree, but we can become in complete control of the quality of our experience, and to a large extent, even the characteristics of it.

Non-attachment is the key. Withdraw the emotional pipeline into a conflict, and the conflict cannot continue. Give thanks for all the good things in your life and, through the power of your attention on the things that make you happy, you will multiply them beyond all expectations.

Happiness breeds happiness, sorrow breeds sorrow, and conflict breeds more conflict. Make your life what you want by Being what you want to Be and Substance will flow into manifestation exactly as you have desired it!

A "Problem" Is an "Opportunity"

All "problems" should be viewed as "opportunities" to put to use your newfound understanding of how to re-create your life. The more attention given the difficulty, the more difficult it becomes, so in meditation and contemplation look for the solution not at the problem.

Each time you find a solution and apply it, you become stronger and more sure of yourself. Every negative force in your life can be made to produce positive results by using the Law of Substance. Knowing that all things are transitory helps to keep your attention on what you want rather than on what you don't want. "This, too, shall pass," is a good motto to keep in mind when dealing with inharmonious situations and people.

The "I AM" position of "Objective Watcher" is never so useful as when contemplating inharmonious conditions around you. In the first place, the objective attitude drains away emotional response, which is one of the avenues through which the situation feeds.

Secondly, being objective allows us to think more clearly about where we are in the NOW and what we want to program for the future. A negative emotion or attitude only muddies the waters and keeps us from making positive, constructive use of the "opportunity" to master our own Beingness.

Remember, also, that other people are in your life for your benefit. They bring you "opportunities" to master your temper, dissolve greed, become unselfish, learn to love, and control prejudice and all the other negative thought-forms that we've allowed to accumulate around us. We may drum a particular person out of our life by forceful action of some sort, but until we've mastered whatever inharmonious responses that person elicited from us, the Soul Self will continue to bring other people into our lives who will re-create the same condition in other times and places.

Counselors have discovered that divorce is rarely the answer to a bad marriage. Statistics show that, nine times out of ten, a person will turn around and marry the same set of problems in a different set of clothes. Until you change the response mechanism in you that thrives on that type of problem, the "opportunity" will return again and again. The value of adversity is that it points out areas in which we are not acting with mental and emotional discipline and balance.

There is an old saying, "No one is your enemy, no one is your friend, everyone is your teacher." Ask yourself what the other person has to gain from the inharmonious experience both of you are in. Remember, you are also in his life for his benefit. His Soul conjured you up out of Substance to create certain results for him, because you have the particular qualities needed to bring certain emotional reactions to his attention. Sometimes we can put a lid on our own response simply by recognizing that whatever is "bugging" him is *his* "problem." Often, when that insight is gained, we can help him understand his own problem and the whole situation dissolves.

One of the most difficult and complicated emotional reactions in my own life is my response to criticism, a response mechanism so entrenched that it has taken most of my energies and attention over my entire life to minimize it.

These experiences taught me many things. Because my own response to criticism was so extreme, I learned how to be tactful when I found it necessary to offer criticism to another. I also learned that, many times, given a proper understanding of the situation, criticism of another wasn't even necessary—the problem dissolved of its own accord. I learned to jump to the defense of the "underdog," to try to discover *why* someone acted as they did, and to present that alternative to others when their criticism reflected emotional reaction instead of reasoned response.

Finally, when enough "pluses" were added to my comprehension of the overall picture, I understood that when another criticizes me, that person is actually expressing a *personal problem*.

I am only the instrument through which they react to their environment in their own arena of experience. When reason comes to my aid, and there is no response from me, the situation dissolves for lack of energy.

Mastering the Use of Substance

Visualization, the use of thought-form as the mold through which energy flows, is only part of the process of mastering the use of Substance. Choosing the correct visualization is perhaps even more important. It has been said, with more truth than jest, "Be careful what you ask for—you might get it!" You can have anything you ask for, often to your sorrow if you haven't chosen carefully or wisely enough. So let us consider what we really want.

One day a woman called me on the phone and said, "I want you to give me a spell so that Joe will marry me!"

Flabbergasted, I replied, "Even if I knew a spell to make Joe marry you, I wouldn't use it, or give it to you to use."

"Why not?" she asked. "I love him very much. I would be a good wife to him, and I do want to marry him. Why won't you help me?"

"Because it isn't Joe you want to marry," I answered. "You have the cart before the horse. If you want to draw upon Substance, you have to search out the primal Idea behind your request. Do you not agree that what you primarily, basically want is someone to love and be loved by, someone with whom to share your life in companionship and empathy?"

"Of course," she agreed.

"Then Joe may or may not fit that picture. Only your Soul Self has access to that kind of understanding about another person. You can make Joe marry you, if you are determined enough, but if he turns out to be something other than what you *really* want from a man, you will suffer great disillusionment, and so will Joe, because you manipulated him into a marriage he didn't want."

"Then what should I do?" she asked.

"First, think about what you want your lifetime companion to be. Write down a list of all the qualities that turn you on about a man, from physical description to character attributes to lifetime goals. Give joyful and happy consideration to the fun times you will have together, and realize that your love can grow through the years into something greater than you can at this moment imagine.

"When you have done that, and *only* when you have done that, then every day in your meditation time, at the Alpha level, give sixty seconds—one minute is all that is required—to total and complete immersion into visualizing your ideal. Hold the picture without wavering in your mind for one minute, and it certainly will be fulfilled.

"Then, if Joe *is* the right man, if he can fulfill your dreams and you can fulfill his, he will ask you to marry him, and you will both be very happy. If not, he will fade out of your life, and you will meet someone else who *will* be all you've asked for.

"One word of caution. Don't hold Joe to this picture. Don't try to make him something he may not be. Be willing to allow him to come into your life, or to fade out of it, according to the will of the higher plan for your life. Be truly willing to release him, realizing that if he does go, someone infinitely better will take his place."

She did as was suggested. Within a week, Joe moved out of town, and thirty days later she met a man whom she married within the year. They complemented each other perfectly. When I met her again about two years later, she thanked me for making her wait until the right man came along.

"I didn't work the miracle," I replied. "It was your own right use of Substance that brought about the right realization of your desire."

How to Use Substance to Create a New Job

When you are using Substance to bring about your desires, expect the unexpected and be willing to allow it to flow easily through your life. Don't hang on to old thought-forms and emotional patterns. Joyously anticipate new things, new avenues, new places, and new people.

One woman whose husband was stuck in an unfulfilling job asked for help in getting them out of the rut their lives had become. Her first impulse was to ask universal Substance to give him a job as an advertising manager at a local department store where the pay and especially the prestige was greater. She believed in her husband and knew that he had the necessary qualifications, but all attempts to get the job were futile, even though both of them used visualization and scientific prayer for over a year.

"Whenever something doesn't come easy," I told her, "take another look at what you are asking for. It may not be right for you. Reconsider the Idea behind what you think you want, and clarify your position. Get your husband to write down what he *really* wants from a job. Prestige and a paycheck are only part of it. The work must be fulfilling and rewarding. He must feel that he is doing a service for others. He must feel worthy and of value to his community, and most of all, he must be true to himself and to the path of attainment his Soul Self would have him follow.

"When he has assessed what he wants from a job, have him write down what he has to offer. List all his qualifications and talents, and don't forget to include attributes that he may not now be using. For instance, his profession is writing, but he can also play the piano very well and isn't using that quality in his present occupation. It might open up another door for him.

"When you have really explored what you want from a job and what you have to give in return, then every day in your meditation time, at the Alpha level, hold the idea that there is a job somewhere in which he will be able to use his talents maximally, at very good pay, that will be rewarding and fulfilling for both of you, and that it will be offered to you immediately."

She did as directed, and six weeks later she came to me in tears. During their annual two-week vacation they had visited a cousin in a distant state. While there, her husband had been offered a job at a tremendous increase in pay, doing the work he loved, as promotion manager of a large music company. "But I don't want to leave my hometown," she wailed. "All my friends and family are here. How can I be happy somewhere else? I didn't intend for Universal Substance to take us out of town. Why couldn't he have found a job here?"

I pointed out that the Divine Plan of her life obviously had something important for both of them to experience, and that she should look forward joyously to the new experience. She was a good metaphysical student. It didn't take long for her to recognize that she was the only one who could block her good, and that the closed door at the local department store was a definite sign that something better was to be found elsewhere.

How to Use Substance to Change Relationships

Substance can be used for the healing of relationships in much the same manner. When two or more people are in an inharmonious situation, one or all of them are in the *wrong place*. If they were in the right place there would be only harmony and happiness.

So how do you handle the person in the wrong place? It's obvious from the Law of Cycles that you can't wish anyone ill or harm, no matter what they do to upset you, for that which you send to another always comes back to the sender. Neither can you go on forever turning the other cheek, or turning a deaf ear to barbs, for after a while even the hardest armor wears thin under perpetual attack.

Most of the inharmonies we live with are just petty annoyances which serve to bring us up short and cause us to re-evaluate our spiritual progress. We need to recognize that any situation in which we react emotionally is a signal that our own responses are not under control. However, some relationships in which we become entrapped can be severe enough that our jobs, our sanity, even our lives may be in jeopardy. The following technique will work whether the situation is petty or severe.

Instead of wishing your adversaries would fall down and break a leg—kick them upstairs! That's right! Wish for them everything they would wish for themselves, and do it with all the sincerity you can muster. If they had the things they wanted, they would be in the right, harmonious place, and they wouldn't be taking their frustrations out on you.

Is a promotion on the job your adversary's highest wish? Take that desire into your meditation time and give it all you've got! Unhappy in a marital situation? Visualize finding happiness, with or without the present partner. It's not up to you to decide if the marriage is to the right partner; all you want for this person is happiness. Let his or her own Soul Self determine how it is to be obtained.

By the Law of Cycles, whatever you wish for them will also come back to you. It may be you who gets the promotion, or desirable transfer to another place, but the end result is the same. The two of you are no longer creating friction, and that was the Idea in the first place!

It just might happen that the loving energy you are directing will change that former enemy into a friend. In which case it is the situation that has been changed and healed, and both of you are then in the right place, moving harmoniously together.

How to Use Substance to Handle Material Losses

By now you are beginning to understand the idea behind the use of Substance. When dealing with creative energies, bear in mind that qualities, characteristics, and whatever adds to personal experience are of more value in trying to assess what you want than the specific physical attributes of a material possession.

Suppose you had a priceless heirloom that had been in your family for generations, one that gave you great emotional pleasure to own. Then suppose this heirloom was lost through fire, flood, or theft. No amount of money could replace this treasured object, but also, no amount of money could take away from you the years of pleasure which its ownership afforded you.

Suppose the loss was caused by someone else through carelessness or theft. Are you feeling vindictive? Are you going to see that "he gets his," no matter what? Is prosecution of the culprit your most attention-consuming thought?

Hold it! Before you pursue that line of action further, ask yourself just what it will draw into *your* experience from the realm of Substance? Remember, the *Law* takes care of its own. No one gets away with anything, even if it seems so on the surface. Everything an individual sends out comes back sooner or later. That Law applies to you as well as the thief, and if vindictiveness is your *NOW* action, the return of that vindictiveness from someone else will be your future result.

Everything you have accumulated in the way of material possessions during this lifetime has come into your experience because your desires created it out of Substance. Whatever you've been able to gather for yourself in the past, you can duplicate that and more in the future, because now you know the secret of using Substance.

All physical things are transitory in nature. They move from owner to owner and from aggregation to disintegration. You'll save yourself many emotional scars if you don't let your possessions possess you. When they move on, out of your life, let them go, and confidently *expect* something new and better to take their place.

Here are two mental techniques to bring back objects that have been lost or misplaced. These techniques have worked even with stolen objects. They work more quickly if you eliminate as much of the emotional stress that accompanies such a loss as you can. Know that if the object really belongs to you, *no one* can keep it away from you.

The "Silver Lasso" Technique

Visualize a sparkling silver lasso in your mind, or a golden one, and send it out to loop over and draw tight around the lost object. See the magic lasso bringing the object back to you, and then visualize the object in your hand. Allow joy to surge up in you over the return of the object. If the object is nearby, you'll walk right to it in a very short time, amazed that you didn't see it before. If the object is farther away, it may take a longer time to retrieve it.

The "Where Would I Be?" Technique

A friend once told me that when his children were little they had a pet turtle which frequently crawled off and got lost. When they begged their father to find it, my friend would say, "Now, if I were a turtle, where would I be?" and invariably he'd walk to a patch of leaves, kick it around a bit, and locate the turtle.

He said it as joke to his children, but marveled at the uncanny accuracy with which he always found the turtle.

I recognized a Universal Law in the telling of the story. We are One with All That Is, One with Universal Substance. My friend had simply merged his consciousness with that aspect of creation which represented the turtle, and in the merging brought about reconciliation.

The Idea delighted me, and since that time, "Where would I be if . . . ?" has become a household phrase whenever something is lost or misplaced. "Where would I be if I were a ring . . . a set of car keys . . . a child's mitten?" Invariably, within a few minutes, the searcher goes directly to the place where the item lies.

How to Use Substance for Healing

Again, it's the Idea behind the request for healing that must prevail if you would tune into Unlimited Substance for healing yourself or another.

Bear in mind that broken bones and broken hearts are not so dissimilar. Frequently a physical distress signal is only a symptom of something much deeper and not so visible, an emotional distress that may not even be recognized by the sick person.

Insurance statistics show that eighty percent of accidents happen to twenty percent of the people. Members of the psychological and medical professions are beginning to understand that many illnesses and accidents are psychosomatic in origin and are often psychological distress signals.

You may use any technique or prayer formula that appeals to you. You may ask God for help, consult a psychic or spiritual healer, use your own affirmations for good health, or tune into the Universal Healing Stream in scientific prayer. All of these techniques will work miracles for the practitioner who understands that, whatever terminology is used, whatever sequence of mental activity is most effective for the individual, behind all requests lies the Idea of whole or complete healing for the patient.

Complete healing must include the causes as well as the symptoms of the ailment. If Aunt Harriet thinks that no one really cares about her and the only way she can get attention is to be ill, then no amount of prayer is going to effect a cure. Her illness is too necessary for her emotional well-being.

If Brother Charles can't cope with the pressures of business, and a well-deserved emotional breakdown is the only thing that will prevent the world from knowing that he has failed, then a breakdown is what he is going to have, and he will enjoy it thoroughly. Not only can no one blame him for failing in business, but the breakdown will be a huge success!

You can never successfully cure a symptom. I once knew an alcoholic who "successfully" stayed on the wagon for almost three years. He attended all the AA meetings and gave his time and effort to help other alcoholics. One day, he was found dead of an overdose of a drug which he had habitually used during those three years to create the "highs" so desirable to him.

Was he cured of alcoholism? I think not. He simply switched one set of crutches for another, ignoring the reason *why* he needed the highs in the first place.

When using Substance to heal yourself or another, keep in mind that the emotional *causes* of the illness or accident must also be healed, or the accident or illness will simply repeat itself— perhaps in another form, but nevertheless, it will be repeated.

Ask for and visualize the whole Being, including all seven bodies, joyously living a vital, enthusiastic, productive Life. You don't need to know what is disrupting that person's emotional health; that is between the person and his or her own Soul Self. You don't even have to know what the physical symptom is, but if you should be told, recognize the symptom as only an end-product, finished and already on its way to disintegration, out of one's life forever.

Visualize Light and Love and total health permeating that person's entire Being—mental, physical, and spiritual. See the energy of health flowing into every new cell that is forming in the body and encouraging them to grow as vital, healthy cells, doing whatever it is they are created to do in a vital, healthy way.

Keep in mind that the end-product you want is health, total and complete. Let Substance flow on its own path to bring about the visualized end-product. Remember that doctors and psychologists are God's channels of healing, also. Perhaps a special doctor with special knowledge and skills may be needed to bring about a complete cure. If that is so, Substance will find a way to bring that special doctor into the life of the patient and through that means bring about the complete cure you visualized. Whatever happens, however it happens, Substance is at work following the prototype you projected.

Spiritual Healing and a Lesson in Forgiveness

A spiritual revelation comes about as a sparking together of two related Ideas producing an expansion in consciousness that creates a whole new concept that had not been known before. Suddenly the impossible becomes possible. I want to share with you a process that produced two remarkable healings for me and led to a new revelation about the mechanics of spontaneous spiritual healing.

I'd planned to spend one Fourth of July weekend with friends from Kansas City, meeting at a resort city in southern Missouri, about 150 miles from my home in Little Rock. The days were hot and muggy, as southern July days can be, so I left late Friday afternoon after work, stopping about 10:30 P.M. at a campground to spend the night, relishing the refreshing coolness under the stars.

The next morning I showered and dressed in the campground bathhouse, but when I left the bath, I slipped on a mat and fell on the hard cement on my tailbone. The pain was excruciating! An X-ray from a local doctor confirmed a cracked bone. The doctor gave me pain medication and suggested I return home rather than continue with my plans for the weekend.

Understanding mind action, I knew that giving in to self-pity was the worst thing I could do to myself, and that even though my activities would be curtailed, spending the time with my friends would carry me through the week-end better than returning alone to my hot and stuffy apartment.

I relied heavily on the pain medication, while I thoroughly enjoyed being pampered and cared for by my friends, who gave me all the loving sympathy I could want. We were all metaphysical students, and we spent a lot of time trying to discover how I had brought this on myself. The whole weekend was fascinating, for I was the center of attention! If my subconscious had created pain so I could get some much needed attention, then it was an outstanding success!

I returned home Monday, driving carefully, getting out of the car often so I wouldn't get stiff from inactivity, and arriving home late that night. Pain medication had gotten me safely through the three-day holiday and the long drive home. Tuesday morning, however, brought a whole new realization. I was scheduled to teach an ESP class that night, and it was shockingly apparent to me that the Higher Mind contact I depended upon was impossible through the drug haze that blurred my mind. I could not continue to enjoy a broken tailbone and teach the class, too. My choices were clear. I could not have both!

I sat down in a comfortable overstuffed chair and went into meditation to achieve Soul Consciousness for guidance. In the "conversation" between myself and my Soul Self, I pointed out that if we were to continue to do the work that had been set for us, the body had to be healed. I spent the time visualizing a healing influence flowing from higher consciousness into the body, resulting in total health and freedom of activity. When I arose from the chair, my mind was clear and my body completely free from pain. I never took another pill, and I had no pain from that moment on. I had made a choice. I wanted to teach my class more than I wanted a broken tailbone! When that choice was made, I experienced an instantaneous healing.

Years later I found myself in a similar dilemma. I had grown spiritually through the years, striving constantly to upgrade my attunement with Soul-Consciousness, making it a reality in daily living, but always wanting more and closer association. I earned my Ph.D., moved from Arkansas to California, and in general felt pretty satisfied with life. Only one thing marred my consciousness.

Before embarking upon a metaphysical career, I had had a painful love affair which had left a disastrous emotional scar. Periodically through the years this man had appeared to me in dreams insisting that it was necessary to forgive him, but I stubbornly held on to the hurt, refusing ever to be vulnerable to love again.

I discovered rebirthing, a method of using the breath to release deep-seated emotional and physical traumas. One day, as I started my rebirthing session, my rebirther said, "You can have anything you want from this session." My soul replied within, "How would you like Light Consciousness?" I was thrilled! My inner reply was "Yes! Yes! I want that more than anything!" I went excitedly into the breathing to allow Light Consciousness to permeate my awareness.

Though I gave my whole attention to the accomplishment of this process, it seemed that the energies in my body went only as high as my neck and stopped there. I wondered if I was being "stiff-necked" about something, and at that moment the voice of my rebirther, which I had shut out, came through with the word "forgiveness." I don't know what else she was saying. I only heard that one word, but it was enough. I knew I had to forgive my past lover or I would never reach my goal. Desperately, I thought, "In this state of consciousness, it should be easy to forgive," and suddenly, the past no longer mattered! After twenty years of emotional pain it had been instantaneously healed! Once more I discovered that healing of body, mind, or soul comes when you want something else more than you want to cling to the old hurt.

This revelation is so profound that I feel no teaching is complete without it. Do you want to be instantaneously healed? Then want something else more than you want the old. Want total health and a pain-free existence more than you want the attention and freedom from responsibility that goes with illness and accident. Do you want Light Consciousness? Then want that more than you want the emotional traumas that keep Light Consciousness from you.

You may be embarked upon a week full of interesting work when a cold or flu germ threatens, and you say with determination, "I haven't time to be sick," going about your daily activities regardless. The cold or flu will diminish or go away altogether, because you didn't have the time to give energy to the thought of being ill.

You may come home tired from an exhausting day at work, thinking only of collapsing before the TV in robe and slippers, when someone suggests an exciting evening out. Suddenly you aren't tired anymore! The prospect of the new activity completely absorbs your mind energy, and you are infused with new creativity and interest.

You are the master of your life. Your mind will give you whatever you truly desire. I heard someone say, "Some people must have traumas, illness, or accidents in order to feel truly alive." Think about it. No one can diagnose your life for you. Are you secretly contented with what is happening in your life?

Even discontent can be absorbing, and will direct mind energies into more discontent. Choose an alternative to whatever is absorbing your mind energies at the moment, and so concentrate your attention on that image that your present place in time and space cannot coexist with the new ideal. That is the secret of instantaneous change.

You Are Power!

This is an excellent exercise to separate in your mind the functions of Soul and Personality.

Say, "I AM POWER. I AM POWER. I AM POWER . . . ."

Repeat this statement over and over until it becomes a realization, not just an affirmation. In doing this exercise, you are not merely trying to reprogram your subconscious mind. There is a special cognition for this statement.

Do not say or think, "I have power." You *are* power. It is not just a tool to be laid down or picked up.

Do not say or think, "I am powerful." That statement or thought only enhances the lower ego, and that is not what we are trying to do.

Say only the words, "I AM POWER." You are expressing a statement of Truth. All things from physical body to personal possessions to relationships are energy-in-manifestation. It takes power to move that energy around. You *are* that power, whether you realize it or not, whether you want it or not. You are, every day of your life, moving energy around to create the world you live in. When you repeat the statement, "I AM POWER," think in terms of actually being the power that creates the life you live, with its relationships, possessions, situations, and events.

Soon you will begin to understand that you really are the master of your circumstances, not the puppet. Then you will be able to exert control over the events and situations in your life, and do so harmoniously, without harm to others, who are also powering their own experiences—experiences that do not need to harm you or influence you in any way.

Keep down any idea or feeling of self-aggrandizement in repeating this statement. *Everyone* is power-in-manifestation. No one has more or less power. Each one only has more or less understanding of the dynamo within. The power remains the same. Remember, you are not seeking to show yourself better or worse than anyone else. Each individual is unique. All you are seeking to do is to open up your realization of the tremendous forces your Soul Self has at its disposal, which the outward consciousness of the Personality can tap into to manifest that uniqueness.

How to Use Substance to Bring Material Possessions into Your Life

Most techniques of visualization that you read about in books will work. It's usually a matter of finding the one that works best for you. If the Soul Self is in charge of our lives, we rarely lack for anything that we must have. Basic needs such as food, clothing, shelter, and love flow easily and naturally through our lives without much effort when we maintain awareness of the promptings of the Inner Voice directing and guiding us.

However, sometimes our "wants" outstrip our "needs." Then we can assert our mastery of Substance to bring the extras into our experience. Do remember to keep in mind that the Idea behind the realization of your desire is *all important*. It's not the object itself that you want, you want what the object represents to you in experience value.

EXAMPLE: You think you need a new car. A car is not a *need*, it is a *want*. There are plenty of alternatives to owning a car. There are buses, car pools, planes, trains, motorcycles, bicycles, and walking—any of which, under certain circumstances, might have distinct advantages over traveling in your own car.

The basic idea behind a car is "transportation," but then any of the above will also fit into that category. If we merely asked for a good means of transportation, someone might give us a book of coupons on the local transit system, and our request would be amply and adequately fulfilled.

So why is a car specifically desirable to you? Probing deeper, you might find that attributes such as ease, comfort, accessibility, economy, prestige, independence, and other qualitative experiences are the *real* reasons why, combined with the Idea of transportation, you want a car of your own. Now we have something definitive to work with.

(World energy problems have given us a new perspective on the automobile. Automobiles, as we know them, will undoubtedly fall victim to the tumultuous changes that are presently upsetting our planet. However, the Idea of transportation will always be at the forefront in the march of civilization, and the concepts presented here will still apply to whatever material form the Idea may take in the future.)

Emotional qualities trigger Substance into creativity. You'll get exactly what you want when you understand yourself sufficiently to deeply analyze what the object *means* to you and *why* you want to experience that particular manifestation.

EXAMPLE: Suppose you want a special set of furniture to decorate your home. The set you have in mind costs about $2,000. Should you visualize the money to buy the furniture? No. The *money* is not what you want. You want the *furniture*, or rather, you want *what the furniture represents to you as an experience.*

Strangely enough, asking for money often does not work with Substance. The basic Idea behind money is "a medium of exchange." For example, let's consider a $100 bill. You can't eat it, you can't wear it. You might put a frame around it and hang it up on the wall for whatever aesthetic value it would have for you, but in itself it has no value whatever. The emphasis is on a piece of paper that is really only an I.O.U. I have given $100 worth of labor or service, and now I wish to exchange it for $100 worth of someone else's labor or service. But on the current world market my labor or service may not be worth as much as someone else's labor or service.

In the realm of Substance there is no standard of how much anyone's labor is worth, and asking for money without the corresponding exchange of labor or other value counteracts the *purpose* of money as an exchange medium of something for something else. The request then results in a non-materialization, because you have nullified the Idea behind it.

You may build a financial empire by using Substance, but to do so you must comprehend the work that money must do and the responsibilities inherent in its use, rather than the money itself. You can build factories, churches, schools, give jobs to people, spread a philosophy, or educate the populace, but behind it all is the Idea of the *experience* of so doing. Money then is the avenue whereby your desire can be made to fulfill someone else's desire, but the end-product is still the only thing that Substance creates.

Concentrating on the money to fulfill your desire can short-circuit other channels through which it might come about. Maybe you'll win a new car, or the furniture you desire. Maybe it will come in some other way. Maybe money is what you'll get, but allow Substance to choose the method, the means, the channel, while you concentrate on the end-product, the experience you desire.

Paying bills usually requires money in hand, but not always, so don't limit Universal ability to give or to create. Visualize the bills paid—the end-product. See yourself receiving the receipts and feel the relief you'll experience knowing that you've fulfilled your obligations.

One time I desperately needed $300 to pay some overdue bills. At that time such an amount of money was completely out of reach, or so I thought. One evening I had an important letter which had to be mailed that day, but when I got to the small post office it was closed, and there were no stamp machines. I stood there wondering what to do, when a woman walked in and I was prompted to ask if she had a stamp in her purse. She did. I purchased it from her and mailed my letter.

On the way home, I was elated because the realization came pouring in that if God could provide so small a thing as a stamp, He could surely bring forth the $300 I needed, for both required a miracle. I relaxed, visualized the bills paid, and waited expectantly for the channels to open up. Sure enough, within the week, I made some unexpected sales and the money came in with which to pay the bills.

While you are waiting expectantly for the realization of your desire, be alert to small things that might be the "lead" you are seeking to the next step towards the attainment of your goal. God usually does not hand us our wishes on a silver platter. Our "work" entails listening for and then following the guidance given by the Soul Self.

We do not dictate the way in which our desire is to be ful-filled. Instead we cooperate consciously with any avenue of fulfill-ment that opens to our understanding, whether it be a "hunch" (that strong sense that we should follow a certain course of action);

a person who tells us of an opportunity wherein the goal might be furthered; or a book that gives us additional insight into our own ideal—the *reason* why we want this realized goal to be part of our experience.

In this way, opportunity does not pass us by while we sit idly dreaming of the wonderful things we think we want. The woman who provided the stamp was a "lead" into deeper realms of faith for me. To "pray without ceasing" means to be constantly aware that the next person you meet *may* be the channel through which your dream comes true. So watch for it and expect it to happen, even if it is only one small step at a time. Take that small step, then wait expectantly and confidently for the next one. It will come. In your program for prosperity, never turn down anything, large or small, new or used, tangible or intangible, that is lovingly offered to you, even if at the moment you think you can't use it. Giving and receiving constitutes the full cycle of prosperity and supply.

Jesus spoke fluently and frequently about prosperity and how to obtain it: "All that the Father hath is mine" (John 16:15); "It is *your* Father's good pleasure to give you the Kingdom" (Luke 12:32—emphasis is mine); "Seek ye *first* the Kingdom of God (the realm of the Inner Self), and His righteousness (right-use-ness; see "The Law of Righteousness," Week 5), and all these things will be given to you" (Matt. 6:33). These are a few of His statements which are very good seed thoughts for your meditation time when working on Substance to create material possessions.

An old adage says, "It is more blessed to give than to receive," but the concept is incomplete. First of all, how can we give if we have received nothing? If we have nothing to give, because we have received nothing, where is our channel for blessedness?

This idea also short-circuits receiving anything, since the adage implies that "receiving" is not blessed.

Thirdly, when we receive something, according to the axiom, we provide a blessing for the one who gives. But, most important, by receiving with gratitude we open up other channels of receiving the material good we seek. In accepting the gift we imply that we are open and receptive to the realm of Substance, where supply is limitless, and we can have all the things we need *or* want.

If the thing offered is useless to you for any reason, accept it anyway. Look around for someone who can use it, and you become a channel for someone else's good. If you reject something that is offered you, you block both the channel for someone else's giving and the channels for your own receiving. Give as you receive, and receive as you give—with love and graciousness.

Desire and Spiritual Progress

Buddha stated that desire itself is an archenemy to spiritual progress. As long as there is desire for anything—material objects, love, rewards, even for spiritual attainment—that desire will bind you to the Wheel of Return in order to receive that which you desire.

Yet to be completely desireless is to become a nonparticipator in the arena of life we came to explore. An author whose name I have forgotten, but whose thought opened up new vistas of understanding for me, wrote, "Desire *is* God's Will pushing to explore, to become, to experience."

Desire is the motivating force that keeps on stretching towards objectives. The desire to experience the goal—the end-product—is the method used by the Soul Self to teach us values. Through this the Soul acquires the perspective that comes with completed experiences.

Once something has been achieved, it becomes an enduring part of the Soul's record of its existence. To seek and to achieve is to grow in strength, love, and compassion—the Soul's way of acquiring necessary wisdom and enlightenment.

The human Spirit—the original Divine Spark—is only a prototype, a blueprint, as it were, an undeveloped Idea of the Creator's that needs to be filled in (full-filled) by the experiences that are undertaken by the entire Entity—Body, Mind and Soul. It matters not whether the experiences are good or bad, harmonious or inharmonious. Each experience undergone brings understanding with it, a learning of the consequences of both good and bad use of Cosmic Law, and it is this "experience-value" that is the criterion by which the Soul judges situations and relationships. To change a situation—to "master" it—we look for the good that could come out of it, the value of the experience to the Soul.

What is often lost sight of is that the goals themselves are a by-product of the need to experience. They are not as important to the Soul as is the *journey* that brings the goals into manifestation. It is the *process*—the way we handle our intellectual and emotional reaction to experiences; our attitudes—that teaches us the lessons to be learned and develops our sense of values. Our adventures along the way provide the basic ingredients that promote the growth of the Soul.

It's a matter of perspective. The detached, impersonal viewpoint of the "I AM" allows you to enjoy fully all the fruits of your creating while maintaining the ability to remove yourself emotionally and intellectually from any or all of them instantly, if needed.

This objective viewpoint also allows you to know when it is time to remove your attention from any phase of participation for the greater good of yourself and/or others. As long as you remain attached to the desire to achieve a particular accomplishment, you remain bound to the ultimate achievement of it by the focus of your attention.

The ability to detach whenever needed is the key to mastery in any situation, but the knowledge of *how* to detach comes when the Soul Self has enough information gathered from its prior experiences to accept personal responsibility for the conscious direction of its own Will.

Fantasy, Illusion, and Other Dangers

I have, up to now, stressed the cultivation of the higher aspects of psychic development while ignoring, in favor of the more positive approach, some of the pitfalls and dangers along the Path. Now it's time to look briefly at some of the illusions that can beset the unwary traveler, and ways in which they can be understood, recognized, and avoided.

1. Desire to Control Others or to Seek Dominion over Others

This ego drive can be very subtle and requires alertness to weed it out when it is found. It manifests in the psychic force as psychological manipulation of the energies and emotions of others. It can be found, for example, in the psychic readings of those who get a personal thrill from statements that shock, tantalize, or create sensationalism.

The purified Ego seeks only to help. It knows when to speak and when to withhold information that another Soul may not be ready to receive. Its most important aim is the uplifting enlightenment of the seeking companion on the Path.

2. Inflexibility of Thought

"Saved, sanctified, and solidified," a minister's wife once said to me, speaking of certain members of her congregation, who felt that all had been done for their salvation, that nothing more need be learned, sought, or achieved. Truth in all forms is growing, evolving, expanding, as the mind expands to become more aware of the limitless nature of knowledge and Cosmic principles.

Individuals who tie themselves to one doctrine, one interpretation of Cosmic Truth to the exclusion of others, tie their spiritual growth to a lame horse. However great the ideals, precepts, and enlightenment in any ideology, there is still more to be learned. No human channel through which spiritual tenets flow can, in one lifetime, express all that is to be learned from the limitless outflow of energized knowledge. Alice Bailey did her best with a prodigious output of thirty books, taken from telepathic dictation by her Tibetan teacher, and even these are subject to endless interpretation and application.

Beware the psychic who makes light of or puts down another's faith, actions, or beliefs. The Navajo Indians say, "Criticize no man until you have walked a mile in his moccasins." Be flexible in your acceptances, constantly striving to increase your own enlightenment and psychic insight. Nothing is the last word in any philosophy.

In great humility, respect the Light of understanding in whatever form it appears, even if it may contradict previously constructed concepts. The true Light never imprisons or blocks one in any way, but serves to broaden and enhance one's scope of understanding, field of service, and personal magnetism.

3. The Temptations of Ego

As our mental faculties develop, our minds become sharper, more penetrating, and more sensitive to the thoughts and emotions of others. These faculties usually appear slowly and are integrated slowly into the personality patterns, and it is this slowness which creates the greatest trap on the path of discipleship.

Aspirants, still involved in the activities of the materialistic world, use their growing mental and psychic abilities in self-pursuits that satisfy the needs of personality and social life. Activities are engaged in that nourish ambition and feed pride and vanity. The Inner Beingness becomes addicted to this type of desire and loses interest in directing energies in the path of aspiration to become the servant of humanity, or even the servant of loved ones.

Psychics who take this self-centered nature with them into esoteric pursuits use their faculties to satisfy these vanities, and often set themselves up as "The Great One," using manipulative language to describe their abilities and talents. All of this creates activities that continue to nourish pride of self.

Such ones may fake a psychic reading rather than admit that nothing is coming through their muddied channel. Their readings will be clouded with phrases and concepts which serve to enhance their personal image, rather than seeking the pure clear Truth for the edification of the client who should be served with care and unselfish love.

The spiritual aspirant must watch closely for these signs of egotism, for they are often very subtle, and individuals are sometimes blind to their own self-interest when working with others. Aspirants will make more rapid progress on the path when they advance their spiritual unfoldment through self-forgetfulness, harmlessness, and the pure joy of service.

4. The Dangers of Meditative Trance

The goal of meditation is not to create a sleeping or trance-like mind, but to build a disciplined, sensitive, and well-organized mind, so that the qualities of aspiration, devotion, and discrimination may become synthesizing, analyzing energies. The mind is disciplined not through inhibition of activity, but by the transmutation or transformation of the energies and thought patterns which flow through it, and through the constant seeking of higher attitudes of mind and Soul, which serve greater ideas and greater goals.

A blank or inactive mind, in which no thoughts are allowed to move, can lead to an inhibition of the circulating thought waves in the mental field and cut off the vitalizing flow of creativity and Life Energy to the brain. Not only that, but malicious or mischievous entities from the astral plane delight in the vacant field of a blank or non-energized brain, bringing their images, colors, sensations, and emotional ploys to delight or frighten the unsuspecting psychic.

My description of an inactive mind is not to be confused with the stillness of deep meditation. The most effective method of quieting the mind is to raise its vibrations so high by means of your aspirations that no lower thought currents or emotional and physical impressions reach it; only ideas, impressions, illuminations, and thought-forms of a very high order are registered from the Higher Mental level.

Spurious "masters," guides, and other entities from the astral realm use the trance condition of the inactive mind through trance mediums and spiritualistic seances. They can be recognized by their attempts to frighten, scold, manipulate, dominate, coerce, bully, or even flatter their listeners into submission. Any control that is activated by fear or subtle emotional manipulation is to be shunned with all the forces at one's command.

True enlightenment and true esoteric principles uplift and create a sense of deep happiness and freedom within the recipient. Even the psychic revealing of personality traits which are detrimental to the progress of the Soul will bring no tears and no chagrin if the message is truly from the higher spiritual realm, for its revelation will strike a chord of aspiration within, which will, with a flood of great joy, impel the listener to release the old in order to clasp the new, and he or she will be directed into better and more rewarding action.

5. Voices, Faces, Colors, Images

Optical disturbances, auditory voices, and the sense of levitation are frequent physical accompaniments of the shifting of the level of consciousness. Beginning students on the mystical Path are usually still at the mercy of their own emotional energies, and their early attempts to use visualization and imagination lead them through the emotional waves of the astral plane with their misleading illusions.

The dimension in which we live, breathe, and experience is created by our imagination at work—by the visualization that is so vital to any occult undertaking. In the beginning, students must use imagination, because only through the calculated use of their image-making faculty can they program the inner mind to open the doorway to psychic development.

But, as they progress, they must become very aware of every thought, of every feeling, of every impression. They must learn to catalog, to analyze every thought which comes through the mind. One simply cannot close one's eyes and just become psychic. It usually requires a period of training as diligent as that of any other skilled profession.

Most extradimensional information seems to come across the top of the head, and unless it is immediately recorded within the inner layers of the Theta level of the mind, it is soon forgotten and not to be recalled. Thoughts, however, that arise from one's own imaginings will come from deep within the brain itself, and seem to rise up to the top of the head, where they come into conscious awareness. Ideals and concepts from the higher abstract mind seem to arrive full-blown in the middle of the head, with a corresponding energy that urges one to put them into action.

Visualization takes place in the frontal area of the brain, near the location of the pineal gland, and it, too, will have a "source" separate and distinct from other types of brain activity. Students must discover for themselves where their sources are, to differentiate between their own lower and higher mind activity, and other thoughts which come from either an ultradimensional source or the minds of those around them.

Imagination is the fire which powers the wheels of creation. However, the lower astral world is peopled with phantasms individually created through the unwise use of Substance fired by someone's unenlightened use of imagination. These distorted fantasies are easily picked up by a beginning psychic who is eagerly seeking psychic "phenomena."

One of the most heartbreaking things any teacher can watch is to see a developing psychic wander off into a morass of fantasy, created by an ego desire to know all, be all, and tell all, at too early a stage in their development. Learning the wise use of psychic power necessitates an understanding of the various levels of personal spiritual development.

The most dangerous time for developing psychics is while their lower bodies are in the first stages of purification, while they are still subject to vanity, pride, ego, and emotional excitement over the emerging talents of mind. This is the time when they are most susceptible to intriguing visions, images, faces, and voices from the astral plane that often arise during meditation, or semi-sleep states, but which may appear at any time.

The voices may even give misleading advice which leads to emotional disturbances. Some aspirants who have not maintained their objective, critical faculties think that the voices they hear are the inner, true Voice, and they blindly obey until they see that it is too late for them to escape. If the emotional state is unstable, the nervous system can be shattered by the revelation that they have been duped, leaving their faith and belief sadly retarded, or even destroyed.

To discriminate between such voices and the true Voice one must use pure reason. You must know that the true, inner Voice of the Soul Self never demands, never flatters, never forces, never says anything to increase a person's vanities, nor the glamour of being important. Also, it *never* suggests fear, negativity, or separation. It prompts toward group responsibility and welfare, and for activity, duty, sacrifice, and unity. From it comes courage, energy, joy, and the will-to-good.

Visions are often holographic—three-dimensional and quite realistic. They seem to appear in material form as solid objects or persons, although sometimes they are ephemeral and ghost-like. They may be frightening, charming or alluring, but whatever their form, it's important to remember that they, too, are usually not real. For the most part, they are merely images thrown off by the brain as it adjusts to the chemicalization created by the merging of higher and lower energies.

I've heard them called "brain excretions," an apt term. They should be observed objectively and given no importance, and they will gradually fade, to be replaced later, perhaps, by true astral vision, which allows one to see forms and entities of the astral plane in their true perspective, objectively and without emotion.

One must maintain one's sense of humor while going through this stage. During that time, I often amused myself by speaking aloud to the faces and forms that appeared before my eyes as real as though a corporeal entity stood there or hung in the air. Invariably there was no response—the blank look remained, the form did not change, and as I watched, it would gradually fade from view.

True astral vision is not a gift for the unwise. It is earned, and then only when one has one's own emotional energies under control, and one is no longer enthralled by the astral plane. Psychics who truly have astral vision and understand its nature do not use it for the seeking of knowledge, information, or wisdom, nor do they seek astral plane entities for guidance or enlightenment. They know those qualities will be channeled to them through their own higher mind, and their contacts on the astral plane are only for the purpose of helping fellow travelers caught there in the web of their own emotional dilemmas.

6. The Dual Life

The spiritual life is a dual life, and successful disciples are those who maintain the balance between the two—the life of spiritual aspirations, beauty, ideals, visions, and the life of daily duties, obligations, and responsibilities. They never become so deeply involved in personal seeking that they forget their primary needs and the needs of those who are karmically involved with them.

Mysticism, to be most effective, must be integrated into our daily lives. It should be viewed not as an objective by itself, but as a vital factor that influences all our undertakings. Anyone, in any position, can do better work and achieve more harmonious relationships if they remain open to the guidance, love, and energy of the Soul Self.

The balance must also be kept between the incoming energies from meditation and spiritual aspiration and the outlet for these energies through ongoing service. Overstimulation of the psychic centers results when there is an excess of inflowing energy with no corresponding outlet. This overflow of energy may stimulate any of the chakras and cause psychological as well as physical problems.

All the emotional, creative, and generative energy produced by the sex center and the solar plexus center, for instance, should be redirected into activities which are creative and productive of good for more than just one's self. Severe problems in social relationships can arise when these centers are overstimulated without channels for the use of this energy.

Religious and ideological illusions arise when there is too much energy in the heart and throat centers without sufficient outlet to use it for the edification and enlightenment of others.

If the head centers are overstimulated, and their energies dammed up without release, then psychosomatic problems and mental complications plague the aspirant. Physical health problems in all areas of the body can be created by overstimulation of any of these highly charged vortexes.

The right motivation for mystical and psychic development lies in serving others, for that is the only way we can serve God. To do this, we must develop three great virtues: cooperation, gratitude, and humility.

Cooperation will engender in the aspirant a sense of group consciousness, of unity, and of the need to work for the highest good of all. It will help you dissolve feelings of loneliness and separateness, and will help you to let go of the preoccupation with self.

Gratitude will focus attention on the higher aspects of all areas of life and, by the energy of that attention, increase the flow of higher mind activity.

Humility will keep you from "storming the gates of Heaven by force," and keep you progressing slowly, but steadily and safely, through the emotional and mental traumas which often mark the upsetting of established modes of behavior. If self-satisfaction becomes a hindering problem, it is good to remember that you are only a worker in the harvest fields of God, and that no matter how great your talents and abilities, there are those whose talents, skills, and abilities outshine your own as the sun outshines the moon. Rather, let that which you *now are* be a stepping stone to a future of progressively greater and greater achievements.

One Important Last Thought

Never, under any circumstances, use your newfound mastery as a means to manipulate *people*. This is turning your abilities onto the path of Black Magic. Remember the Law of Cycles: Whatever you send out into the experience of another comes back to you for your own experiencing.

For the sake of your freedom to experience and grow spiritually, allow others their freedom to do likewise. Never insist that they follow your advice, listen to your teaching, perform certain acts, or even that they be healed or changed because *you* think it would be good for them. Whatever they are, whatever they are doing, is their own experience on the Path of evolution.

This doesn't mean that one should become cold or indifferent to another's plight. If you see someone in danger, you cannot turn away saying, "Well, that is that person's experience, and I must not interfere with Karma." How do you know whose karma you are witnessing? Maybe it's your own. You might need to save someone to compensate for having placed someone else in danger.

The disciple on the spiritual path must respond whenever there is a call for help. You must use your abilities to the utmost when aid is requested. By helping others we help ourselves, and all positive use of Cosmic energy aids in lifting the total consciousness of the whole human race.

However, you must never interfere with another's use of free will. You may guide, instruct, uplift, and inspire, but always allow others to use the energies you place at their disposal in whatever way they choose. The spiritual Law is precise and undeviating if you use your capacities as a means to cause others to act against their will, especially if it is to your benefit, as opposed to their benefit. The limitations you impose on them by so doing will be returned a hundredfold to you, if not in this lifetime, then in one or more others.

When you have the true understanding of working with Substance, you will not need to manipulate others. Places, situations, and events may be changed to suit your desire or whimsy, but bear in mind that God answers prayer (even scientific prayer) *through* His and your Creation, and the *right* people, those who can also benefit by your desire, will be moved into place to create the circumstances you wish.

You need not stipulate who these people will be. There are unlimited numbers of persons who can and will, happily and with great profit to themselves, share your experience with you.

This kind of understanding is especially needed in the sales field, where manipulation is taught as a means to an end. The salesperson is trained to do everything within his or her power to influence the prospective purchaser as desired, to never take no for an answer.

How much better it would be if the salesperson used the power of Substance, instead of the power of Will! During meditation in the Alpha level, visualize the *right* people, those who can be benefited by your product or service, being drawn to you and you to them, in greater numbers than you have ever before experienced. See them happy and prosperous because they found what you have to offer, and see yourself prosperous and happy because you have benefited so many.

This visualization is not so different from those found in sales manuals, except that it concentrates on the Idea of service, instead of the Idea of sales. Through the force of Will you can sell to anyone who can be manipulated into buying, whether or not they have need of that particular product or service, but through the power of Substance you need never meet anyone who cannot use your service, and the sales will be automatically forthcoming. Only those who need, can use with profit, and can afford to buy what you offer will be drawn into your path, for mutual benefit. All others will go and prosper elsewhere.

Workshop #4
Psychokinesis: Manipulating Matter

≈

Mind control of objects has been called *Psychokinesis* and *Telekinesis* by differing authors. The terminology may vary, but the focusing of attention is the same: the control of objects through the force of the will.

The force of the mind can manipulate Substance with comparative ease, and the force of the will can control matter in the same way, although not so easily. As you learn by experimenting how to control objects by the direction and focus of your will, you may gradually come to an understanding of how the mind can work on your own body for healing and how it is that material objects around you must serve your desires.

As with all exercises, each time you are successful, your confidence will be enhanced. The more you practice, the better you will become.

Exercise #1: A Psychic Craps Game

The object of this exercise is to control with your mind the fall of two dice which you will throw.

Your intent with the first six throws of the dice is to throw as many 1s as possible. The intent with the second six throws is to throw as many 2s as possible, and so forth until all six numbers have been thrown six times.

Mark on a score sheet six divisions of six lines each, numbering the first six-line division with a 1, the second six-line division with a 2, etc.

Record your first six throws in Division #1, marking whatever combinations of numbers come up. If a 6 and a 4 come up, mark 6–4. If two 1s come up, mark 1–1, etc. At the end of the six throws circle the number of 1s you have thrown.

Repeat the process with 2s, 3s, 4s, etc., circling the number when what you have actually thrown is what you intended to throw.

You might try throwing the dice from your hand at first, and then using a cup after you become more proficient.

Chance is one out of six. In thirty-six throws, with two dice, you have seventy-two chances of actually getting the number you project. Therefore, a score of more than twelve correctly thrown dice will be more than chance.

Intent, Purpose, Will, and Desire will teach you the subtleties of dice control. Some students hold the visualization and will steady while the dice roll and achieve results.

One student found she did better when she visualized the numbers desired and then, just before letting them roll, took her mind off the desire and didn't think about what she wanted while the dice were in motion. She did this through the simple expedient of looking at another object. The focusing of her eyes elsewhere was effective in drawing her mind to that object so that the dice rolled into the desired position while her attention was on something else.

This follows the metaphysical concept proposed by Unity writers, to "Let go and let God." After you have asked for a manifestation of desire, and have done your meditation work as your part of the bargain, then just let go and allow Substance to manifest what is desired at the proper time.

Exercise #2: Heads or Tails?

Your intent is to force your will on a set of three coins so that they fall in a predetermined pattern of heads and tails. There are four possible combinations: three heads; three tails; two heads, one tail; or two tails, one head.

Mark on your score sheet four divisions of six lines each, numbering the first division three heads; the second division three tails, etc. You may abbreviate heads (H) and tails (T) for convenience. Using the same method as in the dice game, allow six tries for each combination sequence.

Shake the coins in your hand while visualizing the specified pattern in which you want them to fall. Drop the coins, and write down the actual result beside your call. Go directly to the next toss until twenty-four throws have been made.

Count one point for any coin that matches your call. For instance, if your target is three tails on the first toss, but only one turned up, your score is one. Where all three coins match your call, your score is three.

Exercise #3: Pendulum Swing

Hang a pendulum or small object on a string or chain from a nail where it can swing freely. Be sure there is no draft that can nullify your experiment. By force of will, command the pendulum to swing. Use your visualization and see the pendulum moving back and forth. It may take several tries, but keep at it until the pendulum swings. Don't give up easily. The rewards will be worth the effort, not only for the demonstration you will make, but for what you will learn about your mind while you are practicing.

Exercise #4: Pencil Roll

Place a round pencil or pen on a perfectly flat surface such as floor or table top. By force of will alone, command the pencil to roll. On a table, make it your goal to have the pencil roll off the edge.

Exercise #5: Making Waves

Place a shallow dish of water on a flat surface. Command the water to ripple. Speak the command aloud and with emphasis, slightly rolling the R's: "R-r-r-ripple!"

Treat the pendulum, pencil, or the water in the same way you would train a pet. Be persistent and firm with the expectation that it will obey.

Exercise #6: Needle Float

Fill a glass with water to the top edge. Place a small object like a toothpick or a needle on top of the water. By force of will make the object move around on top of the water, from edge to middle, from edge to edge, from middle to edge, etc.

Hold your hand one to two inches above the object and Will the object to move by following the discharge of magnetic energy from your palm. (A needle works faster than a toothpick, although both will obey.)

Exercise #7: Sailboat

From a piece of waterproof material such as foil or waxed paper, cut a strip about ½" x 1", and bend one end upright. Place it in a shallow bowl of water on a solid surface free of drafts. Point your index finger at the upright portion, very close but not touching it. Be very careful not to breathe on it. You might even wear a mask to prevent your breath from forming air currents around the delicate little sail. By concentration, you'll find you can repel or attract it just by the power of the Will.

Exercise #8: Pyramid Tent

Stick the eye of a needle into the center of a small base made of a piece of cork, sponge, or other material. Cut a 2" x 2" square of paper. Fold it pyramid style from corner to corner, two ways. Place the center of the paper fold on the point of the upright needle to form a tent. Make sure the folded paper swings free, and that one corner or side does not touch the table.

Cup your hands around the paper, keeping the palms at least two or more inches away from the paper. With your Will, command the paper to turn to the left on the needle point. Command it to stop. Then reverse, so that the paper now turns to the right.

This exercise uses the magnetic flow from the palms of the hands as well as mind energy and is perhaps the easiest of all the exercises to perform successfully.

Exercise #9: Spin The Bottle

This is an exercise to experiment with group mind control, using five to ten people. Form a circle around a large table, or seated on the floor. Make sure the surface is smooth, with no coverings such as a tablecloth or rugs. Choose a large soda pop bottle, wine bottle, or other bottle-type object, such as a bowling pin, that will spin easily. Place it on the floor or table with its neck pointing towards someone chosen as a target.

As someone spins the bottle, all circle members concentrate on the thought that the bottle will stop with its neck pointing towards the target person.

Each member of the circle takes a turn, with five spins to make a hit. The next spinner may choose a new target. Each time the bottle stops with its neck pointing to the target is considered a hit. To count as a hit, it must be right on target. If the indicator falls on a line between the target and another player, spin again.

In a circle of ten players, fifty spins would require five hits to meet chance expectancy. If the hits run above chance expectancy, there is definite possibility of group mind control.

Exercise #10: Paper Feather

This exercise precludes any possibility of influencing the target with anything but the mind. Cut a half-inch square of tissue paper. With a tiny drop of glue, attach a long, thin thread to one corner. Using an ice pick or other sharp instrument, punch a small hole in the cap or cork of a clear glass bottle and pull the loose end of the thread through the hole from the bottom until only four inches remain dangling. Fill the hole with glue or melted wax.

When the glue or wax is dry, cut off the excess string. Lower the square of tissue paper into the bottle. Screw on the cap and wait for the paper to stop swinging.

Sit across from the bottle and stare at the paper, while imagining a strong wind blowing against one corner of it, in an effort to get it to move. Try for at least fifteen minutes at a time before giving up, and then try again at a later time. Sooner or later it will move!

Exercise #11: Help A Friend

Use your newfound understanding to help a friend manifest something he or she desires. Do so with permission, of course, and ask the friend to visualize, too. Be sure both of you understand what emotional experience or intent is the *real* goal behind the desire.

If this is a long-standing situation that needs to be changed or harmonized, spend some time visualizing all the stumbling blocks and causes being dissolved and Substance being re-molded into a new situation.

Do not blame or find fault, even with yourself. Realize that existing circumstances are part of the total experience pattern of the individuals involved, and that all things work together for good, if you look for the good to be found in the experience.

MEDITATION PRACTICE: OCCULT MEDITATION TECHNIQUE

By this time you should begin to have some control over your thoughts, emotions, and body sensations during your meditation time. Don't be too concerned if you haven't come along as rapidly as you think you should. Remember, people develop at their own pace, and your pace is right for you. Your meditation exercises may be bringing forth information from many past lifetimes of spiritual development, and therefore you may progress rapidly at first. Or this may be the first time you've turned your attention toward spiritual things, and the new energies and thoughts must forge new pathways of action. In that case, you may find the going more difficult. Don't judge yourself on speed, only by the changes taking place in your life, which will be uniquely your own and not like anyone else's at all.

Choose a short-range goal for yourself, something that you want to have happen during this week. Use the following occult meditation technique to make it come about. In this meditation, both mental and emotional energies are under the conscious control of the "Objective Watcher." You, from the "I AM" point of view, are *watching* the action of the meditation at the same time that you are *causing* the action to take place. You are both the observer and the doer.

Occult Meditation Technique

Sit comfortably, with straight spine. Cleanse your body from head to toe with the White Light.

Make the physical body completely still. Go directly to the Alpha level of mind.

Now still the emotional center. Do this by observing that somewhere between your diaphragm and heart you will find a whirling vortex of energy. This is your solar plexus center, the center of your emotions.

Speak to it, requesting that it be still. Then turn your attention to a quiet, pleasant scene somewhere, a brookside, a lakeside, your own quiet retreat, wherever it may be.

When both emotions and body are stilled, think about your goal for the week. Place a mental image of what you want into the third eye center. See the image in detail, just behind the forehead, or on a screen projected a little above the level of your eyes.

When this image is complete, send a shaft of White Light from the crown center of your head shooting up into the air, to fall like a giant web down and around the world and back into your feet. Know that this shaft of energy will go out into the world, touch the persons who can be benefited by bringing your image into manifestation, wherever they may be, and bring them back into your world.

Now return to the third eye position, and hold the image you've created for sixty seconds without allowing the image to waver. Your previous practice in holding the focus of your attention will pay off here.

At the end of one minute, allow the image to fall backwards into the heart center. There allow emotional desire for the experience to rise up from the solar plexus to surround and bathe the image, as seed planted in the ground is watered by moisture and rain.

Release the image completely. Expect it to manifest, and watch for opportunities to help bring your desire into fulfillment. If an anxious thought comes to your mind unbidden, dismiss it with the knowledge that whatever forces are required to bring your desire about are at work, and that it will manifest in its own good time. *Don't* allow worry or anxiety about the outcome to nullify your work. Adopt the attitude that *whatever* happens will be exactly right, because your own Soul Self is in control, and it knows how to make all situations work together for good.

Finish the meditation with a visualization of the protective White Light, while slowly returning to Beta consciousness.

WEEK 5

≈

The "Mystery Laws" of the Universe

As we attempt to understand our Cosmic or spiritual connection to the Universe in which we live, move, and have our Being, it's only natural we should formulate in words principles which seem to exist throughout all interrelationships.

These principles have been called "Mystery Laws." It remains for our scientists and psychologists to uncover the details of how and why these principles exist, and how and why they operate as they do. When they do, I'm sure their language and verbal symbols will be quite different, but the underlying Truths will remain the same.

The metaphysician talks about vibrations, universal rhythms, and Cosmic Law; the scientist uses such terms as radiation, electromagnetic fields, and the conversion of energy into matter; the psychologist talks about the Id, the Ego, and the Universal Unconscious. To the discerning mind the Ideas expressed by these word symbols are interchangeable.

Your personal acceptance of certain basic concepts of Beingness-in-the-world as workable Truths, whether they are as yet scientifically expressed or not, will facilitate your growth as a knowledgeable spiritual entity, and give you a foundation from which to analyze realistically as well as spiritually the events that occur in your experiencing. Expanded sense perceptions are part of this enlarged concept of Beingness.

It is believed that in ancient times these concepts were more easily accessible to the common people. But because of political intrigue and personal disagreements between priests about interpretations of doctrine, which resulted in wars, violence, and the destruction of temples, schools, and recorded literature, the Mystery Laws went underground and became the sole property of the priests of the ancient religions.

"Mystery Schools" were then founded, in which the secrets were jealously guarded, and passed on to initiates only after long and careful screening and tutoring. Among these Schools or Orders, the most well known are the Rosicrucians, the Golden Dawn, Freemasonry, and the Sufi and Hindu mystical traditions. The oath of secrecy among them is still prevalent today, and some concepts are still not available to the general public.

This veil of secrecy has been cherished for so long that the original necessity for it has become shrouded in tradition, and much of the distress of the world today can be laid at the feet of individual ignorance of personal divinity. The priests and gurus waited to be asked for their knowledge before passing it on, but who was there to ask for it, when few people in the world even knew that it existed?

It is, however, also true that the Mystery Laws underlie the teachings of Jesus, Buddha, Zoroaster, and all the great avatars of the world. All the Mystery Laws and spiritual Truths which I tell you here can be discovered in Biblical references, some of which I will give to you as we go along. It requires only meditation and singleness of purpose to seek them out.

Today, science is rapidly undermining both the veil of secrecy and the religious myths that kept the people in bondage. The language of science, however, does not yet include the motivating power of a First Cause, a Supreme Intelligence, which permeates the emotional and intellectual as well as the physical aspects of this vast Creation. Therefore, many of the ancient Mystery Laws are now finding their way into print and are becoming more readily accessible to the average person, so that a balance may be maintained. I believe that science and religion will one day walk hand in hand to restore harmony and fulfillment to the evolution of humanity.

If we accept the theory of reincarnation as a workable premise for the expansion of human spiritual awareness, then most of us who are now interested in mystical lore have probably been members of a Mystery School or community at some time in the past. All that we learned then is still stored in the superconscious area of the mind and filters down from time to time in response to the needs of our situation in the form of intuition, insights, and inspiration.

The Beta level of the brain cannot use this information consciously, however, until it has once again been expressed in verbal form and returned to our awareness through the sense impressions of hearing or seeing. It then becomes a part of the memories stored from this life's experience and can be drawn upon at will.

According to traditional esoteric belief, the earth itself is now entering the final stages of a 25,000-year period of evolution. The last days of the Piscean Age are upon us. The new Aquarian Age, beginning somewhere around the year 2000, will present completely new vibrations and a different force-field in which to live and experience.

The last 7,000 years have served to develop and refine the emotional nature. The next stage of evolution must develop and refine the mental body. We must learn how to think with discipline and to put our intellectual powers to constructive use.

These last days of the old Piscean Age and the first days of the new Aquarian Age will act as a period of purification, when all karma still attached to the emotional bodies of individuals must be balanced out: old debts must be paid, relationships harmonized. All the traditional institutions of society, i.e., government, marriage, education, etc., will undergo violent and radical change.

The old forms which served the emotional growth of humankind must now be subjected to the scrutiny of the intellect, and new forms will naturally take their place. Since change is often accompanied by turmoil, we can expect many of the revolutionary prophecies of the Book of Revelation, Nostradamus, and other seers to now come to pass.

This need not alarm us. If we remain centered in Soul Consciousness, we will always be in the right place at the right time, doing whatever is right for the moment. Remember that all things work together for good for those who love the "Law" (Romans 8:28), and this period of purification is no exception. Only good can come out of whatever turmoil faces us if we look for and expect it to work for our benefit, since the Law requires that we get what we expect.

Thirteen Tenets of Arcane Wisdom

The ancient Mystery Laws are again being disseminated throughout the world to aid us in our emotional struggle in the ensuing years and to provide a foundation for the new intellectual growth to come. Even orthodox churches, which have traditionally barred all metaphysical information from their doctrines, are now beginning to accept some of these precepts and to give them out to their congregations under the guise of psychological or scientific understanding.

These Mystery Laws are not the same as the metaphysical laws we've been discussing up to this time. Metaphysical laws deal with things you can *do* to make life better, the use of mind power to change your environment, the "think-yourself-rich" type of philosophy. For a more modern term, the Mystery Laws might be called Universal Laws. They deal with ways you can *Be*, with attitudes and understandings of Cosmic Forces that act with or without our cognizance of them.

The Laws that I relate here deal only with the growth and development of expanded consciousness, and are designed to bring about an externalization of the superconscious aspect of mind. Their purpose is to take the student along the path to Self-Realization, that inner illumination of the Soul Self.

Following are the essences of thirteen of these Cosmic Laws, gathered from the writings of the Rosicrucians, Theosophy, Science of Mind, Astara, Unity, the Kabbalah, and the works of various authors, as well as my own claircognizance as I studied them. I have never found all of them gathered together in one book before, although this might exist. Of course, there may be more than these thirteen Laws, but if so, it will be your delight to find them out. The so-called Greater Mysteries of Planetary and Hierarchical Evolution are not within the scope of these lectures and therefore are not treated here.

The first six Laws are mundane and deal with the quality and manifestation of the affairs of life on the material plane. The seventh Law I call the "Pivotal Law," because your understanding and use of this Law determines whether you take the Left-Hand Path or the Right-Hand Path in your development. The next six Laws are transcendental or spiritual and deal with the quality and manifestation of Being or Spirit.

Any of these Laws could provide enough material for a full study by itself, or even an entire book, but I'll content myself with a brief discussion of each one.

1. Energy Follows Thought—
Thought Molds Substance

This is the First Law of the Universe, and we've dealt with it at length in the first four sessions. Ann Herbstreith paraphrased it this way: "Where your attention goes, your energy flows."[12] The secret of the "Mystery" is that God *is* the Creative Energy of the universe. Or maybe we can say it better: The Creative Energy that flows through the universe—that creates the universe and holds it in place—*is* God. The two terms are synonymous. Creative Energy is another name for God.

If you need further personal understanding of this Law, turn your meditation upon these words of John: "In the Beginning was the Word, and the Word was with God, and the Word *was* God" (John 1:1).

To become "one with God" is to become one with Creative Energy. Jesus said, "With God (Creative Energy) all things are possible" (Matt. 19:26). Awareness of this Law will permit us to consciously tap this energy flow and channel it into our own creative enterprises, which is what is meant when God says, "Call upon me and see if I will not pour you out such a blessing, there shall not be room enough to receive it" (Mal. 3:10).

Thought is our contact with this Energy, and when thought is followed by the spoken word and directed by personal Will, then the Energy we have contacted becomes visible as our own personal world. We are making this contact involuntarily at all times. "As a man thinketh in his heart, so is he" (Proverbs 23:7), and so are the manifestations of Energy and Substance around each person. The secret of mastery is the voluntary and directed use of Creative Energy by thought and by the spoken word.

2. The Law of Above and Below as One

Wisdom students have always been intrigued by the legend of the Emerald Tablet of Hermes Trismegistus, said to have been a piece of emerald on which Phoenician characters were engraved. One tradition has it that this precious tablet was found by Sarah, the wife of Abraham, in a cave guarded by the corpse of Hermes Trismegistus, believed in legend to be the grandson of Adam and architect of the Pyramids.

Another tradition names its discoverer as Alexander the Great, while yet a third maintains that Hermes Trismegistus, alias Tehuti, the Egyptian god of Wisdom, presented the tablet to an alchemist, Maria Prophetissa, who is believed by some to have been Miriam, the sister of Moses. Still another states it was found on the body of Hermes at Hedron by Isarim, an initiate.

The words on the tablet itself, from the Latin rendering, are in part: "That which is above is like that which is below, and that which is below is like that which is above for performing the miracle of the One Thing."

This means that a precept, to be a Universal Law, must operate in the same way on all levels of the Cosmos: in the visible and the invisible, and in the spiritual, the astral, and the physical planes.

The construction of an atom is exactly like a solar system, and the construction and attributes of a solar system reflect the construction of the galaxy which is its habitat, and so forth, to the outermost limits of the Cosmos.

The figure of a man is sometimes superimposed on the Tree of Life, used in the Kabbalah as a symbol that the microcosm of the individual is an exact replica of the macrocosm. The teachings of the Kabbalah show that by studying ourselves we can better understand the workings of Nature and from this understanding learn something of God and the divine scheme of things. One can affect the other, since each is subject to the same Laws.

Instruments show us that color and sound vibrations, governed by the laws of matter, extend beyond the range of our physical senses, and we know that there are living intelligences on other levels of Being than ours. This gives us a basis from which we can make further extrapolations.

It becomes, then, a matter of reasoning from the known to the unknown, the visible to the invisible, the human to the divine. If God created all things out of His own Substance, then that is the same Substance that we use in our own creating, for that is the only Substance that is available for any use. Therefore, we must reason that all things use the same Life-Force which flows through animals, plants, humans, Beings that exist in other dimensions, and even seemingly inanimate objects.

In esoteric philosophy we are told of seven Planes of Being: mineral, vegetable, animal, human, astral, angelic or devic, and monadic (spiritual), each becoming progressively more ethereal in composition. On all planes of Being, from the densest to the most rarefied, you will find these three things: (a) substance or body; (b) motion or active energy; and (c) consciousness or awareness.

Let us consider the first element: substance or body. It is easy for us to see that rocks, animals, plants, and humans have bodies, because we can see them with our eyes. The body of an etheric being, however, cannot be comprehended through the input of data from the senses. It requires deductive reasoning. People who travel astrally report that the body they inhabit feels solid to them, and that other things on that plane feel solid while they move in that level of Being. Reports coming through mediumistic channels indicate that "Beings of Light" can be seen inhabiting the more etheric realms. Reason can then accept that this precept is probably true: substance or body, no matter how fine, surrounds all created forms on any level of Being.

The second principle is that motion or active energy operates on all levels of Being. While we can easily understand the movement of energy through space, it required the invention of the microscope to show that atoms of the densest material were also constantly in a state of motion. The more slowly they move, the denser the material, but reason asserts that the continual movement of the atoms may be the prime cause of the ultimate breakup and deterioration of every formed thing, as the atoms which compose its body struggle to regain their freedom and return to the original *Substance* from which they came.

"As above, so below." If even the atoms of the rocks struggle to return to the Substance from which they came, who can deny that humanity, too, struggles unendingly to return to its own

Source, the Mind of the Creator, and that other elemental and spiritual Beings, imprisoned in the focus of their own evolution, are also striving to perfect and evolve whatever attributes have been given them to unfold?

The third precept is that consciousness or awareness is to be found on all levels of Being. We are inclined to think of consciousness as being an attribute of mind, and to believe that the lower stratum of the known world is essentially mindless. But by deductive reasoning we must assume that if the atoms of a mineral form are in constant movement, there needs to be some kind of elementary consciousness strong enough to hold them in position for the lifetime of the form. We could say that it, too, is in the process of evolving, since some minerals deteriorate into soil for the benefit of plant life, and others evolve into precious gems, or living radioactive crystals. You have only to look at certain kinds of rocks under ultraviolet light to see their energies radiating through their gorgeous colors.

Every chemist is aware of the affinities between certain chemicals, how some chemicals attract and others repel one another. Machinists know that a machine which is operated twenty-four hours a day without rest will break down sooner than a machine which is periodically stopped to allow a respite in its activity. Both these examples indicate a certain kind of consciousness at the mineral level.

Experiments done with plants show an elementary emotional reaction to forces which threaten their existence. Seeds placed in pans of soil, watered and cared for identically, show definite and different responses to love and rejection. Those seeds that are given love and attention grow abundantly, those that are cursed and reviled wither and die, just as a human baby will die if no one gives it love.

An experiment with far-reaching implications was done several years ago by Cleve Backster at his School for Polygraph Examiners in New York. He attached the electrodes of a sensitive galvanometer to common house plants, in a method not unlike using an encephalograph or a lie detector, and his instruments showed that the plants reacted violently whenever he dumped live brine shrimp into boiling water, as if the death of the little creatures was somehow felt by the plants themselves.

However, one day, in an extension of the experiment, he spoke to the shrimp, telling them that in fifteen minutes he was going to put them into the boiling water. At the prescribed time, all of the shrimp were motionless, and there was no answering response from the instruments attached to the plants.

The American Indians offered a prayer to the Great Spirit for good hunting and then offered an apology to the spirit of the animal whose life they planned to take, asking in advance for forgiveness, and thanking the animal for its sacrifice.

Vegetarians deplore the inhumane slaughter of beef cattle, claiming that the terror of the animal prior to the slaughter contaminates the meat with fear toxins that poison the body of the consumer. Communication with the animals beforehand could have calming effects. Also, the custom of giving thanks before a meal may have greater benefits for our bodily health than we know.

Mind reacts upon mind. Blessing creates harmony in inanimate as well as animate things, while anger and resentment create inharmony between all the forms involved. Jesus cursed the fig tree and it withered and died. Nothing more is said in the Bible about this incident, but since we know He taught His disciples the ancient secrets, we can assume this was one of His demonstrations of the interaction of mind upon mind.

Peter and Eileen Caddy, with a group of like-minded people, have made a garden at Findhorn, Scotland, where the life-forces of plants and trees are recognized as Devas and are talked to as if they had an intelligent consciousness.[13] As a result, blossoms and vegetables grow more profusely there than anywhere else in Scotland, and people travel from all over the world to study and admire this. It is reported that when one tree had to be removed, they told the inhabiting Deva within the tree that it would be cut down the next year. Within six months, the life-force had completely left the tree. It was dead.

3. The Law of the Whole and Its Parts

Although the Whole is the sum of all its parts, it is greater than its parts, since the parts cannot grasp or comprehend the Whole. However, we, as parts, can comprehend larger portions of life than we now do.

All aspects of Creation, whether material forms or vibrational forms, are part of the whole of Creation and partake of the Consciousness that created it. Images, thoughts, and vibrations flow freely from mind to mind through the One Mind and can be understood and interpreted by any mind that tunes into the larger part.

This Law says that Mind reacts upon mind, influencing and being influenced by its many parts.

William James said that the vibrations of a pebble tossed into a pond would affect the farthest star. Such a statement may be the height of hyperbole, since it is a moot question whether the activities of the earth plane can pass beyond the sphere of earth to influence the activities of such remote planes of existence, but it serves to illustrate a very important Law. On our own planet and, to a certain extent, within in the solar system in which we exist, we definitely do have an influence, physically, mentally, and emotionally, and we, in turn, are influenced by the actions and reactions of other parts of Creation.

When we speak of individual parts of Creation, we usually think in terms of human beings, but a vein of ore is a differentiated part of Creation, as is a tree, a goldfish, or a cow. Each of these has a vibration peculiar to its own Beingness that can be measured by instruments and/or your own sensory apparatus, and all of these interact one upon the other: you, the vein of ore, the tree, the goldfish, and the cow.

Through magic and alchemy, people down through the ages have attempted to influence and exert dominion over their environment, often only to be buffeted by the forces they strove to control.

Some occult magicians attempt to call upon elemental spirits of parallel lines of evolution, and make them subject to the will of the magician. Needless to say, this is a very dangerous activity. Evolution on all planes proceeds only as we learn to serve one another, but service is not servitude. To make another Being your slave is to invite retribution from the Law of Karma—you receive what you send out.

Mastery, or dominion, is achieved through detachment, discernment, and discrimination. When we become mentally and emotionally detached enough from our own workings to discern possible future effects and/or reactions from that part of Mind we are touching, then we will be discriminating enough never to harm another Being. This is true mastery.

A better method is cooperation with others for the highest good of all, so that no part of evolution is harmed or held back by us. The lower kingdoms willingly serve the higher kingdoms, but the greater our own evolvement, the greater the responsibility towards the lesser ones.

Nature works in an ecology of togetherness, ensuring the survival of all. The Hierarchy of Advanced Beings work to elevate the consciousness of humankind. We, in turn, must take responsibility for the expansion and advancement of consciousness in the forms below us. The new Aquarian Age is an age of brotherhood, and mental compatibility will ultimately take the place of emotional interaction or self-serving exploitation.

The mastery of alchemy is achieved through transmutation, transcendence, and initiation, which bring the lesser evolved parts of Creation into a higher level of experience.

We can become more psychically aware of the vibrations of coexisting parts of the Whole, and expand our own interaction with these various parts, by an extension of the senses and/or an instrumental aid. A simple pendulum or a dowsing stick, sometimes known as a divining rod, will often aid in locating underground streams or bodies of water, lost articles, veins of ore, even missing persons.

The psychic gift of *psychometry* uses the Law of the Whole and its Parts. Psychometry is the ability to take an object in your hand and, through a mental attunement with that object, know something about the person who owns it. Psychometry is one of the easier psychic gifts to develop and can be useful in many areas of life. In some cities, psychometrists have helped police solve crimes by holding an article belonging to the victim and, through their psychic insight, providing previously unknown clues. These, when added to information already known, has helped to uncover the guilty person.

Some people have the gift of "water-witching," or dowsing. The dowser cuts a forked branch from a hazelwood, willow, hawthorn, cherry, or dogwood tree. The piece should be roughly half an inch in diameter and about ten inches long. The two

Figure 10. Dowsing with a Forked Willow

long ends of the fork are held in the hands, with equal tension on each side.

The hands are held palms up with the branch grasped firmly in clenched fists. The single end of the twig, which is from one to two inches long, points either upward or roughly parallel with the ground. This position bends the two arms of the fork outward and creates a tension like a strong spring. The operator paces off the ground to be surveyed, concentrating on the idea of water. The Y will suddenly snap downward when the dowser stands above water.

Some operators can even tell how far below ground the water is by allowing the branch to slowly bob up and down, the number of bounces corresponding to the number of feet down to the water. The designation will seldom be off by more than one or two feet, and more frequently it is right on target.

More sophisticated dowsing rods have been manufactured of various types of metal, and these are used by psychic researchers to find veins of ore, buried pipelines, cables, underground tunnels, mine fields, and other types of underground caches. Special divining rods have even been manufactured to measure the human aura. The advancement of this science in today's language is called "radiesthesia."

The oldest known picture reference to dowsing was uncovered in Mesopotamian ruins (*circa* 1300 B.C.). It is believed that one of the ancient records etched in stone depicts a priest using a divining rod. Also, we can probably assume that Moses used some sort of divining rod when he smote the rock that brought forth water to quench the thirst of his fellow desert travelers.

There are numerous cases on record of dowsers locating water in places where geological surveys have failed. This ability works even at a distance. Without ever leaving his home in Maine, Henry Gross has located water in Bermuda, Ireland, and Nigeria by simply holding a pendulum over a map! Some dowsers have not only located water at a distance but were able to determine the depth of the water as well, by letting a small dowsing stick bob over the map.

Researchers are now using pendulums and dowsing apparatus for experimental medical diagnosis, determining the suitability of various kinds of food, and checking types of allergies, among other things. They use such terms as radiation, vibrations, radio waves, electromagnetic fields, etc. The most interesting aspect of this work is that the *same* instrument, whether pendulum or divining rod, can be put to such diverse purposes as locating underground springs, oil pockets, mineral lodes, lost children, and even determining the sex of an unborn child or an unhatched chick.

Although the instrument undoubtedly responds to the magnetic energies in each of these situations, the driving or discerning force has to be the operator's mind. When *willed* to do so, the divining rod will find minerals instead of water, but will find water just as readily when the *Will* of the operator changes.

4. The Law of Rhythm

The rhythm of the Universe is unmistakable, from the earth going around the sun in a 365-¼ day cycle, to the entire galaxy swinging in majestic glory through a 25,000 year orbit around some far distant central point. There is the constant, predictable motion of the ebb and flow of the tides, and the procession from civilization to civilization of human evolutionary advancement. The ceaseless motion of Life moves in timeless rhythms of birth and death at all levels of expression from the densest to the most etheric. This law is sometimes referred to as the "Law of Cycles," or the "Law of Periodicity."

The Book of Genesis, generally attributed to Moses, states it this way: "While the earth remaineth, seedtime and harvest, and cold and heat, and summer and winter, and day and night shall not cease" (Genesis 8:22).

A son of David, known as "The Preacher," concluded in his study of wisdom that: "to every thing there is a season, and a time to every purpose under the heaven. A time to be born, and a time to die; a time to plant, and a time to reap; a time to kill, and a time to heal; a time to break down and a time to build up; a time to weep, and a time to laugh; a time to mourn, and a time to dance; a time to embrace, and a time to refrain from embracing; a time to get, and a time to lose; a time to keep, and a time to cast away; a time to be silent, and a time to speak..." (Ecc. 3:1–8).

There is a season for all things. A time for activity and a time for meditation. All of us know times when the hunger for spiritual teachings is so great it seems we cannot be satisfied. At other times, it's as though we've reached a saturation point or some kind of plateau, and we need time to digest what we've learned, while returning to the world of mundane activity again.

Nature on planet Earth follows the twenty-four hour cycle of a day. All creatures, from an abalone to a zebra, follow a daily pattern of work and rest, sleep and activity. True, some creatures (people included) are more like owls, working at night and sleeping during the day, and others are meadowlarks, "early to bed and early to rise," still we all seem to live in twenty-four hour segments.

Responding to the infinite rhythms of the universe, our lives ebb and flow in rhythms of their own. Our physical, mental, and emotional natures follow definite, predictable rhythms. The Rosicrucians postulate seven fifty-two day periods during the course of a year, ranging from birthday to birthday, in which activities are more sure of success at certain times than at others.

There are also seven-year cycles within the human lifespan that are predictable. The first seven years are geared to learning how to use the physical body—how to walk, to talk, to coordinate the muscles. During this time the nature of the child absorbs without discrimination the feelings and attitudes of others.

·The mental and emotional bodies are attached only embry-
onically to the individual at birth, and part of the spiritual discipline of each incarnation is learning how to draw information
from the Soul that is needed to successfully negotiate the path
chosen. So the second seven years mark the beginning development of the mental body. The child starts to school, and begins to
use the memorizing and reasoning capacities of the brain.

The third seven years begin the process of developing the
emotional body, and a search for personal identity, with much
rebellion against authority and established "isms." Puberty occurs,
and biological functions create an attraction to the opposite sex.
It is during this time that the individual is the most physically
attractive. The plainest girl and the homeliest boy exhibit a glow
from within that reflects the pure beauty of Spirit. Occult tradition says that the Soul first takes responsibility for the actions of
the Personality at age fourteen, or the onset of puberty, which
action creates both beauty and unrest within the developing child.

With the fourth seven-year cycle the individual begins learning to coordinate all three of these energies—physical, emotional,
and mental. This is a period of social learning, of searching for
maturity and how to function as an independent entity within
social structures.

Astrology gets into the act, too, with the rhythms of the
planets and their predictable influences upon the human being.
The planet Saturn, called by astrologers "The Teacher," or the "Lord
of Karma," makes a complete revolution around the horoscope
every twenty-eight to twenty-nine years. "The Teacher" triggers
events that have been set up within the mental and emotional
fields of the individual and brings about the rewards (or punishments) in the form of external activities previously visualized.
Both prayer and fear can actualize events under Saturn's timing.

(Saturn was once thought by astrologers to be the influence
from which the word "Satan" was devolved, because, like the Law
of Return, we are more apt to remember the bad returns and forget
the good. Since Saturn triggers events which bring about rewards
and punishments equally, astrologers currently have a more positive outlook on Saturn's influence.)

The end of the twenty-eighth year of life, marking the end
of the fourth seven-year cycle, astrologers call "The Saturn

Return," meaning that Saturn is now in the same position it was in at the time of birth. As the person starts into the fifth seven-year cycle, there are frequently great upheavals in the physical and emotional life, and extreme changes take place. There may be divorce or a change of occupation, often a change of location; almost certainly a change in lifestyle will occur at this time.

During the process of this fifth seven-year cycle great philosophical growth and change takes place, while the individual reviews and revises attitudes towards life, fellow human beings, and ethical and moral codes.

The sixth seven-year cycle, beginning about age thirty-five, often marks a tremendous spiritual transformation. Spiritual insights occur, and frequently a shifting of religious basis takes place. Many of the people who pioneered today's metaphysical movement began with revelations which happened to them about their thirty-fifth year.

The years between forty-two and forty-nine mark a greater awareness of the ability to consciously direct energy. The responsibilities of earlier years either change in character or are released entirely, and there is a greater freedom of thought and action that had not been possible earlier in life. From this arises the expression, "Life begins at forty."

The years from forty-nine to fifty-six constitute a cycle of inventory-taking. The individual searches for deeply philosophical and spiritual meaning to existence, takes stock of talents and accomplishments, and reassesses values and priorities. Mental and emotional energies are directed toward determining and laying the groundwork for what the individual wishes to do with the rest of his or her life.

This period also ends the second twenty-eight-year cycle, or the second "Saturn Return." Once more, individuals must assess their value systems and prepare for a new, frequently different, future. Unlike the end of the first Saturn cycle, when changes were often thrust upon the person seemingly without volition, the end of the second cycle places the responsibility for change and adjustment directly upon the free will of the person. If the opportunity for change and reassessment is not acted upon, then the individual starts to lose vitality, strength, and life energy. Debilitation, inertia, and impotency set in, and the end of life may come quickly.

For those who take advantage of the foundation laid in youth to consciously redirect their Life Forces, the remaining seven-year cycles will reflect progressively deepening philosophical, spiritual, mental, and moral insights. These can truly be "golden years," the greatest and most rewarding of one's life, drawing upon all the wisdom bought by experience. If one is thrown off in the timing of this cyclic program through mental or emotional blocks, immaturity, or childhood conditioning, there are set up within the psyche composites of guilt, insecurity, fear of success or fear of failure, and feelings of lost time and opportunities. There arises an urgency that "it is later than you think," and the person either plunges into despair or seeks out opportunities for education, religious experiences, or other activities that expand the inner Self.

An in-depth study of the seven-year cycles of life would take a book in itself, and it would pay the serious student to put some personal time into this type of research.

The most well-known rhythms, of course, are *biorhythms*,[14] which chart the course of our physical, emotional, and mental ups and downs.

The physical biorhythm cycle is the shortest, at twenty-three days. During the first half of the cycle, the first eleven and a half days, physical aspects are ascending, and we give off the strongest amounts of energy during this time. We can work our hardest and for longer periods of time. We are more resistant to disease, better coordinated, and generally in better physical condition.

During the second eleven and a half days, which is the low side of the cycle, the body is recharging and energy is being accumulated. We tire more easily, need more rest, and are unlikely to behave vigorously. This is the most likely time for a physical slump, and we are more vulnerable to disease.

The emotional cycle of twenty-eight days is sometimes called the "sensitivity rhythm." This cycle has a positive phase of fourteen days in which we are inclined to react in positive, happy, and constructive ways to most events. We get along better with other people and with ourselves, so this is the best time for undertaking projects requiring cooperation, a positive attitude, and creativity.

During the fourteen-day low cycle, the negative side of our emotional nature often brings out the worst in us. Feelings affect judgment, so the days when we are recharging our emotional powers can be poor ones in which to perform dangerous tasks that call for swift reaction and sound judgment. Accidents are more likely to occur during a person's lower emotional phase. We tend to be testy, short-tempered, and negative during this time, so these are not the best days for teamwork or for making job or family decisions.

The thirty-three-day intellectual cycle is divided into positive and negative phases of sixteen and a half days. During the positive phase our minds are more open, our memories more retentive, and our ability to put together separate ideas to achieve new understanding or a new inspiration is at its best. The positive phase is a good time for tackling new, unfamiliar situations that call for quick comprehension and adaptation, such as a new job. Efforts at self-improvement through reading and education will also be more fruitful during this period.

During the sixteen and a half day negative phase, we are less inclined to deal openly with new subjects or situations. We often simply close our minds during this period so that we can recharge the brain cells. It is not easy to concentrate or to take the time and trouble to think things through clearly.

That we are all subject to the Law of Rhythm goes without saying. A human being is a complex organization of cells, rhythms, vibrations, energies, and magnetic fields, all of which have their individual cycles and are subject to influence from many external as well as internal pressures. Much research needs to be done in this field, so that we can all gear ourselves more productively to the interacting up and down swings of these cycles.

Shakespeare put it this way: "There is a tide in the affairs of men that, when taken at its flood, leads on to victory." There is a time to act, and a time not to act. The wise person discovers and acts upon his or her personal timing.

5. The Law of Use
(Right-Use-Ness or Righteousness)

The ideal human being is one who has experienced and mastered (or achieved dominion over) all aspects of the area in Creation where he or she exists.

This includes evil. Some New Thought movements like to pretend that evil does not exist in the world, that it is only the absence of good, as darkness is an absence of light. In one sense they are right. The absence of good does allow evil or inharmonious vibrations to manifest. However, to pretend that evil doesn't exist is to refuse to face up to the responsibility that we may have created an end-product that was not what we desired.

The same Law that works to give us health, wealth, happiness, love, and spiritual advancement can also work in opposition to bring us sickness, poverty, and lack of love. It is the same principle, misused through ignorance. Evil is live spelled backwards. To master or to overcome evil simply means that, through our experiences, we have learned to recognize and to use a higher aspect of the Law, instead of a lesser one.

Occultists believe that humans originally had access to all the extrasensory power we are now striving to regain. If so, then the "fall from Grace" (the Garden of Eden allegory) can be interpreted as a result of becoming so fascinated by sensory perceptions from the physical world, symbolized by the eating of the fruit from the Tree of the Knowledge of Good and Evil, that our attention was focused only on what could be seen, heard, touched, tasted, or smelled.

This, then, led to reliance upon outside advice from sources other than our own Inner Consciousness, such as from priests (represented by the serpent who pretended wisdom). The serpent is an ancient Egyptian symbol for the Kundalini, a power most often gained by priests and spiritual students, so the serpent that pretended wisdom would be a symbol in allegory for external sources. The failure to *listen* to the God-awareness that is within each individual, that unerringly directs us through and away from emotional, mental, and physical trouble, leads to atrophy of those inner senses.

When Eve "ate" (consumed; took in; experienced) the "fruit" (results) of the Knowledge of Good and Evil, she gave to humankind the gift of duality. It is this gift that lifts us up and makes us different from the animals, for animals have no choice but to follow their instincts, whereas we have the possibility and the capacity to so direct our thoughts and activities that we can literally become God-like beings.

True, like Pandora's box, this "gift" released into the world much pain and sorrow, heartbreak and struggle, but it also gave us the right—and the opportunity—to prove we are capable of controlling the mighty forces of good and evil. Once we have experienced evil, and recognized it as the result—the end-product — of thought manipulation of Substance, then we are in a position to do something about it. The sometimes painful school of experience leads to wisdom, and wisdom leads to mastery.

Since thought creates form, human thought has created evil, or negative, unproductive thinking which, intensified by many minds, has achieved a life of its own; and that life feeds off the same kind of thoughts that created it. Through the Law of Attraction we attract other people's negative thought-forms with our own. The evil of the world then multiplies within our own thinking, and becomes a semi- or quasi-living Beingness (not really a Being, but a Beingness) which we call the Devil. It feeds from our own thoughts, which amplify it. Multiply your own negative thoughts by the millions of people in the world and you'll understand where the "Devil" comes from.

Humans will learn to transcend the apparent evil of the world by changing their creative thought. Then the Devil, or Evil, will "become chained" (Rev. 20:1-3) because it cannot exist when it cannot feed, when it has nothing to feed upon.

It is even possible that these masses of negative thought-forms could become powerful enough to take embodiment in a human body. Such a Being would be soulless, but powered by the negative thought-forms of the people, like a robot.

This would be an excellent description of the Anti-Christ prophesied in the Book of Revelation. It would also explain why it is supposed to have such charm and to be so attractive to all who hail it as their leader, because it is literally the embodiment of all their own thoughts, beliefs, and ideals.

A leader comes up out of the consciousness of the people and reflects the general attitude of those he or she governs. The Anti-Christ, it is said, will be hailed by the whole world, and the masses of people who are ensnared will be those who have contributed to the thought energy that gives it life.

After a brief period of popularity (three years, according to the Book of Revelation), the Anti-Christ will be toppled from the throne. Anything that is wholly negative or evil will soon self-destruct, since only Good can stand up under any onslaught. Those people who endorsed the policies and philosophies of the Anti-Christ will learn from bitter personal experience about the effects generated by the causes they endorsed. It will be a period of "lesson-learning" by extreme hardship throughout the entire world, but out of it will come a new knowledge of the causes and effects of both good and evil. A better world for all people will be created by the chastened, more loving thoughts of every individual.

(The Anti-Christ might also be likened to a lightning rod, drawing to itself all the negative thinking that now permeates the world, so that it can be destroyed. From this perspective, it could also be considered a "savior," albeit a bitter, hard one.)

Fundamentalist theologians expect the Anti-Christ to be a literal embodiment of the Devil, but deeper reflection can carry the translation even further. We, as metaphysicians, strive to be in tune with the Presence of Christ within us, or the Soul Self, as we call it. By that definition, the Anti-Christ would offer a leadership that is strictly human, or human-based, following the reasoning of human logic (like the Garden of Eden serpent), rather than the intuitive knowingness of the inner God-Presence.

Such leadership would be fraught with peril because it would not be warned of erroneous reasoning by any inner guidance. It would be self-serving, rather than promoting the upliftment of the human consciousness. Most of our present leaders, while intoxicated with the power they possess, still try to function at the highest level of consciousness they can attain, and do their job for the greater good of the greater number of people, according to their understanding. Even this will be gone when the striving for greater good is not present.

The Law of Use (or Right-Use-Ness) indicates that the need to experience evil can be transcended by the overcoming or transmuting of inharmonious tendencies within ourselves. Usually we cannot master something until we have experienced both its good and bad qualities. We *know* that evil exists. But, in the same manner, we can *know* about our own counterpart of good—our ability to transmute the end-product we've created. The essence of the Anti-Christ exists in the world wherever human needs are not met. In contrast, each person who follows the Inner Guidance will strive to uplift others and bring the presence of joy and fulfillment into their lives.

Metaphysical students should have as their spiritual goal the cessation of personal warfare within themselves, knowing that when this tendency toward negative thinking has been reversed, it is no longer effective in manifestation. What has been accomplished by one can then be multiplied throughout the One Mind of humankind, and more and more individual minds will find the strength and understanding to follow suit. In this way, the time of world peace as well as the time of personal spiritual growth will be hastened, and the Law of Right-Use-Ness, or Righteousness, will be fulfilled.

6. The Law of Opposition

In our experience, there appear to be *two* forces at work in the Universe: the Force of Light, or Creation, and the Force of Darkness, destruction, and death. As I have shown, these are actually two aspects of the same Force. A diversion of the Creative Force of Light for destructive ends becomes an apparent force for darkness, a perversion of the Creative Force. The relationship between the forces of good and evil can be expressed as the Law of Opposition.

Since we have the choice—and the chance—to use both of these forces constructively, let's examine them more thoughtfully. Sometimes the appearance of evil, death, and destruction is deceptive, since destruction must often precede reconstruction.

When a form has served its purpose, it is no longer useful and it must be supplanted by another form. Old buildings must be torn down so that newer, more modern and efficient buildings can take their places. Forms such as cancer are elements out of control, operating in opposition to the health of the host, and therefore must be destroyed if health is to be restored.

Institutional aspects of society, such as government, marriage, religion, and education, need to change with the changing needs of evolving humanity. Many things that would be considered "sins" in our present society, such as genocide, infanticide, polygamy, and polyandry, have been an integral part of social structures in the past and were considered good for the greater welfare. As humanity evolved, human rights and human dignity gained more importance in our social mores, and new, more humane social interactions were selected while old forms were dropped.

The institution of marriage, for example, is undergoing radical changes today because the social structure is under pressure to meet the changing needs of people. Instead of considering this an activity of the forces of darkness and sin, as some religionists do, we should try to find what is lacking or no longer needed in the old forms of marriage. This will help us discover how the new form of marriage that will arise out of this transition will provide for a greater good.

All things, good and bad, are part of the whole. In our personal lives we sometimes find the forces of destruction and darkness seemingly at odds with things we hope to accomplish. When that happens to me, I take what I call the "Eternity point of view," and try to discover the overall picture of what is happening in my life. I've found that never has one door shut to close off a path of experience but another door has opened up to a greater good or a greater experience in another direction.

As I look back over my life, I also see that every event which seemed at the time to be an irreversible tragedy has, over the years, turned out to be a blessing in disguise, teaching me invaluable lessons of humility, love, and greatness of spirit, often bringing into my life people who have enriched my experience immeasurably.

To those who love the Law, all things work together for good, and the Force of Darkness is no exception. This is not just a "Pollyanna" attitude of looking for the good in everything that occurs, although that is a powerful law in itself. It is a dynamic expansion into attunement with the Greater Plan for your own life, and also into the Greater Plan for the evolvement of the human race, of which we are "parts of the whole." Joseph said to his brethren who sold him into slavery, "Ye meant it for evil, but God meant it for good" (Genesis 50:20).

Dion Fortune, in her book *The Cosmic Doctrine*,[15] speaks of good and evil as opposing circular forces which bring Creation into manifestation. The force of good tends to concretization, or aggregation of Substance, creating static particles or forms. The force of evil, moving in the opposite direction, tends to dissolve or diffuse particles.

Ms. Fortune deserves much credit for her addition to occult thought and her clarity of understanding of these two opposing forces. She admits that the words "good" and "evil" are truly unsatisfactory to explain the workings of these influences that play upon Creation. I would like to suggest another interpretation. Let us call them positive and negative electrical poles, the Yin and Yang of the universe. The positive electrical force is an expressive, repelling energy, and the negative electrical force is a receptive, aggregating energy.

Astrologers label these same forces male (positive) and female (negative) in an attempt to define the alternating energies found in the planets and astrological signs. Section Thirteen of this session (The Law of Polarities or Sex) will show how these dynamics are applied in human sexuality and life energies.

It is only because these two forces flow in continual opposition to each other throughout the universe that evolution, movement, and differentiation—and therefore Creation itself—can take place. Without opposition, the force of negative energy would become static in the immediate present, continually building up without differentiation. Without opposition, the force of positive energy would return all forms to the Unmanifest from whence it arose and, if unchecked, reduce all forms to nothingness.

Forms which are considered "good" for a lengthy period of time ultimately become static and non-evolving, and must be diffused so that their Substance may be reused for something else. All evil that builds up within a Universe is attracted toward diffusion by its very nature, and is therefore self-destroyed, because the very idea of "evil" implies a force which tends toward nonexistence.

The two forces, forever opposing each other, create stability, a foothold, a purchase on space as it were, says Ms. Fortune. Jesus said, "Resist not evil" (Matt. 5:39). Resisting or opposing evil tends to aid the force of good, or the clinging, aggregating energy, which holds the evil inert, or static, keeping it from following its normal course into nothingness. Without the change and tension caused by the growth which these opposing forces permit, the Cosmos could not progress to its own finality. Good and evil are not alien to each other, but proceed out of each other as part of the One Force. That which is in opposition is not necessarily an enemy.

Dion Fortune says, "Never oppose evil which you mean to destroy." Instead, make a vacuum around it, and by so doing prevent opposition (good) from touching it. (As we have learned, the best way to destroy evil or inharmonious structures in our lives is to turn away all thought energy from them.) Then, being unopposed, it is free to follow the laws of its own nature, which is to become diffused and to return to the Unmanifest, the undifferentiated raw material of existence, where it ceases to be organized or to have qualities. It starts afresh at the beginning, transmuted through neutrality into good.

As Shakespeare put it: "There is nothing either good or bad, but thinking makes it so." Both Forces can be used to bring good into our lives, if we handle them with conscious awareness.

7. The Law of Intensification

Hundreds of books and thousands of words have been written on the subject of how to use your will power, mind power, imagination, and/or visualization to get what you want out of Life. In the previous section we discussed the Laws of Manifestation and Substance, but there is additional information which should be included here.

Any strong feeling, action, or thought-process impresses itself upon the realm of Substance, and the Law of Manifestation is automatically set into motion, with or without your awareness of the part you played in bringing the manifestation into being. To increase the intensity of the initiating action, the use of magic rituals, sacred words, or any object of representation provides effective mental or emotional links from thought to result.

Kingdon Brown, in *The Power of Psychic Awareness,*[16] says it in this way: "Strong feelings, plus a Link, directed at a Target, equals Results." A link is usually, but not always, a visible object which represents some aspect of your desire.

Using a link to obtain what you want brings the Law of the Whole and its Parts into action. Any "part" of the Whole can be used as an object on which to focus your attention, but usually some tangible article which is imbued with the vibrations of the target is selected.

The link serves to sustain the emotion and thought-image for a longer period of time, giving it the added intensity of duration. Magic rituals have the same effect, and for the purpose of this example can be considered the same as a link.

Lighting a green candle for prosperity, for instance, serves to keep bringing your thought back in a positive, expectant manner to your desire for prosperity, as long as the candle remains lit. Church altars have candles that can be lit in prayer for the salvation or preservation of a loved one. The candle can be used by the mind as a physical link to bring about an outer result.

To effect speedier healing, for instance, one may obtain something the sick person has worn, such as a piece of jewelry, or some item of clothing. You can then direct the force of your thought, emotion, and action into the object while mentally linking up with the person.

Psychics who give readings through the mail, or over the telephone, often ask for a handkerchief, a photograph, or some other item belonging to the individual, prior to the reading. Sometimes the handwritten letter itself will serve as a link.

Initiators into the sacred mysteries, even the instructors of Maharishi Mahesh Yogi's Transcendental Meditation techniques, will ask for a gift of fruit, flowers, and a personal item, such as a handkerchief, before bestowing an initiation or a secret mantra.

The link is a powerful tool of association with the object of your desire. A pendulum or dowsing rod can be considered a link. So can a photograph. Some research has been done by psychic healers who place a photograph of an ill person under various colored lights to intensify the power of the prayer for healing.

A researcher from one of my classes tried an experiment with an aerial photograph of a field he used for a cattle pasture. He smeared thin strips of a chemical fertilizer on the photograph, alternating strips of fertilizer with bare strips. He did nothing else with the field. He did not plow it, water it, or interfere in any other way with the natural activity of the land, not even with Mind action.

In early summer, he took me to the hilltop pasture where I saw with my own eyes the strips of slightly greener grass growing in long rows down the field, corresponding to the strips of fertilizer he had placed on the photograph.

In Genesis, humanity was given dominion over all the elements of Creation. When the storm threatened the little boat in which Jesus was sleeping, He merely held up his hand and said, "Peace. Be still," and the storm abated. Someday, humanity, following the Way-Shower, will learn how to use their dominion over all the elements for the benefit and blessing of humankind.

Mid-Arkansas is the center of much tornado activity, high winds, and floods. An important part of research activity at the Parapsychology Education Center was the prevention of destructive weather by mind control. All members of our classes automatically became members of "Operation Weather Control." Wherever they were, whatever they were doing, whenever destructive weather threatened they went immediately to work, using their minds to dissipate and dissolve destructive elements that might be brewing.

Most of the psychic work had apparent positive results, but because weather in all its aspects is most capricious, no one dares to make positive claims to total power over the elements. However, three instances stood out as exceptional.

One night, *five* formed funnel clouds (tornadoes) were sighted over the city of Little Rock. The Weather Control group, listening to the police radio, went into action with the first sighting and *not one funnel touched down!* A pretty impressive percentage, even considering the capriciousness of tornadoes.

One of our class members had a soybean crop in the field ready for harvest when a thunder storm blew up in the west. She called for help, and one of the researchers fitted a plastic shield (a link) over an aerial photograph of her field, leaving the surrounding fields untouched. The class member swore that the rain came up to her fence line on three sides—leaving her field dry until the beans were in—and then came down in a deluge.

The third incident was perhaps the most spectacular of all! In the mid-1970s, Hurricane Carmen threatened to overrun the Louisiana coastline. Mr. W. H. "Bill" Moore, one of the directors and cofounder of the Center and a most active researcher in weather control, had a daughter and her family directly in line with the threatened storm, which was circling in the Gulf of Mexico at 180 miles an hour, moving towards shore at about 30 miles an hour. Evacuation of the city was contemplated when our squad went to work, using the emotional contact with the daughter as a link.

We visualized a brick wall between the Louisiana coast and Hurricane Carmen. Mr. Moore put his thumb on a map of the Gulf (a second link) precisely where satellite photos showed the hurricane to be centered and declared, "This destructive energy will stay right where it is until the wind velocity decreases and its energies will dissipate harmlessly, so that when it reaches land it will be no more than a tropical storm."

The rest is history! National newspapers carried the story of how, unprecedentedly, Hurricane Carmen stalled for *five* hours in its forward speed, about twenty miles offshore, and when it finally reached land the winds had calmed to a mere thirty-five miles per hour. It veered westward into relatively unpopulated marshlands instead of into the heavily populated Lake Pontchartrain area, as had been earlier predicted.

What caused the most jubilation among members of the group was a local TV weatherman's remark that night, "It was as though that hurricane had struck a *"brick wall!"*

The consistently positive results of our many experiments caused Bill Moore to formulate a new equation: "$R = R^P$" (R = R Prime, or "the Representation is equal to the Reality.") A map, a plastic shield, a White Light circle of protection, or a green candle for prosperity will equal the reality in psychic results.

As with all the Laws, this, too, can be used for evil effects. The classic example is the effigy or Voodoo doll made with a lock of hair or a fingernail paring from the victim, which can be used to cause disaster or the death of its target. In my personal experience, I know of a death spell using magic rituals that was cast by a sick mind in a personal vendetta, and three sisters (the person's aunts) were dead within a year.

Sybil Leek, in *Diary of a Witch*,[17] describes state murders committed using witchcraft in the name of "public good" (although she does not say if she participated in any of them).

I consider this Law of Intensification the pivotal Mystery Law. On your understanding and use of it will rest your spiritual position (and progression) during the coming Age. It is where the Left-Hand Path into black magic forks from the Right-Hand Path leading to compassion and love.

Emphatically let me repeat: If you use this or any other Law for the manipulation, destruction, or coercion of any other person, the boomeranging results will bring equally disastrous consequences for you.

Its use raises questions of ethics, as well as of morality. What about the group of people (or just one person) who use their minds to prevent a much-needed rainfall just because they wish to have a pleasant weekend? Consider also the possible consequences for two opposing groups of workers—farmers, whose livelihood depends upon rainfall, and construction workers, whose paychecks stop when the rain comes down.

The manipulation of weather is the easiest of all natural Laws in which to achieve mastery, but it carries great karmic implications if such mastery is not used responsibly. It is through the conscious and unconscious use of this Law, combined with the Law of Karma, that we learn the virtue of harmlessness in our spiritual journey.

8. The Law of Silence

Within the deepest state of mystical consciousness is a place of great stillness, where the individual is no thing and all things. It is sought by Eastern mystics as the place of Union where the Soul loses its identity in the all-enveloping embrace of God.

Western mystics identify it as an awareness of or an immersion into the total Beingness of Omniscience, everywhere One with All That Is. It is at once a Becoming and a Completion, a total union with the Stream of Life flowing ceaselessly through all manifested and unmanifested forms, omnipotently existing forever within an omnipresent Consciousness without beginning and without end.

The experience usually happens spontaneously, but can be induced through fasting or prolonged meditation. It always leaves the person completely changed. Drug-induced mystical states can also awaken a person to the awareness of and desire for greater spiritual consciousness, but this method leads to dependency rather than to mastership.

As with all true Mystery Laws, the principle of "As Above, so Below" applies. The archetypes of all Creation are found within the stillness of the Mind of God. (Some people also hear the "Music of the Spheres," which is the sound of Creation coming into manifestation.)

So it is with the minds of humans. The possibilities and potentialities of each life are found within the stillness of the individual mind, and it is only in the stillness of meditation or introspection that the potentials can be discovered. It is only *after* discovery that they can, through the force of Will, be consciously acted upon.

We must, through the stillness of our inner Selves, discover the capabilities inherent in us. There is an extension of this Law. When once a project has been set in motion through prayer, visualization, or meditation, the Law of Silence must be enforced. *Do not talk about it!*

Talking about a project or an end that we wish to accomplish channels the energy out into useless waves of air. Worse still, the as yet unsprouted seeds of our desires may fall on the antagonistic soil of a hostile mind, which could attempt to destroy the desire before its fruition.

Whatever your grand dream, there is always someone there to counteract it with a derisive comment: What a bunch of hogwash! You know that's never been done! What makes you think you can do it? Yes, but it'll never work! You know your parents (friends, teachers) won't like it . . . .

These minds do not recognize themselves as enemies. In fact, they masquerade as well-wishing friends and relatives who do not wish to see you disappointed. Or, because they themselves cannot envisage your goal, they honestly do not believe it is possible to attain.

Your uniqueness lies in the special capabilities that are yours. If a desire, and the enthusiasm to fulfill it, come through into your mind, know that the energy and power to make that dream come true are also there. No matter what anyone else may think or say, it is the Law. But we are also very susceptible to the thoughts and words of others, especially those we hold dear. Therefore, hold your heart's vision in silence until it is closer to fruition and cannot be destroyed by vagrant words.

There are two times when the Law of Silence may be broken. One is when you feel you need the power of another mind to help you envision your goal. An example is the power pool that is formed when two or more people gather together to pray for the health or healing of someone who is ill. When doing this, choose someone whose metaphysical understanding matches or exceeds your own, and you know that person will work for you instead of against you.

However, when you have received an instantaneous healing or remission, or if you have been healed by a spiritual healer, do not talk about it to *anyone* (not even a spiritual friend) for at least forty-eight hours. It takes that long for Substance to become "set" in the new pattern. During the first forty-eight hours it is still vulnerable to the doubts and negative thought-forms of others and must be protected by your silence.

The other time when silence may be broken is when you feel you are with someone who can help you attain your goal. For instance, holding a vision that you will get a certain kind of job is fruitless unless you tell the prospective employer that you want the job. The employer probably will not offer it to you unasked, although that does happen sometimes. More often, though, you must be assertive enough to go after it.

Watch expectantly for avenues to open up in which your desire might be fulfilled, and then speak up. At these times you will find people around you being cooperative, but don't discuss it idly—or even enthusiastically—at times when there is little or no chance for its fulfillment. That is almost certain death for the idea, or will, at best, result in extra efforts being needed to overcome the discouragement that is sure to be thrown your way.

Above all, do not talk about negative situations which you are trying to overcome unless the person to whom you speak can be of positive help with the overcoming. The Law of Silence is especially effective here: it helps to turn your thoughts away from a situation you do not wish to further energize, and also you do not add another's negative beliefs to an already bad situation.

9. The Law of Reincarnation and Karma

Buddha is said to have remembered over 500 of his earth lives, and he felt that two great Laws were the real keys to the Mystery of Being. These he called the Law of Reincarnation (or the Law of Rebirth) and the Law of Karma.

Karma comes from a Sanskrit word meaning "action." Today's usage aligns it more closely with the fruits or results of action. Karma, then, is usually considered to be the Law of Action and Reaction, or, as it is more frequently called, the Law of Cause and Effect.

Much has been written on the mystery of karma. We usually think of it as the results of bad action or bad judgment, and therefore think of karma as being bad. But the word itself is neutral. There can be good karma as well as bad karma. In fact, as I heard one of my students say, "There are no rewards, and no punishments, only consequences."

Karma is more than just the sum of a person's actions, which are the causes, and the results of those actions, which are the effects. It also includes the impressions or tendencies created in the subconscious mind by those actions. In lifetime after lifetime we tend to react in a certain way in response to certain circumstances. It is these tendencies, which we carry over into each life, that are so hard to eliminate from our personal behavior.

Patanjali, the great Indian codifier of Yoga science, said that exercising control over the senses, studying inspiring literature, and turning one's attention to the highest Self within are the actions which will secure mastery in life. To understand this further, you might enjoy reading the Yoga Sutras of Patanjali, sometimes called the Yoga aphorisms. They deal with meditative techniques for quieting the lower mind of the Personality and awakening to the higher mind of the Soul. One should practice these disciplines with the goal of gaining tranquillity and lessening the afflictions of body and mind, Patanjali says. The best American translation of this work is, in my opinion, *The Light of the Soul* by Alice A. Bailey,[18] but there are other excellent translations as well.

Patanjali identifies five afflictions of body and mind that disciples on the spiritual path need to deal with: (1) attachment; (2) self-conceit; (3) hatred; (4) ignorance, or absence of awareness; and (5) false pride.

Attachments come through desire, love, and self-gratification. They create input of data from the senses that we feel we cannot live without. For example, we usually love others as a means of self-satisfaction, rather than as an opportunity to share ourselves in service to or with them, or to know another so intimately as to become one in spirit. Often we love another because he or she fulfills our own needs, rather than learning, through loving them enough, how to put their needs before our own.

Attachments are the passions of the mental body, which control and dominate the thinking process. These passions, though they are intensely felt, are only partial activities, using only a portion of the whole Being.

Self-conceit—a more modern term for this may be "self-centeredness"—embraces all the passions: anger, lust, selfishness, and self-hate. What happens to us when we become angry? We are enveloped in a violent tantrum of ego and self-indulgence, an abnormal mind-engulfing state. Discipline, tranquillity, and self-control are all lost. These passions are emotional maladjustments, giving the emotional body the upper hand over the activities that frame our lives. Like the other passions, these engulfing attributes restrict the full use of the whole range of Being.

By intensifying awareness of the "I AM" focus, we gradually gain control over our emotional and mental natures. All decisions, judgments, and evaluations are then projected from the Soul Self, which allows each experience to be an attribute of the whole Being and not just of a portion of the Self.

Hatred is usually based on fear—fear of pain, emotional hurt or loss, or the unknown. When something is really understood it is no longer feared or hated, but accepted and placed in its proper perspective. The thing formerly hated is then allowed its own expression of life on its own plane, whether that is the plane of devolution or evolution. It is no longer resisted, but given freedom to move as its own nature dictates. If the thing hated is truly evil, then, as we have learned, it will tend of its own nature toward dissolution. The withdrawal of resistance will allow it to move outward into its natural state of diffusion. If it is only our ignorance which labeled it "evil," then its inherent goodness will become known and its purpose in our lives understood.

Ignorance, or lack of awareness, is particularly self-perpetuating, because we do not know what we do not know. From this grow arrogance, limitation, prejudice, and restrictions. The blinding scales of ignorance begin to drop away only when we finally turn within and, with humility and sincerity, seek for knowledge and enlightenment.

False pride is ego-centered. Understanding the real nature of the ego is a stumbling block in the spiritual growth of many people, especially Westerners. We tend to be more dynamically oriented than Eastern peoples, who traditionally relate to life in a more accepting fashion.

There is lower ego, which is of the Personality. It is our "Will-to-do." We could not accomplish anything worthwhile in life, even spiritual progress, without this ego. We cannot destroy this ego—to try to do so is not only foolhardy but dangerous, since it can only be repressed, not destroyed—but we can expand it and our understanding of it.

The Higher Ego is our spiritual Identity, our "Will-to-become," the "I AM" Presence. The lower ego should be the voluntary servant of the Higher Ego, desiring only to do whatever is willed by the Soul Self.

It is the lower ego of the Personality that indulges in pride, acquisitiveness, and self-acclaim. It is always willing to be flattered, to be exalted, to be cajoled. To achieve this it will often sacrifice integrity, honor, even health and wealth. It is this aspect of the ego that must be held in check, or rather, transmuted into the higher qualities of self-respect, ethics, integrity, and sensitivity. This transmutation takes place when the Soul Self, through understanding and rightly controlled desire, places its priorities in order and wills the energy of the lower ego to be directed into proper channels.

I believe this submission of the lower ego to the Soul Self is what is meant when spiritual texts speak of subduing the ego. Any other action against the ego is a psychological perversion, a violation of the essential self.

Untransmuted qualities of the Soul create the negative actions and reactions in our lives. A repeated action tends to perpetuate the emotion that created the action; a negative reaction will often, through ignorance, create further negative emotional responses, which in turn create further negative activity. These cycles are carried over from lifetime to lifetime. Some remain deeply impressed upon the subconscious, so that it takes much introspection and self-analysis to find and correct an offending characteristic.

Of course, the opposite is also true. Continued positive and constructive use of energy creates tendencies within the Soul to react in positive ways to events and situations in our lives, so that by conscious use of positive responses we gradually build up subconscious tendencies to react in a positive way to life's exigencies.

A corresponding action is not always needed to remove the effects of "bad" karma from the Soul's pattern of action. For instance, a person who kills another person in a fit of anger takes on the karma of the unfulfilled life-pattern that he caused to be short-circuited. This indebtedness may be fulfilled when someone in turn kills him, thereby short-circuiting his own life energies, or he may be given an opportunity to save a life, thus restoring the balance.

Nor is it necessary for the one to whom the karmic debt is owed to receive the repayment, or to do the repaying. In other words, the one that was killed does not have to kill the slayer in repayment. Should the one who is killed decide to invoke the Law of Forgiveness, then no further debt is owed, and the slate is wiped clean between these two. Further lifetimes will not hold any karmic ties between them in regard to this particular action.

However, the impulse toward hate or anger which created the bad karma in the first place may remain an aspect of that Soul for several lifetimes, giving rise to other actions which bring retribution in one form or another until the Soul is purged of the desire for anger.

Karma is not intended by the universe as a weapon for punishment. It is a tool for learning and for purification. It is only by experience that we learn to transmute the Soul's attributes into higher and finer qualities, until finally complete detachment from the fruits of one's action unbinds the Soul from the Wheel of Rebirth on the earth plane and it is free to go on to other levels, other dimensions of experience.

"Good" karma can be as much of an attachment to the earth plane as "bad" karma. If we fail to forgive ourselves or others, and carry our "tally sheet" of payments and repayments from lifetime to lifetime, we create and maintain the need for these types of lessons or experiences. If we do good for the sake of reward, we will have to return in order to claim the reward.

The true lesson of karmic adjustment is to learn to live harmoniously and graciously within the illusions of the Earth plane, letting each experience be its own reward, giving generously of our time and talents without calculating how, why, or if our gift may return.

The mysterious Law of Cycles takes care of its own; therefore, perfecting the experience of the NOW moment should be the only concern of the aspirant. In this manner we may, in one lifetime, dissolve all past mistakes and create a clearer reflection for a more perfect future.

10. The Law of Progression and Change

The Universe moves circularly forward from the unmanifest to the manifest and back to the unmanifest, constantly creating, un-creating, and re-creating itself. It is this movement which creates time and space.

Some movements are more rapid than others. Called "vibrations," they create the background which we recognize as the world (space) around us, and provide input of data for the senses. In the eternal NOW only the background seems to move, giving us the sense of time, a term for the progression and chronological recording of events. The Soul is relatively unmoving in relation to the world of the senses, but it, too, progresses and changes throughout eternity.

Although not all change is progress, all progress *is* change. Another old cliché says, "Nothing is changeless except change itself!" We must recognize and accept this force of change in order to accomplish anything we set out to do. You cannot create new circumstances in your life and at the same time maintain the status quo, like the woman who wanted a new job for her husband but was unwilling to move to another city to accept it when offered. When you start moving Substance, anything can happen.

In some cases, this force of change creates tremendous upheavals and even chaos in one's life in order to effect progress. Fortunately, this extreme case doesn't happen to very many people, but it happened to me, and I've seen its influence in the lives of some of my students, so I feel it should be dealt with here.

My own personal makeup is that of a very fixed person. I have a Leo Sun, with six "fixed" planets in my horoscope, so astrologers will understand when I say that the energies I work with are solid and long-lasting in comparison, say, with a Gemini, who fluidly moves from project to project with little hold on the past.

The ideas and ideals impressed on me by parents and teachers as I grew up were as though set in cement about me. To change any of these almost required an "Act of Judgment," and that's exactly what I got.

When I first began to study metaphysical principles, I *knew* intellectually—and maybe spiritually—from depths inside myself that these were Truths, and that I wanted to put them to work in my life. But every time I attempted an affirmation for better conditions, I'd get a reverse effect.

In other words, when I tithed or prayed for prosperity, I'd lose my job, or some calamity would put my family even further behind the financial eight-ball. Whenever I prayed for or affirmed good health, one of my family members would end up in the hospital, or another illness would strike.

We moved three times in two years, buying a home in each place, expecting to stay and put down roots, only to have the "rug yanked out from under us," having to sell our home for a loss and move to yet another location to start over.

Those years were the most chaotic of my life. If there hadn't been deep within me some stubborn, unreasoning, intuitive feeling that the Principles were right, and *had* to work no matter what they seemed to be doing to my life, the tender seeds of new conditioning would never have survived those two years. I'd have returned to the old comfortable, familiar way of Being that didn't pose a threat every time I turned around.

That was my first recognized contact with the "I AM" within me, although at that time I did not yet have a name for it. I only knew that that part of me which pushed me on in spite of chaotic conditions was Something apart from that which was happening to me, Something that could not be touched by intellectualizing, Something beyond the reasoning force of my mind.

I made my first contact with metaphysics in the Unity Church, somewhere around age thirty-five. By that time, attitudes and conditioned patterns of living were deeply entrenched in my sub-conscious. It figuratively took "dynamite" to blast them loose.

As I said earlier, age thirty-five marks the start of a seven-year cycle of new spiritual beginnings. In my life, the "dynamite" was probably long overdue, but I didn't know that then, and the emotional trauma was great. Finally, in desperation, I asked my Unity minister about it, and he gave me this illustration which I hope will help you as it did me.

He said, "Consider a rain barrel that has been sitting in the sun. The water looks clear on top, but on the bottom are dregs, dirt, and debris. What happens when you put a hose running fresh water into the barrel? Immediately all the dregs are stirred up, and all that sediment must arise and pour out over the top of the barrel before the water can be truly pure and fresh again.

"Everything that's happening to you is the dregs from your subconscious. All the fears and negative thought habits that you've harbored through the years must now be washed up and out into manifestation so that they will be finished and done with. Once manifested, they will never bother you again."

So I learned to recognize these inharmonious conditions of my life as end-products, manifestation that had been speeded up, perhaps, by the intensity of my enthusiasm and desire for a new life. As such, I knew they should be only temporary in duration.

Whenever I got a reversed effect from an affirmation or a prayer, I learned to take it as a sign I was moving Substance, and all the debris had to be cleaned out of the way before it could manifest as desired. Then I would give thanks that it was over and done with and continue to wait expectantly for the results originally asked for, which I soon discovered were never far behind.

The "reversed effect syndrome" remained with me with dimin-ishing consequences for about five years before gradually fading out of my life. Once in awhile a small reversed effect appears even today, perhaps when I touch some conditioning more deeply buried than others. Then I say, "That's great! I'm glad that happened! It means I'm moving something!" I feel honest joy that one more negative conditioning is going out of my life—manifested out as an end-product, never to return.

It doesn't take a "blockbuster" to change the lives and habits of most people, and for that we can give thanks, but if you find it happening to you, be gratefully expectant. It means you're moving Substance, and your true desire will soon manifest, so just hang on and don't give up.

There's still the Law of Grace to consider, and if I'd understood at that time in my life how Grace functions, perhaps I needn't have suffered so much.

11. The Law of Grace

It is not necessary to pay every jot and tittle of one's karma. If that were so, humankind would be so deeply buried under the results of our misdirected energies that we would never be able to progress.

I don't know if the Law of Grace was given to humanity as a special dispensation by the Christ, or whether He simply brought it to our attention. Whichever it was, the Law of Grace transcends the old Mosaic Law: "An eye for an eye, and a tooth for a tooth" (Ex. 21:24), which kept people in bondage to their karma.

The word "repent" gives us a clue. Along with the words "pensive" and "penitent," it derives from the old French word, penser, meaning to think, to engage in deep thoughtfulness. To repent, loosely translated, means to re-think. When we repent of our misdeeds, we literally re-think the consequences of our actions, thoughts, and motives, re-evaluate our priorities, and determine to pursue a different course of action in the future.

This re-thinking—repenting—changes the course of our destiny. Because the old causes are no longer in force, new effects are created.

Attitudes and habits relating to the environment are buried deep within the subconscious, and are largely unconscious to the Beta mind. Most of the time we are really unaware of the true motives behind our actions. Psychologically, we often hide so-called sinful or unacceptable motives even from ourselves, blaming others for our failures and shortcomings.

Fortunately for us, psychoanalytic programs, guided fantasy games, group therapy, and other types of self-analysis are becoming increasingly popular in our culture, so that more and more people are awakening to take responsibility for their own moral, spiritual, and psychological health and growth.

The Law of Grace has to do with forgiveness, both of ourselves and those whom we have allowed to harm us. To face squarely the idea that we have been hurt emotionally, physically, or mentally, and to realize that we, ourselves, allowed the hurt to happen in the first place—that it could not have been thrust upon us if we had not in some fashion accepted it—is a major step toward self-awakening. Therefore, not only is it politic to forgive the one who filled the thought-mold which brought us this experience, it is also imperative that we forgive ourselves for having condoned the action which took place within.

Let us examine how the Law of Cause and Effect works in this matter. Our "sin" is not the action we commit (although the harming of another does bring its own consequences). The *motive* behind the action is the real culprit. This is usually one or more of the five "afflictions" listed by Patanjali: attachment, self-conceit, hatred, ignorance, and false pride.

For example, suppose that the hidden attribute which is creating the inharmonious condition in life is hatred of a particular person, race, ideology, or whatever. As long as this hidden motive remains unknown and unchecked, life will continue to pile incident after incident into your experience upon which this hate can vent itself. People will seem to do things deliberately to excite your animosity. You will continually run into the type of person you despise. You may gradually come to believe that the majority of people are dishonest, untrustworthy, liars, cheats, "out to get you," and that if you don't "look out for your own interests, nobody else will," maybe even to the extent that you feel you have to "do unto others *before* they do unto you."

Now suppose that through therapy, insight, revelation, or metaphysics, you suddenly realize that all the incidents which you blamed on other people could be traced back to this one

hidden attribute in you—the ability to hate—and your acceptance unto yourself of the consequences of that ability.

You repent. You re-think the consequences of your actions
and motives. We'll assume that the revelation is deep enough and
cleansing enough to purge you of all hatred for other people.
(Actually, it rarely happens that way. Instead, we learn slowly
and painfully through many individual thoughts and actions. For
the sake of this example, though, we'll assume that the revelation
and purging is complete.)

Now you have a sense of forgiveness for those you previously
despised, and a warm, compassionate feeling of gentleness and
tolerance overcomes your animosity. Now a new cause is set up.
Your new insight will reveal to you a warmth and gentleness of
human nature you never even suspected before. People will go
out of their way to treat you well. You will be showered with
love and kindness because only love and kindness is going out
from you, and the new cause creates a new effect.

However, prior to your "conversion," there was a gigantic
load of unpaid karma set loose upon the world. The effects of
that vibrational level still remain, even though you no longer
harbor it yourself. This is where the Law of Grace come in. As
long as you remain within your new set of attitudes, the old effects will never touch your new vibration.

You will be truly free of those consequences, and they will
gradually move out and dissolve into the unmanifest, where they
will be transmuted back into neutral energy again.

In reality, life is never that black and white. We seldom can
turn over a new leaf immediately and let the old be as though it
never was, much as we would like to. Usually, our new insight
gives us enthusiasm and energy to use in new ways, and for the
most part we consciously act in the way we would like to become
accustomed to, changing the old tendencies by slow but sure increments of thought and behavior, transmuting the Soul Force
into upward action.

However, deep inside are the old subconscious habit patterns
which need to be broken down, dissolved, and replaced. One
day in a fit of pique, we say something spiteful to Aunt Minnie,
and before the day is over, someone says exactly the same thing
back to us. Metaphysicians call this "instant karma." In reality,

we've fallen back (backslid) into the old vibrational level, and there, waiting to slap us in the face, are the still undissolved consequences of our prior thought and action.

We can consciously call upon the Law of Grace to help us over these rough spots, and if we are really sincere and have truly forgiven we will find the way becoming smoother and our personal insight becoming greater. One always goes with the other. Grace is given freely—we do not have to earn it. It comes for the asking. It is the Divine Forgiveness which allows us our mistakes and gives us new opportunities to try again—and again, if needed.

To loose the bonds of karma, I feel that it is helpful to find the causes first, to know what we are doing wrong, so that it can be consciously corrected. I have a friend, a Religious Science minister, who disagrees violently with me on that. He feels it is not necessary to do all that inner probing, that by simply calling upon the Grace of Jesus Christ we can be freed immediately from all our "sins," known and unknown, and be reborn with new freedom of thought and action, the kind which presumably leads to "good" karma rather than "bad" karma.

He may be right. It is not wise to argue with another's experience. I know the Law of Grace works no matter how difficult the situation, and only the individual can know how much or how little he or she needs to know about the subconscious Self and its workings.

12. The Law of Eternal Life Energy

God (the Substance from which we were created and in which we live, move, and have our Being) is eternal Life Energy. The expression of life is eternal, or at least as eternal as our finite minds can grasp. As long as God exists, we will exist, for we are God expressing Himself in these particular identities, yours and mine.

God, existing in and through all aspects of Creation, is that Creation in its totality, the sum of all its parts yet greater than its parts. We, individually existing within the Creation, are parts of the whole, and as parts of Infinite Life we have the ability to draw upon the eternal Life Energy to the fullest extent of our capacity to comprehend *what that Life really is.* The expansion of that comprehension is the development of *Self*-Realization.

If we are God expressing Himself as us, how can we be lost from God, as some doctrines teach? We can lose sight of our divinity and our right to live harmonious lives, but that doesn't mean that the divinity is not still there. The very fact that we continue to exhibit the Creativity that is God-in-Expression, even if that Creativity produces inharmonious results, is God-in-Action, God learning to know Himself through His creating and His Creation.

Meditation on the opposing principles of "good and evil" (positive/negative) as outlined by Dion Fortune[19] will help us to understand the finite illusions we experience as we use these creative energies: the Law of Good, which tends to aggregation, and the Law of Evil, which tends to dissolution. Both are necessary in order to create any kind of manifestation and both are part of the eternal life pattern.

We, in pursuit of Self-understanding, must get outside of an experience and into our intuition, and as the Knower ("I AM"), perceive the manifestation for what it is: an experiment in the use of negative/positive principles of creating, an experiment in living, or action.

By so doing, we put the manifestation in proper perspective, and can make valid judgments about whether we wish to pursue that line of action or take another course. We can either breathe additional life into the present circumstances or extinguish them by turning our energies elsewhere.

Jesus said that He came that we might have life, and that more abundantly (John 10:10). He meant that He came to show us how to receive life more abundantly by following His precepts and learning to understand His own comprehension of Eternal Life. Peter said that God is not willing that any should die, but that all should come to repentance (re-thinking), and that all should have abundant Life (II Peter 3:9).

Paul, in one of his letters to the church at Corinth, stated that when Christ (meaning the principles taught by Christ) had finally put all the world under its dominion, the last enemy to be overcome was death (I Cor. 15:26). We can hasten that eventuality by beginning now to study the concept of what Life really is, and to expand within ourselves more and more the joyous thrill of true living, or living true.

Young people have a joyousness, a vibrancy and love of life that is so natural to them that they are mostly unaware that they exhibit these characteristics. It is not until the negative returns of ignorant and unwise thinking have hit us again and again that we lose this joyous going forth to challenge life. As joy fades, life fades, and this condition is known as old age.

The fish swimming in the water says, "Water? What water? I don't see any water!" Only when it is taken out of the water can it appreciate what it left behind. So it is with us. When finally we experience the slowing down, the physical ills that signify the rigidity of approaching age, only then do we appreciate the fluidity of motion and energizing enthusiasm that mark youthfulness and the vigor of life.

Paul said, "I die daily" (I Cor. 15:31), and we do. Death, in all its forms, is the dissolving of one set of circumstances to be replaced by another. Recognizing death in this light, it ceases to be an enemy and becomes a friend. Without the death of the outworn, the outmoded, the no longer useful, we would remain static in a static world with no opportunity for further experience. Without the death of the unneeded, we would be unable to shake off anything we had created. It would continue to cling to us like a festering sore, stripping us of dignity and renewal.

Even death of the body is not an enemy. The body, made up of the elements of the sphere we have chosen to satisfy our need to experience, is a mirror that reflects our wise or unwise use of the energy of that sphere. The aging process is proof that we have not yet learned how to stabilize the negative/positive processes. This balance will eventually come when science and religion join forces for a mutual understanding of the mechanisms of life.

At our present state of evolution, death of the body is a blessing, for it releases us from an outworn vehicle which can no longer function with the living vibrancy it once had. Then the Soul, which is undying, has the opportunity of starting over again with a new body, under renewed circumstances.

All that science can tell us now is that there is no known reason for the aging process. The body was meant to rejuvenate itself, and it would if the individual understood the Eternal Life principle.

Jesus' grasp of the Life principle was so great that He was able to call it forth into the dead and decaying body of Lazarus and also to raise His own dead body from the grave. His ascension was the culmination of His personal application of the Law of Eternal Life, a dramatic revelation that orthodox churches have ignored because of the lack of a basis for interpretation.

When Jesus said, "Those that follow me, I give unto them eternal life" (John 10:27, 28), I believe He meant what He said, even to the ascension of our own rejuvenated and totally vibrant, living physical bodies, when our evolution ultimately catches up with His. He did say, remember, that "all these things I do, you can do, also. And even greater things than I can you do, for I go to the Father within."

That day can be hastened. Many people down through the ages have made that same ascension, although very little is recorded about it, except in some obscure books which the consciousness of humankind as a whole is not yet willing to reveal.

In fact, one woman and her husband made the ascension in this century. In 1957, Annalee Skarin ascended as Jesus did 2,000 years ago, and she did it in the documented presence of eight reliable witnesses, who legally swore they witnessed the event. Later, in private, her husband followed her in his own ascension, and both have been seen in their glorified bodies since that time, appearing in the middle of a room, unannounced, just as Jesus did to His disciples.

Before her ascension, Annalee wrote the book, Ye Are Gods, giving us some vital understanding of the Life Principle as she knew it then. Since that time seven more books in the same writing style of Annalee Skarin, and with her byline, have mysteriously appeared in manuscript form on the desk of her publishers.[20]

I'm ashamed to say that I read four of her books before the revelation came of what she was trying to say. She kept repeating over and over that "Love, Joy, and Gratitude" are the emotions of Life. It follows that they are also the key to the ascension of life in its completed perfection onto the plane of the Masters.

We have talked much about what negative emotions can and have done; now let's examine these three positive emotions, Love, Joy, and Gratitude.

Love can be defined as communication between you and your fellow creatures. As true Loving flows out in greater and greater quantities, the negative counterparts gradually find less and less room in your emotional makeup.

Love is also a freeing agent. The more completely your responses reflect genuine love and compassion for the creations of God that make up your environment, the more you will find that you can allow them to proceed on their own way without deterrent, and the more easily you'll be able to detach yourself from the pain of inharmonious relationships, situations, and the people that create them. You are then free, and so are those around you, for negative, painful emotions are the elements that bind us to the Wheel of Rebirth. Non-possessive love, and compassion for all creatures releases both the one who loves and the ones who are loved to flow with the eternal Life Energy, on their own evolutionary paths. This is the true meaning of "Divine (impersonal) Love."

Joy can be found most readily when we are in communication with God, or under the direction of the Soul Self. If one's activities make one more joyful, then this is a criterion of progress. Suffering comes from limiting or narrowing the focus of consciousness, and reflects the principle of "lessness." Joy comes from the expansion of consciousness and illustrates the principle of "moreness." As we open up the inner life and bring forth the God-Self within, joyous living becomes more of a reality in our experiences.

Gratitude multiplies that which we are grateful for. If energy follows thought, then that on which we keep our thoughts centered will magnify and multiply itself according to the amount of energy we give it. If we are grateful for the blessings in our life, it follows that we will have more and more things for which to be grateful.

These three emotions, if actively cultivated, can supplant *all* other emotions in your life, and you, too, will bring forth greater and greater realizations from the Soul Self within.

Achievement of Self-Realization, or the realization and externalization of the Soul, must ultimately become the ruling factor in our lives. With it comes an ascension in consciousness over the manifestations we ourselves create, and an objectivity that permits no negative quality to distort our perception of ourselves as miniature "gods-in-the-making."

Abraham Maslow, in his book *Motivation and Personality*,[21] was the first psychologist to deal extensively with what he called "self-actualizing people." Most psychologists deal only with states of mental abnormality. Maslow called his research "A Study of Psychological Health."

Most people, says Maslow, are "deficiency-oriented." That is, they are very concerned with procuring and keeping objects and states that are expected to fulfill basic needs. Self-actualized people, on the other hand, are "goal-oriented." They have the capacity, drawn from some source within themselves, to deal lightly with lacks and shortcomings in their surroundings.

Although they recognize the spurious, the fake, and the dishonest in personalities, they are relatively free of overriding guilt, crippling shame, and extreme or severe anxiety. They find it possible to accept themselves and their own nature without chagrin or complaint, or for that matter, even without thinking about it very much.

Self-actualized people live life with spontaneity, simplicity, and naturalness, both in their behavior and in their inner life, thoughts, and impulses. They are essentially unconventional in behavior, although they do not commit overt acts of unconventionality for effect. Their unconventionality is not superficial but essential or internal. Recognizing that the average person may not understand or accept this, the self-actualized person has no wish to hurt others or to fight with them over trivial things, and often goes through conventional rituals with good humor and grace.

Thus conventionality is a cloak that rests lightly upon the shoulders of self-actualized people, says Maslow, and they seldom allow convention to hamper or inhibit them from doing anything they consider very important or basic. Their assurance is an integral part of themselves, which they can adopt or discard at will according to the needs of the moment and the type of people they find themselves with.

Such people are autonomous, creative, self-starters, and responsible for their own destinies. They maintain a certain inner detachment from accepted modes of enculturation and have an essential need for privacy.

Other words for "autonomous" are self-deciding, self-governing; being an active, responsible, self-disciplined, deciding agent rather than a pawn helplessly "determined" by others; being strong rather than weak. These people are ruled by the laws of their own nature rather than by the rules of society, but those rules allow for the need not to harm or unnecessarily injure others by one's actions. Their values are high-minded, kind, and thoughtful, and there is a constant struggle for perfection within themselves.

Abraham Maslow was an independent-thinking, scientifically oriented researcher in human behavior. His definition of "self-actualized" people corresponds remarkably with our definition of "Self-Realization," or being in tune with the Soul Self. Maslow said he could only find six people who fulfilled his criteria, and even those six had qualities which were in some degree inharmonious.

As Paul put it, "All have . . . fallen short of the Glory of God" (Rom. 3:23). Self-realized people, however, accept the challenge of their shortcomings and strive for closer and closer attunement, that "ye might be perfect, even as your Father in Heaven is perfect" (Matt. 5:48).

13. The Law of Polarities or Sex

Within all manifestations of Nature are the negative/positive polarities of sex. This is a subject which has caused much confusion within religions, social customs, political structures, and even in educational fields. Taboos have grown up around various sexual customs and activities, from outright prohibition of certain practices to rigid social structuring of types of sexual interactions between humans. The present-day swing of the evolutionary pendulum is toward the opposite extreme of much more leniency.

Let us take an esoteric view of this much misunderstood energy and see if more clarification can be attained.

Sexual energy is really another name for the vital Life Force that flows in abundance through all living creatures. It *is* you! Without this creative sexual energy, the organism will not live. Perversion, repression, or misdirection of this energy results in warped and misshapen lives.

Sexual energy has a positive and a negative electrical or magnetic force. By this I do not mean positive and negative in the sense of "right" and "wrong." I am talking about polarities, like the negative and positive poles of a magnet. The positive pole or energy is a projective force: it pushes objects away from it. The negative pole is a receptive force: it pulls objects toward it.

As an analogy, a battery has a negative and a positive pole. Which of these poles do you think is the stronger? Which one do you think the battery could do without? Neither. The poles are equal in strength, and if either pole becomes weak or lacking in energy, the battery will not fire.

These negative/positive energies flow throughout the Cosmos, which strives to bring them into balance. Within the Father/Mother God of Creation, these two forces are equally balanced. The Father-God Principle (positive) projects energy outward toward the Creation. The Creation Itself (the Mother-God Principle, or negative) receives this energy into Herself, and "becomes fruitful and multiplies" Herself (positive), and creation is perpetuated eternally.

Within the human being are both positive and negative energies, but because, individually, we are still learning how to use them, each person is essentially more of one or the other. Very few persons have completely harmonized the two energies within one body as yet, so each lifetime is given over to the energy of one or the other. Men, and other male creatures, have the positive or projective force in greater quantity. Women, and other female creatures, have the negative or receptive force in the greater quantity.

A man, being essentially positive, gives off his energy in a projective fashion into external activities. This is a natural use of his essential life force, and he doesn't even need to think about how he does it. It just *is.*

The receptive female force, however, is needed to balance this projective activity. If a man does not, in some fashion, receive the female energy back into himself, he soon does not have any energy left to give out to the world. Then you see a man who is dull, impotent, unimaginative, and lacking vital life force.

A woman, being essentially receptive, receives energy into herself without necessarily being aware that this is the natural expression of her life force. She, contrary to the male, needs to consciously think about projective (productive) use of this vitality in order to live a balanced life. If she does not, the energy within her will stagnate, and soon you will see a bitter, shrewish, discontented, bitchy type of woman.

Negative and positive energies, like the poles of a battery, flow naturally back and forth between men and women in the ordinary activities of daily living. It is not necessary that sexual union take place between two people for this to occur, although national insurance statistics show that married couples, on the average, live longer than single people. This would indicate that the normal give and take of energies between a man and a woman is enhanced by their living in close proximity in a stable companionship.

Sitting in a roomful of women only, one notices how there is an immediate sparkle of enthusiasm when a man walks in. This means that the energy normally generated by females is somehow recharged with the entrance of the projective vitality of the man.

The same holds true when a group of men who have been alone suddenly come into the company of a woman. There is an immediate sparking of new energy within the group.

This exchange of energy takes place at the chakra levels and varies, depending on the individual. The person whose thoughts center primarily on sexual activity would find the lower chakras aroused with the entrance of a person of the opposite sex. An individual who has succeeded in opening into activity some of the higher chakras would find those centers sparked into action with the entrance of a person of the opposite sex.

In fact, the higher the most developed center, the more selective the response. A person whose mental center has fully awakened usually responds more favorably to another person with an active or awakening intellect, and probably not at all, or only cursorily, to one who is physically or emotionally controlled. Tragic mismating can take place if there is too great a disparity between the individuals at the level of the highest awakened chakra.

If you know and understand this Law of Polarities, you can willfully recharge your own energies at any time, simply by giving thought to the accumulation of the opposite type. I, as a woman, can deliberately draw vitality from the presence of a man who attracts me, to recharge myself. I do this without being coy or flirtatious, and the man is not even aware of what is happening, as a rule. Because it is his nature to project or give out this energy, nothing is being taken away from him. I simply make myself a conscious receptacle for forces which are flowing naturally.

A man, on the other hand, needs to be aware that, while to lust after a woman may be "sinful," to admire her and to enjoy the pleasure of her company is not. On the contrary, the pleasure he feels in her presence is evidence that the recharging mechanism is working. Recognition of this natural law will help eliminate much anxiety found in ordinary associations. Do not repress your natural love of the opposite sex. Consciously direct it into vibrant channels of external activity.

Sexual union itself is a powerful discharge of energy that can have both good and bad effects. Some religious orders in both the East and the West maintain that the highest spiritual achievements are attained when one sublimates the urge for sexual activity. This is true only if the sexual energy, which is essentially generative, is redirected into actively constructive, creative, and productive channels, and is not merely repressed. If this power is repressed instead of redirected then considerable damage can be done to the Soul Force.

At the Parapsychology Education Center, we did much research into developing conscious remembering of past lifetimes. An interesting sidelight that came out of this research was that most persons who had been monks, nuns, or hermits, or experienced other forms of voluntarily cloistered life in the past, had a double burden of family responsibility in their present lifetime. This would indicate that the sex-energies of that past life may have been erroneously repressed or otherwise misdirected.

The Eastern terms for these two energies are Yin (feminine/negative/receptive) and Yang (masculine/positive/projective). In the fully Self-Realized person, these interacting forces flow in balanced action. The tension generated as he or she accumulates the vital life energy (negative action—Yin) is used to project outward into creative efforts (positive action—Yang), which in turn revitalize the life force of the person. All projective creative acts should be performed with enthusiasm, love, and undivided attention in order to provide an avenue for the return of negative (receptive) energy.

The more balanced these two actions become within the individual, the less desperation is felt in the need for interaction with the opposite sex. Companionship is always desirable and enjoyed whenever possible, but times alone or periods without interaction do not create intense longing, anxiety, or loneliness. The energies normally expended in paying attention to one's companion are, instead, used for internal study, meditation, and development, or are discharged in external, productive ways along with social (nonsexual) interaction with both men and women.

Let's look at two words taken from the Bible which have caused a lot of confusion and misdirecting of energies down through the centuries. No one knows what meaning they may have had in local custom when originally written down. The two words are "adultery" and "fornication."

To adulterate means "to dilute" or "to make less pure." You can adulterate milk with water. A partner can be far more guilty of adulterating a marriage by constant harping and criticizing, or with the common "put-down," than by an actual act of extra-marital sex. Mental or emotional cruelty in any form is deadly to the harmonizing of polarities between a man and a woman.

Fornication, on the other hand, simply means "sex without love." How many marriages do you suppose there are where there is no more love? The two stay together for whatever expediency seems logical to them, and the only sanction for sex between them is a paper making it legal. Is this not fornication as much as any prostitution on the street?

Sex can be the ultimate in communication between male and female when performed under optimal conditions, or it can be the most degrading and debasing experience that can take place between two individuals. Performed without love, the act of sex is a discharge of the vital life energy without any return. It is "spent in riotous living," so to speak, which drains rather than revitalizes, and if repeated over a period of time, ultimately renders the body a deteriorated vehicle, devoid of vitality.

To achieve the most in sexual experience, both partners should strive for emotional, mental, and spiritual union as well as physical union. There should be a conscious considering of, or listening to, the inner reactions of the partner; a mental and emotional merging with what is taking place on all levels. This recharges the life force, and instead of being drained, new vitality is created within both partners. The result is a healthy, vibrant body instead of a degenerated one, and the positive/negative recharging cycle is not short-circuited.

When the act of sex achieves procreation, the child that is born partakes of the mental and emotional attributes of the parents at the time of conception. A loving, spiritually aware union will attract a loving, spiritually aware soul. It follows that the converse is also true. If only the sacral centers are activated during sex, then an earthy, unevolved soul is the one most likely to be attracted. Of course, this is a generalized statement and need not hold true in all cases, as other factors (such as karmic ties) also enter into the attraction between child and parents.

The only sanction for sexual union between two people should be a shared regard for one another and a mutually conscious striving for spiritual as well as physical union, so that the forces exchanged are jointly energizing to both.

If the Law of Polarities were understood in this way universally, there would be no more manipulation of one person for another's enjoyment; there would be less anxiety and fear, and fewer guilt-ridden personalities filling our hospitals and psychologists' offices or living out their lives in self-loathing, in the mistaken belief that they have "broken God's Laws."

Instead, let us lift our aspirations in the true understanding of Love, which is meant to free rather than to bind.

Workshop 5
Psychometry, Radiesthesia, Dowsing, Pendulums:
The Law of the Whole and Its Parts

≈

Individual aspects of the Whole maintain their individuality only when perceived through the external senses. Once the barrier of sense perception has been crossed, the transient, externalized manifestations of time and space are perceived as part of the eternally changing flow of Creation, which leaves behind a record of its passing in its interacting influence upon the Whole, and especially upon surrounding forms within the Whole.

In other words, the energy radiations that emanate from all things in the universe create an unending flow of vibrations or forces that react upon and influence everyone and everything. Many of these can be discovered by psychometry even after the force or form that created them has long since passed from existence.

Radiesthesia is the name for the detection of this radiation. It comes from two Greek words that mean "rod" and "divining." Dowsing is another word for this ability to successfully employ a divining rod. A forked stick is the instrument most often used to point the way to water, minerals, or lost treasures. This is one of the oldest forms of the mystic wand.

Through practice and understanding, a person with no other known psychic abilities can use one of the methods of radiesthesia to find answers to questions that usually only telepathic or clairvoyant individuals could answer. It is as though one becomes a human radio set that can tune into electromagnetic waves and force fields, with the instrument acting as the antenna or directional finder.

Exercise #1: Psychometry

This exercise can be performed by any number of people, or just two.

Choose a partner, preferably someone you do not know very well. Give your partner some object that you have carried close to your person for a long time, such as a necklace or pendant, earring, eyeglasses, wristwatch, ring, or good luck piece. At the same time, take an object from your partner in exchange. Metal objects usually serve as the best conductors, since their atomic components are denser than other materials, but vibrations may be taken from any object.

Your purpose is to discover something about your partner that you might not normally have known, by tuning into the radiation waves given off by the article.

Hold the object in your hand as you relax your mind down to the Alpha level. Images and activities will flit through your mind. Sometimes the images will be isolated, such as a set of keys or a spotted dog. Sometimes you'll see the person actually doing something.

Say to your partner, "I see a set of keys. Did you lose a set of keys, or has something happened recently that involved a set of keys?" The person usually will respond by telling you exactly what happened that made the keys important enough to leave a vibrational imprint. Later, as you become more adept, you may be able to tell your partner why the keys were important instead of waiting to be told.

Sometimes the image sparks no recollection in either of you. If this happens during these early trials, be kind. Do not say to each other, "No! You're wrong!" This is not only detrimental to developing confidence, but there may be another answer.

Instead, respond with something like, "I don't have that information." Perhaps the incident occurred a long time ago and you have forgotten about it. Later, after the session is over, you may remember the incident, and then you should call the person and report that he or she really did make a hit. It will make your partner feel better and more confident.

Sometimes the incident that is recorded on the object happened to someone else who had the article before its present owner. And sometimes that which you see is something that is going to occur in the future. This doesn't happen often, since your *purpose* is to see something that has already occurred, and your mind usually responds to your purpose.

In any case, if you draw a blank, dismiss it, and try for something else. You will almost certainly get one out of three tries, at least, and you will definitely improve your odds with practice.

Practice every time you get a chance. Friends, relatives, and even strangers are always delighted when you can tell them something about themselves.

Exercise #2: Dowsing

Although willow and hazelwood branches are preferred by "water witchers," you can make a more than adequate dowsing rod from an ordinary coat hanger. Bend the cross bar of the hanger up towards the hook, forming two double arms of a Y. Grasp one end of the Y in each hand, forearms extended forward from the elbow, palms up, fingers bent inward pointing to the body, thumbs overlapping the ends of the Y. Hold the rod firmly but not too tightly, pulling the ends slightly outward to create tension.

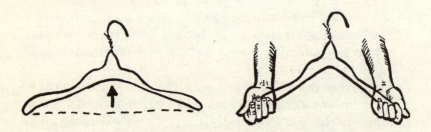

Figure 12. Wire Hanger with Lower Wire Bent Upward

If you'd like an experiment in which there is no possibility of influencing the divining rod with subconscious information, you can make angle rods held in a hollow wand or tubing so that your hands never touch the rods at all. Cut two metal coat hangers as shown below, and, for safety's sake, smooth off the cut edges with a file.

Figure 13. Wire Hanger "Rods" for Hollow Holders

For handles, you may use hollow metal tubing cut into two six-inch lengths, or you may use four empty thread spools. Glue two spools together one on top of the other to form two hollow handles into which the hanger wires may be inserted.

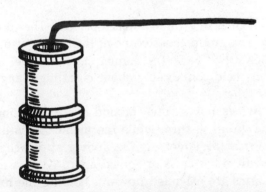

Figure 14. Two Spools Glued Together to Make Holder

Five inches from one end, bend the coat hanger wires at a ninety-degree angle. Insert the short end into the spool or tube handles from which the wires can swing loosely. Hold one handle in each hand, level and relatively parallel to each other and to the ground. Walk smoothly and steadily to keep the rods as stationary as possible. When near or over the target, these rods will either cross each other, or swing widely apart, according to the energies of the dowser.

The following exercises may be used with any type of dowsing instrument.

**Figure 15. Bent or Angled Rods Move Freely
in Hollow Holders**

Form a circle of eight to a dozen persons. The "diviner" leaves the room. The group chooses one of their number to be the "target." When called back, the diviner stands in the middle of the circle, arms held comfortably about chest high, angle rods held in hollow tubes.

The diviner moves slowly around the circle, facing each member of the group in turn, while the members "will" the rod to point towards the target. As the diviner approaches the target, the rods will either cross or spread apart. (With a forked dowsing rod, arms are extended upward, holding the rod in tension head-high, or overhead. The point of the rod should suddenly dip towards the person chosen.)

If you wish, the circle can break up, with the individual members scattered about the room but still concentrating their mental force on the person chosen as the target. This exercise uses both clairvoyance and telepathy, but the dowsing process is an important factor.

Practice with the divining rod in your backyard, trying to locate sewer and water mains, buried telephone cables, etc. As your confidence grows, try more sophisticated exercises, such as locating underground streams, buried objects, etc. If you know the location of an underground stream, try following it with your dowsing rod for a mile or more. Your rod will tell you when the stream changes course or you have walked away from it.

Exercise #3: Programming The Pendulum

You can buy an elaborate, sophisticated pendulum, or you can make your own from any object heavy enough to swing from a string or a chain, such as a ring, key, or bead. Precious or semiprecious stones such as natural quartz crystals, attached to gold or silver chains, are favorites. Some people like to use their birthstones. I've seen intricate ones handcarved from special or exotic kinds of wood. The material in the pendulum is strictly a matter of personal preference, and often has sentimental, esoteric, or religious significance.

The pendulum swings by muscle movements governed by the parasympathetic nervous system of the subconscious mind. These are the same muscles that govern involuntary actions of the body such as digestion, respiration, and heartbeat. The string or chain should be about six to eight inches long, a comfortable length to respond to the minute movements of your hand and fingers so that, swinging freely, the direction of its swing can translate your psychic impressions into clearly understood information. If it is too long it is unwieldy, and if it is too short, its swing will be jerky. Adjust the length until it is comfortable.

Some teachers train their students to *command* the pendulum to move as directed by the conscious Will: back and forth for "yes," a circle for "no," etc. I've found in my research that a larger percentage of people have success with the pendulum when cooperation by the subconscious is *requested* rather than ordered. The effect may be largely psychological, but who can argue with the results? Occasionally, a subconscious that has been dominated by a very strong Will needs to be commanded to move in a prescribed direction, but most people can follow the procedure below for programming the pendulum to respond to the operator's direction.

Acting on the assumption that there is nothing in the subconscious area of the brain except memories of that which it has previously experienced, and on the belief that subconscious behavior patterns are learned from past experiences, we first create

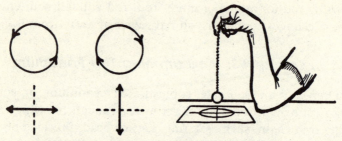

Figure 16. Programming the Pendulum

the experience of the moving pendulum. Hold the string or chain of the pendulum between your thumb and forefinger at a comfortable height, with your elbow resting on the chair arm or table. First, deliberately swing the pendulum in a clockwise circle.

Stop the movement with the other hand, and then deliberately swing the pendulum in a counterclockwise circle. Then move it in a side to side swing, and then in the opposite to and fro swing, stopping the movement with your free hand between swings, so that each action is separate and distinct.

The order of the swings is not important, as long as all four swings are deliberately introduced for recording in the subconscious mind.

Now the subconscious is aware of what you are talking about, and you can question it in this manner: "Which way will you swing to answer 'Yes' to my questions?" Wait and *expect* it to move in one of the four ways shown to it.

When the movement has occurred, ask each of these questions in turn: "Which way will you swing to answer 'No' to my questions?" "Which way will you swing to answer 'I don't know' to my questions?" and "Which way will you swing to answer 'I don't want to say'?" Always wait until a strong swing has been made and then stop the movement either with a command or with your free hand before going on to the next question.

In this way, the subconscious has an active participation in seeking out the answers you request, rather than a submissive one, as is the case when "ordered" to swing in a certain way to reply. The swing will always remain the same for each answer, and if you should forget which swing means what, simply ask the question again. The subconscious will gladly respond. You may question the pendulum aloud or mentally.

The pendulum is an invaluable aid in searching the subconscious mind for hidden motivations or unknown conditioned behavior patterns, but that is a separate study in itself. The pendulum gives the usually unheard portions of the lower mind an opportunity to develop a communication with the external or conscious aspect of the mind.

In this case, the answers, "I don't know," and "I don't want to say," become extremely significant. The "I don't know" means that the answer to the question asked may lie in another region of the mind, or even in the superconscious. In that case you can ask the subconscious to go to the area of the mind or even the area of God-Intelligence where the answer can be found and bring it back to you. Or you can raise your level of aspiration upward and ask the questions to the superconscious aspect of yourself. Your desire is the motivation that brings the correct response from the proper area of consciousness.

The "I don't want to say" answer means you've touched upon some traumatic area deliberately or willfully hidden, perhaps some painful memory which you have literally told the subconscious mind that you don't want to think about any more, a deeply repressed incident.

You might find my book *Rock Crystal: The Magic Stone*,[22] an interesting addition in your study of the pendulum.

One of the most outstanding researchers in this use of the pendulum is Bevy Jaegers, who began her research in the early 1950s. She has successfully used it to find the missing bodies of murdered persons and to pick rising stocks in the stock market, building her own portfolio and that of others to a substantial sum.

Many of the following exercises can be found in her books *Mark I ESP Training Manual, Mark I ESP Advanced Training*, and *The Extra Sensitive Pendulum*, recommended by the American Society of Dowsers in Danville, Vermont.[23]

Exercise #4-A: Male and Female

Test the pendulum over a man's or a woman's head or hand. It may swing in a circle over a woman and in a straight line over a man, but let your pendulum choose its own swing.

Occasionally we find a pendulum which wants to swing in the opposite way. Whichever it chooses, that is your answer always to male and female, wherever found. You can use it to determine the sex of an unborn child or unhatched chickens.

(There is an infrequent, strange phenomenon that creates an apparent contradiction of the programmed male/female swings. You may hold the pendulum over a man's head or hand, for instance, and get a female swing, or over a woman and get a male swing. This may indicate there is an essentially female soul residing in a male body, or vice versa. If true, then further questions which can be answered Yes or No might bring interesting new information. There are still vast amounts of research to be done in this area.)

Exercise #4-B

Place a number of objects on a table. Hold the pendulum over the objects, each one in turn. If it belongs to a woman, it will swing in a circle; if it belongs to a man, it will swing in a straight line (or in the direction your pendulum has chosen for male and female).

You can make this more difficult by sealing the articles in envelopes so that they cannot be seen and you cannot subconsciously influence the swing of the pendulum.

Exercise #4-C

Use a number of photographs, showing an equal number of men and women. Place them face down on a table, and mix them up. Use the pendulum to locate the females. When you have done this, remix the photographs and use the same technique to find the males. Next try an equal mixture of human and animal pictures, letting your pendulum decide which is which.

Exercise #5: Pendulum Detective Games

Choose five playing cards of the 8, 9, and 10 denominations. Four should be black and one red, or vice versa. Mix them up, or have someone do it for you, and place them face down on the table. Hold the pendulum over each card in turn and ask it to find the lone card, red or black, by swinging in the Yes position. Mix and repeat the experiment. The more you practice, the better will be your control.

Practice until you are always accurate in finding the single card. Then increase to seven cards, with five black and two red. When you have become expert in finding the two cards, increase the total number of cards until you are finally working with a whole deck at once, locating the red cards only. Then remix and use the same system to find the black cards.

Exercise #6

Secure three lidded, opaque containers, such as plastic storage boxes. Put several inches of water into one, leaving the other two empty. Have someone else mix them up, or do it yourself if you are working alone and leave the room for a period of time, until you are not sure which is the one with the water. Suspend the pendulum over each container in turn, asking that it circle over the one which holds the water.

Exercise #7

Under one of three or four inverted-identical teacups, paper cups, or opaque glasses, place a metal object such as a ring, coin, or watch. Use the pendulum to locate the object after the cups have been mixed up.

Try using different metals under each cup, and program a different swing for each metal before you begin.

Exercise #8

Write or print thirty-five to fifty common words on 3 x 5 cards, one word to a card. Use well-known words with eight to ten letters each, and deliberately misspell about half of them.

Shuffle the pack of cards, and lay them face down on the table. Place one card at a time face down before you and ask the pendulum to answer Yes or No to determine if the word on the other side of the card is misspelled.

Exercise #9: Choosing Good And Bad

Allow the pendulum to choose whether it will circle for good and swing straight for bad, or use its Yes for good and No for bad. Be sure your directives to the pendulum are clear and its response will always be equally clear, once the communication system has been worked out.

Have someone mix up a number of objects on a table or stand, with one of the articles being "bad," such as several small batteries, one dead; some electric fuses or light bulbs, one burned out; an empty spray can among several full ones; three or four pocket mirrors face down, one cracked; or, several cups of water with one salted. Allow the pendulum to tell you which of the objects is "bad."

Vegetarians and people interested in health foods often use the pendulum to determine if certain foods contain pesticides or additives. Ms. Jaegers says she has been using this system since 1968 to identify phony or counterfeit money, jewelry, coins, and art.

Exercise #10: Finding Lost Or Missing Persons

This exercise requires contact with higher levels of consciousness than the subconscious, so before starting, center your attention on the highest level that your "I AM" can reach, and try to make mental or heart contact with the highest consciousness of the person you wish to find.

Clear the desk or table of all other objects, then rest your elbow on it and ask the pendulum, "Is X (name of missing person) alive?"

Then stand up, holding the pendulum comfortably in your hand, and ask, "Is X (or X's body, if dead) in the direction I am facing?"

If the response is No, turn slightly, maybe one-eighth of a full circle, and repeat the question. When the answer is Yes, continue to face that way and seek to find the distance. Start by asking, "Is X less than 100 miles from here?" If the answer is No, change the question to 200 miles and so on until you get a Yes reaction.

When the answer is Yes, begin to narrow down the distance, in fifty-mile increments, until you find the exact mileage. You will then know the direction and how far. Go to that place and proceed with the pendulum as before for direction, then distance. Only now you ask in feet, not miles.

The most successful time for doing the latter part of the exercise is late at night, when the person is probably at home asleep. The pendulum will locate the person wherever he or she may be *at the moment* the question is asked. When awake, the person may move to another location in the course of normal daily activity.

Exercise #11: Finding Missing
Persons by Pendulum Map Dowsing

You may combine this exercise with the one above for pinpointing a person's location. Suspend the pendulum over a map near the place in which you feel the missing person might be located. Ask the pendulum if you are correct or not. If the answer is Yes, move the pendulum to one of the compass points of the map. Ask it to swing toward the missing person. Draw a straight line exactly on the pendulum's swing.

Then move the pendulum to another compass point and repeat the request. When you have finished all four compass points, you should have four straight lines on the map, converging at a certain point. Where these lines come together, you will find your target. You may continue this exercise with more and more detailed maps of the pinpointed area until you have precisely located the missing subject. This can be brought down as specifically as a certain house on a certain street.

Exercise #12: Finding Lost
Objects by Pendulum Map Dowsing

You can use the same procedure for finding an object that is not in your immediate vicinity.

If the pendulum indicates that the object is still in your house, ask Yes and No questions to first locate the room the missing object is in. Then sketch the room, clearly indicating such things as closets, shelves, drawers, etc. Then use the pendulum as in the above exercise to locate the exact position of the missing object.

Be sure to see the article quite clearly in your mind's eye when you question its location. Don't have a confused or changing image, or you will have a confused result.

≈   ≈   ≈

You may find the movements of the pendulum slow to get started in the beginning, but you will become more and more accurate the more often you do it. As with all other skills, practice is the key.

One more suggestion. You can charge up your psychic energy level by taking three deep breaths before beginning an experiment, and if it should continue overlong, repeat the breathing technique to "recharge."

MEDITATION PRACTICE:
THE POINT-OF-POWER TECHNIQUE

Dr. Russ Michael, author of several books on esoteric philosophy, gives a meditative procedure called "The Point-of-Power Technique" in his seminars.[24] This meditation concentrates on the "I AM" point of awareness to bring the individual to conscious realization of the fullness of his or her own potential to transcend Time and Space. Try this every day for a month and you will have established a point of mastery which will bring poise and balance into your daily life. You'll never again feel yourself a slave to time/space barriers.

You might put this meditation on a tape, so you can listen to your voice guiding you. Where a sentence trails off, remain silent for a moment. Give yourself enough time to do each suggestion before going on to the next.

The Point-of-Power Technique

Sit with your spine straight. Cleanse your Being with the White Light. Turn your attention to that point of consciousness that you recognize as the "I" within you. Relax fully, and let all tension in your external body slip away. Focus your thoughts upon the NOW moment in time, and let this awareness of the NOW permeate the rest of this meditation.

Expand this point of awareness to include all the cells and atoms of your body. Feel the body, vital and alive with health and energy....

Now expand this awareness to include everything and everybody who may be in the room with you, knowing that you are *one* with the universal life and energy that permeates every atom and molecule manifesting in that room in whatever manner it has chosen to express.... Realize that this Oneness influences you and you influence it; that because you *are,* somehow all things are different than they would be if you were *not*....

Extend this awareness now into the city or countryside surrounding you. Feel your affinity with the life and energy that is expressing through everybody and all things that manifest in this area....

Now extend this sense of *oneness* to the continent on which you reside. All existence is in the NOW. You are part of the NOW. You are part of every atom and cell that makes up all of the consciousness expressing in the NOW, in whatever place it may be, or whatever form it takes, and it is influenced by you and you by it....

Extend your consciousness now to include all the peoples, and nations around the globe. Feel yourself a part of the world, the earth, the whole planet and all its people....

Extend yourself into the space around the globe, into the galaxy... into galaxies beyond galaxies... until you feel yourself expanded into and encompassing the entire universe. This is the point of power—the source of life for all existence. Hold this awareness for *one minute,* then relax....

Begin to pull this *oneness with the Whole* gradually back through the galaxies... the earth... your continent... your state... your city... this room... and finally back to its original point within the "I" consciousness of yourself. As you do, realize that the powerful energies and potentials you have just contacted are always available for your use, and are limited only by your capacity to put them into action. Realize that that capacity has now been expanded, and that each time you do this exercise it will be expanded more, until your understanding of Universal Law has been expressed in full dominion, and you are indeed master of your total environment.

≈   ≈   ≈

This is an excellent way to energize a project you may be working on. You will have brought so much energy back with you that your entire body will vibrate with it, and you may even feel that your body cannot hold that much energy. If so, then mentally "dump" the energy into whatever project you are working on, knowing that in so doing you are turning the entire creative force of the universe into your project.

When the energy has been dumped, refill your body with the protective White Light, while slowly returning to Beta consciousness. The results of this meditation will surprise you!

WEEK 6

≈

The Evolution of Spirit

The ancient Wisdom deals with energy and with Consciousness as a form of energy. Consciousness, it is said, exists in all things, but in the mineral, Consciousness is sleeping. In the plant, it is asleep, but dreaming; in the animal, it is awake, but it is not yet aware of self. In the human being, Consciousness is, at last, fully awake, and for the first time, aware of self—and it is this awareness that takes us one more step up the evolutionary ladder, that indeed makes us truly human.
—*Adapted from the teachings of the Kabbalah*

All people, when they have grown fully aware of Self, begin to wonder what lies beyond death. Does this Self, which is so wonderful and so vital, simply return to dust, as the leaves which fall from the trees? Do we live on only in the memory of our children, or the great and noble deeds we have done? If so, what a waste are the precious, often agonizing days of our lives.

The spiritualist churches have done one excellent thing to further the advancement of our esoteric knowledge about ourselves and our potential. They have presented rational evidence that some portion of our awareness, or personality, *does* survive after death, and that in some instances it can communicate with those who are still working out their experiences in the physical body. I feel we need no longer question whether this is wishful thinking or, indeed, truth.

Those pioneers who dare the astral realm to bring back evidence of the survival of the personality brave as many dangers as any intrepid explorer of another unknown land. Many suffer obsessions, psychological horror, ego distortions, fantasy, and even untimely death. On the other hand, some have won through to new spiritual truths and have helped to open humanity's eyes to the fact that most of our religious doctrines today leave us short-changed.

When I first became aware through a personal experience that it was possible to make contact and even communicate with unseen personalities, the only place of additional knowledge available to me was a spiritualist church in my city. I became a regular attendant at their worships and "reading" sessions, and for eighteen months faithfully sat in a weekly circle for medium-ship development.

However, I had a "hang-up." I refused to give my conscious-ness over to spirit control. This was *my* body and *my* mind, and no one had a right to use them but me, I felt. It seemed logical that if contact were possible, then with my cooperation, I should be able to hear audibly or mentally, and/or see mentally or visually, whatever was being projected by other minds, whether encased in visible or invisible bodies.

While others in the group were developing trance medium-ship, I was learning how to read the vibratory energies within my own mind. I learned to speak from "inspiration," listening to and repeating whatever was said in my head. I developed the rudiments of a passable telepathy and I learned how to interpret symbols that appeared in my mind whenever I asked for a mes-sage for someone else in the circle. Once or twice, I even brought forth some bit of evidence unknown to me, verified by another member of the circle, that I had actually contacted the mind of a departed relative or friend. (Or had I simply contacted the memory banks of the individual for whom I was reading? I was never truly certain about that in my own mind.)

Gradually, however, it dawned on me that the content of most "messages" was trivial and unimportant, even banal. Dear Aunt Mary would come through and say, "God bless you, my child. You are going to have a surprise tomorrow," or "Spirit is with you, just hang in there, and all will be well." Few things that were definitive came through that could not be explained as psy-chometry, telepathy, or just a desire to help. Not that these aren't great gifts, because they are, but I felt that unembodied entities often got credit that should have been accorded to the inner mind of the reader.

What became more and more obvious was that these "entities" were very, very human. They were not infallible in either their advice or their predictions. There was even evidence in their messages, sometimes, of human ego, and of jealousy, possessiveness, or anger. It became clear that Grandpa Sam was not much further along the spiritual path than he had been in life, other than having a tendency to say "God bless you," with unvarying frequency.

Most of the people in my group hung like children on "advice from Spirit," often refusing to make decisions for themselves for fear of making the wrong choice. Whenever spirit advice turned out to be less than perfect, the reader always claimed that it was his or her channel that was faulty, not the "great ones" who sent it.

One time I received a message by automatic writing, unmistakably from a recently departed friend, who directed me to do something in connection with another person that was very much against my better judgment. Still new at the "spirit game," and mindful of my teacher's admonition that "spirits can see more about a situation than you can," I set about my task, and got myself into a humiliating and embarrassing predicament that I shall not soon forget.

Years later, when the hurt and humiliation had lessened somewhat, I received the understanding, probably from the entity who had directed me, "You were the only one who loved enough to try to help."

The point I am making is that both of us interfered. My own intuition told me that it was none of my business, although I loved this person very much, and so did the entity (who had been a relative of his on this side of life). He was trying to prevent my friend from getting into a situation that both of us believed would cause him great distress. This was a case of direct manipulation by a discarnate spirit, and I couldn't blame misinterpretation by a "reader," for I had received the message myself clearly and directly, from a recognized source, and had acted upon it against my own inner warnings. What was worse, this action did nothing to change the course of events.

What would you do, if you sought the advice of a dear friend who still lived in the body and the same thing happened? Would you act rashly on that advice, assuming without just cause that the friend knew more about the situation than you did? Of course not. You would weigh their words against good common sense, add it to the store of information that you already have, and if it gave you a good feeling, a new insight, or a new approach, wonderful. Then you would have something you could use. If it didn't, you would gently say, "Thanks, Tom, for your help. I know you love me, but I still have to work this out for myself." Wisdom dictates that one should receive "spirit" advice in the same manner.

Some miraculous healings took place in those eighteen months. Under the leader's guidance, each student in the circle carefully developed a personal "spirit band" for instruction, healing, and protection. The "guides" gave us their names, very often American Indian or Far Eastern, although my own spirit doctor called himself "Dr. Thompson," as American as anything could be.

One day my oldest daughter was in an automobile accident with a semi, and wrenched her back severely, pinching and paralyzing nerves from the waist down. We formed a healing circle, and each member sent his or her own spirit doctor over to the hospital to help her get well. A couple of nights later I found myself hovering over her bed, and I saw her turn over by herself, a feat she had previously been unable to accomplish without help. I called early the next morning to be sure I hadn't dreamed it, and she verified that this had actually taken place. That, to me, was probably the most exciting thing that happened during all those months!

Questions still nagged at my mind. These entities had given ample evidence that they were just as human and fallible as we were—if indeed they were entities, and not just figments from our own levels of mind.

But, in order to heal, they had to be able to tune into the Healing Stream of Consciousness within the One Mind and direct it wherever they chose. If they could do that, then why couldn't I? Why did I need a mediator, other than the obvious, "where two or more are gathered together . . . ?" I decided I was falling down on my spiritual job. I was using other minds, or at least giving credit to other minds, for that which I should be doing myself.

That gave me the final push. I left the spiritualist church and started the long path of return to my own indwelling potential. Not that I don't still call upon help, for "in like minds, the energies are intensified," but I no longer demand that any special person do the helping.

When I need help, I call upon the Soul Self, and the *right* person, living or discarnate, brings the action into being. The sensitivity developed during that year and a half is still with me, and I often feel the presence of an "inner message" from some other mind. Then I never fail to say "Thank you," as I would to any other friend, but I do not deter them from being about their own fulfillment.

From my own and others' experimentation, as well as from reading often differing accounts from spirit-dictated books, I've reached some conclusions that may account for both the differences and the similarities experienced within the realms of astral matter.

The astral plane seems to interpenetrate the physical plane and is subject to the same physical and mental laws, except that thought becomes form instantaneously. To set out on a journey on the physical plane requires much preparation after the thought initiates the impetus to go. To think about being somewhere on the astral plane is to be at the desired destination simultaneously with the thought. There seems to be no time lapse between thought and action, so that differentiating between action and cause of action might be very difficult.

When you pass over in death, you apparently find what you expect. If you are looking for a Heaven with golden streets and angels with harps, that is what you will find—for awhile, until you are bored with golden streets and harp-playing angels. Then you will experiment with other wish-fulfilling pictures.

It is reported that newly arrived souls build a home and environment just like they've been used to on earth, so they are comfortable with the familiar. If we expect nothing when we die, then we will float for a long time in nothingness. This experience of nothingness has been vividly remembered in regression exploration into past life and the periods between incarnations.

This suggests that the astral plane has a high degree of creative emotional matter, which is simply atoms in a less dense form.

The heavier physical level has a slower rate of vibration, therefore there is a lag between thought and manifestation and this gives us a chance to discipline our life, to see *how* it works, and to add intelligent action to emotional desire.

Books and teachers talk about "planes" or levels of awareness in the astral realm. The truth is that these same levels of awareness exist on this side of life, also. Some people are very spiritually oriented, while others are only barely aware of themselves. On the Earth plane we are inclined to feel more comfortable with someone who shares our level of thinking. So it is on the astral plane. You *are* where your mind *is*.

The only light found in this finer density of matter is that which comes from your own Being, because like the outer reaches of Space, the density of atoms is too sparse to collect and hold the light from the sun. If you have developed a greater awareness than the average, you will have a greater Light, for you then become a bright and luminous Being which projects Light out from itself. The greater your awareness and spiritual development, the greater the luminosity you project, a light by which others can see who have no understanding of their own to enlighten them. Because you are automatically drawn to others who have a similar degree of Light or radiance about themselves, the plane you find yourself on will have a great deal of Light.

However, if there is little or no Light within you, then the energy level of you and your companions will be grey or murky; there will be no radiant energy within any of you to brighten where you are. Only in physical bodies can Souls mingle and share this inner Light with one another.

Test it yourself. Do you find it easy to communicate with someone whose interests do not parallel your own? How then can you hope to understand each other unless you both share the same desire to know and understand? On the astral plane you won't even get the chance, unless there is discipline enough in your mind to allow you to look for other Beings within their own pictured environment.

Exploring the astral plane can be exciting and, as a new frontier of the mind, may deserve attention for the information it offers us. But spiritual growth resides there only for the individual who uses the time between earth lives to review and consciously evaluate his or her level of attainment. It is a common belief that most people do that, and that those who do not pay the penalty in lost time and repeated Earth experiences.

Our spiritual growth time can be found only in the NOW. If you are NOW in the physical body, you grow and profit from whatever experiences are afforded here. If you are NOW in the astral body, you grow from whatever experiences are created there.

Both areas are still part of the physical plane of matter, even if in varying densities, and if you find yourself bouncing back and forth between them, in and out of earth lives, then in the cosmic scheme you are still bound to planet Earth. There is nothing wrong with that, because that is where we are in the NOW, but we need to bear in mind that there are still many things to be learned from the *physical* plane before we spend too much time on the astral.

Soul Development

"I teach my Soul." I do not remember where I read or heard that phrase, but it opened many levels of understanding for me. The Personality or lower ego, that which I know as "me," conveys messages to the Soul by the input of data through the five senses, thereby enriching the Soul's knowledge about its present experiences.

The Soul Self and the High Self are two separate identities, or units of energy. Everyone has a Soul Self, but not every incarnate being has a High Self. Called by some writers the "Solar Angel," the High Self is a highly advanced Being that responds to the Soul's desire for spiritual growth.

When the Soul begins to break free of the hypnotic entrancement created by enchantment with the experiences of the dense planes of earth, a very highly evolved entity comes to offer help. While this entity may stay with the Soul for countless incarnations, in the overview of Eternity this is not a permanent attachment.

The High Self aids in the evaluation of knowledge produced by the Personality and sometimes acts as a sender and receiver of messages between the Soul and the Personality. As the Soul gains in strength and wisdom, the High Self has less and less work to do and ultimately the Soul stands alone, fully rewarded for work well done with complete fulfillment of its centuries of activity on planet Earth. At this point, the Soul is ready for its new assignment somewhere else within the universe.

Let us try to clarify the evolution of the Soul.

The Four Spheres of Consciousness: "I AM THAT I AM"

On the Earth plane are four visible evolutionary kingdoms: the mineral, vegetable, animal, and human. Some believe these are vertical, that is, we grow upward from the mineral to the human, and some believe they are parallel kingdoms, evolving in ecological symbiosis, each serving the other. Whatever the Truth may be, in the NOW we find ourselves in the human kingdom. This is what we must concentrate on, so that we may make the most of this opportunity and thereby more quickly move on to adventures in other areas.

In the human kingdom there are four areas of consciousness—perhaps we could better call them "points-of-interest" which capture one's attention, for each Soul is deeply intent upon one or more of these levels. For want of better terms, we'll call these areas of consciousness "The Physical Sciences," "The Mental Sciences," "The Psychic Sciences," and "The Spiritual Sciences."

The Physical Sciences: "I"

This is the first externalization of the "I," the person who is very much involved with physical Beingness: the senses, appetites, personal health, and the immediate environment.

This individual may take great joy in physical prowess or may be deeply involved with the latest scientific findings in the physical world. He or she may be concerned with "natural" health care, diet, yoga-type exercises, etc., or may be aware only of self and centered on gratifying the physical appetites.

All of these things are part of our learning how to beautify, refine, and purify the Body Temple that houses our Soul, and none must be scorned, for we rise by degrees in discipline and understanding. Time goes in a spiral, and we find ourselves repeating old lessons, but in a continually refined process, going from the gross to the etheric. Some part of our Being must always remain on the physical level until our knowledge about our bodies and the physical world is complete.

The Mental Sciences: "I AM"

This is the beginning of the "I AM" stage. You know that you are not merely a self-aware unit functioning independently. You become more people-oriented, working to elevate human consciousness, standards of living and of education, involved with the traditional philosophical, political, and religious doctrines of society. Intellectualization and awareness of mind functioning is high for the person who is focused at this level.

New metaphysical students often find themselves on this level as the scythe of the mind begins to cut away the debris of tradition and enculturation.

The Psychic Sciences: "I AM THAT"

This is the area of "developing potential," the "I AM THAT." The individual has begun to turn within to the Psyche, the Soul, and to accept guidance from the Inner Wisdom—to "render unto Caesar the things that are Caesar's and unto God the things that are God's" (Matt. 22:21). The material world is recognized for what it is, and the spiritual world begins to hold more attraction. All that has been learned from the physical, emotional, and mental levels can now be applied to spiritual concepts.

In this context, I define "religious" concepts as those which are prevalent within the culture or society of the individual. "Spiritual" concepts seek to discover the larger ideas behind the religions and the philosophies of humanity.

The Spiritual Sciences: "I AM THAT I AM"

This is the completed Being—THE I AM THAT I AM (I am *what* I am). This individual has once again reached "un-self-aware-ness." It's difficult to explain this level, because here are your perfected thoughts, deeds, and virtues. You are what you *are*.

There is no longer duality or questioning of Self. You react in *Love* because there is nothing else in you *but* Love. There is no question about whether you should or should not Love, you *are* Love personified. Within you the virtue of Love is perfected. You are not aware of the virtue because it is never questioned, nor are there any of the opposite emotions against which this virtue might be reflected, deflected, or compared. There is no question of duality, because *Love is what you are.* Someone may say to you, "You are the kindest person I know," and you react with an inner shock, because you haven't even thought about *being* kind; you just *are* kind because that is the perfected virtue within you.

That is why I call this level of consciousness "un-self-aware." The cycle is complete, duality is finished, and no more thought or attention is given to it. All earth-found virtues ultimately achieve this state when our journey through earth lives is completed.

(Of course, we are often unaware of our faults as well, but the negative feedback from the environment in response to those faults is the scorpion's sting that keeps us alert to the need to keep reforming those aspects of our Beingness.)

We are, for the most part, working simultaneously through various positions within all of these areas of consciousness, rising higher like bubbles in cake batter, or retreating back to pick up something that we missed last time or to refine that which we already know. Each level must be fully explored before we can stand and say, "It is finished."

Spirit: The Divine Potential

"Spirit *is*."

Into our vocabularies are only now beginning to come the words to express to others something of the realizations that occur within us when we make conscious contact with that highest aspect of ourselves: *Spirit*.

And even those words are but a dim, unexpressive reflection of the glory that is felt when one first stands "between Heaven and Earth" from the vantage point of Soul awareness, seeing the full range of consciousness from the Personality below to the God-Self above and realizing oneself as a whole and complete Being.

The words of the ancients who tried to express this glory are colorless in comparison and unrevealing; and so will be these words of mine to you, until you, yourself, push with unrelenting devotion into the realm of consciousness reserved only for those who have an all-consuming desire to know the fullness of *Self*, a desire greater than any other goal in life.

The following is an attempt to clarify some of the most confusing aspects of the mystical concepts surrounding the Spirit and Soul, the seven bodies or energy fields that make up the total human being, and how human evolution began. The first Western authors on these subjects tried to translate Hindu and Sanskrit concepts into Western thought when there were no clear English terms to define the Eastern philosophies. Authors had to invent their own words and names to express these unfamiliar ideas, so they oftentimes expressed the same concept in different ways and in different words.

None of the interpretations were easily understood (at least by me, a neophyte), and none of them were complete, since each author wrote only about the aspect that he or she had personally assimilated. I went through many years, and dozens of old books, before I could gather enough data to form the following composite, weeding out what seemed like implausibilities and putting together similar abstractions to create a whole. My goal was to provide as clear-cut an idea as possible of the position and purpose of each force field which makes up the total Being. This should also lessen your confusion when you read the works of other authors. If you like, refer to "The Trinity of Self" chart to aid in interpreting the following information.

Spirit *is* . . .all things in potential.

In the books of wisdom it is said that out from the Mind of God in the unknown days of the beginning, all the Life that now expresses came forth in seven bursts of creation. Each individuated Spark of Consciousness that is now reflected in humanity had its beginnings in one of those bursts of creation, called "rays" in esoteric literature.

In that beginning, each newly individuated Spark of Divine Spirit that was sent forth from the Mind of God existed in perfection of the originating thought—a prototype, a blueprint, as it were, for what it could ultimately become, but it was not yet de-

Figure 17. The Trinity of Self

Seven Bodies	Function as	Also known as
SPIRITUAL BODY	SPIRIT (The God Self) 1. Life 2. I AM 3. Awareness	Monad Identity Divine Self Divine Atom of God The Divine in you Mystical Awareness Spark The Father Within (The Creator of all that we are)
MENTAL BODY	(Mental Energy Field)	
EMOTIONAL BODY	(Emotional Energy Field)	Desire Body

ASTRAL BODY
(Lower Mental Body)
	SOUL
	(Your ability to control
	   your Destiny)
	1. Consciousness
	   (Knowledge)
	2. I Know
	3. Thinker (Ego)
		The Christ Self
		(Paul called this
		   "The Christ in You")

CAUSAL BODY	(Memory Field)	Electronic Body Akashic Records Treasures stored up in Heaven
ETHERIC BODY	(Regulates Healing Processes)	Magnetic Body Vital Body Subtle Body

PHYSICAL BODY
Coat of skin—
Body made
   of "dust"
   (elements) of
   the earth
	PERSONALITY
	(Your capacity to expe-
	   rience or to perform)
	1. Form
	2. I Will
	3. Thought (Conscious
	   and Subconscious)
		Lower Self

Note: Although one may be focused in thought and awareness within any one of these consciousness levels, it is important to conceive of yourself as a Total Being: Spirit, Soul, and Personality.

veloped into the fullness of that potential. Unique in its own possibilities (no two creations of God are ever alike), the individual Spark of Spirit had as its tool for development only the *desire* to become fully and completely what it was capable of becoming (i.e., to "know God" in His fullness).

That Desire was the motivating force that pushed the Spark into the stream of experiences which would be its school throughout eternity. The Force was God seeing Himself as the final, completed whole and desiring to express or fulfill Himself as that unique, ultimate vision, living simultaneously within Himself as all parts of His creation, experiencing and becoming One Perfected Unit of eternally evolving Existence or Beingness.

Spirit is—all things in potential. What an eye-opener!

Our minds at this point cannot grasp the original Vision of God, and what He determined as the Perfect Potential of His Being. It is enough that we struggle to grasp what it was He "imaged" for us, the individual cell within the whole. It is mind-boggling enough to know that whatever we are, or whatever we can at this moment know of our future potential, it is only a tiny, tiny portion of the greater concept of what it is that we can *really become* as we strive for ever-expanding awareness throughout our eternal journey.

Our own tiny fragment of God Life has been called a Spark, the Monad, the Divine Essence, and the Divine Atom of God. It can also be called "The Father Within"—the originator of all that we are. The most common esoteric term is Monad.

This bit of *Life* was differentiated in the Mind of God from all the other movements toward individuality, and that fact created a sheath around it known esoterically as the Spiritual Body. It was that portion of God Substance that had its own line of development to fulfill, its own Spiritual Identity to attain.

Soul: The Will-to-Become

The *desire* within the individual Monad to *become* what it had the possibility of *Being* stirred into movement, and created the first glimmerings of activated intelligence. The *Idea* of *individual Beingness* was both the motion within God that created the Monad and also the Substance within the Monad which could be drawn upon for the Monad's own special experiences.

From this Substance, two energy fields known as the Mental Body and the Emotional Body (or Desire Body) were created around the Monad—those bodies of energy consciousness that make up the forces of creation, at least as we know them on Planet Earth.

These mental and emotional energies, activated into movement, created a force of strongly individualized consciousness in which was focused the quality of *Will*—the Divine *Will-to-Become*. This Force of Will can be called the Soul. It was capable of taking charge of the emotional and mental fields of energy and directing their creative activities. As the Soul grew in strength and purpose, it developed a body of its own called the Astral Body (sometimes called the Lower Mental Body). The Astral Body had the further capability of being able to move outside the Spiritual Body, into denser realms of matter.

Esoteric theories are long and complicated about how those individual Souls used the creative forces to build the world of effects which we now experience as the universe, which is known as "the long *involution* into matter," but that does not concern us here. Suffice it to say that out of the trial and error method grew a conglomerate body of knowledge stored in the memory banks of each individual.

Around this body of knowledge is a sheath known by many names: the Electronic Body, the Akashic Records, the "treasures stored up in Heaven," etc. It is most commonly called the Causal Body, for it is from this reservoir of knowledge that the Soul chooses which experiences it will focus on next.

In Week 4, we used the concept of "chairness" to express the Idea behind an object that may be both functional and decorative, although coming in a variety of forms. In the development of the individual, the term "Humanity" can be our equivalent for "chairness." Each separate Monad is an individual aspect of humanity (or "humanness"), which is the Whole.

Unlike chairness, in which there may be hundreds or even thousands of individual chairs looking very much alike, individual humans on the material plane of planet Earth have only "shape" alike, i.e., a humanoid body with one head, two hands, two feet, organs placed in similar positions, etc. The inner Monad/Soul is made up of the results of whatever experiences that particular Monad/Soul has undergone. Although we hold many experiences in common, the reactions of the Monad/Souls are as diverse as the individuals themselves, no two being exactly alike, however akin their outward appearance.

Reactions are products of past experiences, and these experiences, although similar, come in increasingly complicated equations offering different conclusions. For example: Experiences A and B and C may be experienced in any order, such as ABC, ACB, BAC, BCA, CAB, or CBA. Each different series or grouping of experiences affects the ultimate attitude and judgment of the experiencer. It is through this process that the Soul becomes individualized and unique.

Personality: The Activating Force

Over the long ages of involution, the Souls built denser and denser realms of matter, concentrating their attention upon the experiences that each succeeding density created until finally the concentration became so intense that a new medium for more fully exploring these densities was required.

The Soul, following its own blueprint, took a portion of itself (as God did from His own original Substance) and created an entity which we now call Personality, but which was first called "Adam." This Personality had the capacity to move within the denser layers of physical adventure and relay back to the Soul what was found there.

When the first Personalities in allegory, Adam and Eve, tasted of the fruits of their activities, their growing knowledge revealed that they were "naked." Allegorically, this means that their bodies were too tenuous and probably without sensors. They did not have the capability of experiencing in depth all that *could* be experienced in this high concentration of matter. They required bodies made up of the same dense physical elements before exploration would yield all that could be gained from the undertaking.

So, as Genesis tells us, "God gave them coats of skin," which can be interpreted as a body made of "the dust of the earth" (i.e., the elements of the area they wished to experience). He "breathed into them the breath of Life," the umbilical cord from the original Source of Life, Spirit. (Spirit, Breath, and Life are synonymous in esoteric symbolism.)

This, however, was dangerous business. To maintain residence in a physical body as dense as the "coats of skin" given to Adam and Eve, a portion of the Will also had to be included. This Will, being composed of the original Substance of the "Desire-to-Become," must inevitably develop into the "Will-to-Do." This energetic faculty became more and more dominant, and is now known as the "lower ego," which developing metaphysicians struggle so valiantly to bring under control.

When they put on the "coats of skin" (physical bodies), the new Personalities found their perceptions sharply focused through the physical senses which were their antennas, so to speak, into the denser matter around them. This new experience drew more and more of their attention, so that, increasingly, they no longer "walked and talked" with their creators, the Souls. As a protection, the gods decreed that they should not partake of the Tree of Life (immortality), lest they become immortal "like us" (note the plural), and live forever in their iniquity (Genesis 3:22). (The plural is also used in Genesis 1:26: "And God said, Let *us* make man in *our* image, after *our* likeness . . . .")

Unlike the original Monads, which were perfect images (or "images of perfection"—completeness) in the Mind of God, the Personalities were only a small part of that Image still on its way to the fulfillment of that perfection, and were, therefore, still incomplete or "imperfect." Their "iniquity" was not their "sinful nature," as interpreted by many theologians, but the "imperfection" itself, which could create only partial (incomplete or imperfect) experiences for them.

At this point there is a difference of opinion among those who purport to be able to trace our evolution back to its beginnings. Some say that the Soul, having relinquished part of its Will into its new projection, the Personality, settled down into being merely a recorder and evaluator of the input of data from the projection, and gradually gave over its sense of purpose and power of direction to this busily evolving aspect of itself.

It is said that the Soul fell into such a deep sleep of unawareness of its purpose to be the directing force for the filling in (fulfillment) of the potential inherent in the Divine Image, that other entities (masters, teachers, guides, angels, guardians, and other superior Beings such as the Solar Angel, or High Self) were dispatched to maintain a focus between the Soul and its divine mission, lest it slumber forever in its absorption of the experiences it was creating.

Others suggest that the intensification of Will within the personalities served to sever relationship with the Soul (banishment from the Garden of Eden) and to draw more energy into the projection. This left less energy for the growth of the Soul Force, which resulted in an unbalanced rather than a completely developing unity.

We could also speculate that it was all part of the original plan to allow the Personalities full play until each one could attain maximum development.

Others say that the Intelligence which became the human that we know today developed from the tiniest grain of consciousness such as an amoeba, or maybe even a mineral form, and evolved up through all the physical levels of matter, and that it is only through the intervention of these superior Beings that we are just now beginning to develop a Soul at all.

In regards to these speculations, it is really immaterial whether our present state of evolution is an advancement or a degeneration. Either has its advantages and values to the Soul in terms of the total lessons learned by experience.

The Role of the Etheric Body

Personalities are projected into earth-type experiences for the purpose of accumulating knowledge about the use and mastery of the laws governing this particular and unique area of the universe, whether the "laws" be exoteric or esoteric (scientific or spiritual). In so doing, they add another dimension to the expanding capacities of the total spiritual Being.

The Soul, like some huge calculator, draws from the accumulation of knowledge in the Causal Body whatever attributes it needs to acquire further experiences in this level of density. Most of the properties gathered are positive, but some still contain "minus" aspects, which means that more development is required.

Those qualities which make up the new Personality to be projected are gathered together into a sheath called the Etheric

Body (called by some authors the Vital Body, the Subtle Body, or the Magnetic Body), which is an exact blueprint, or duplicate, of the new physical body to be created. It acts as a transmitting and distributing agent for the life force which flows through the physical body, and holds the physical atoms together something like a jello mold. The radiations from the Etheric Body are seen as the aura. The Etheric Body also acts as a focus or vehicle for the new Personality.

Like a giant computer in time and space, the "blueprint" finds and draws together the parents with the right kind of genes and emotional qualities, the astrological time and place for conception and birth, and whatever else is needed to bring these characteristics into full expression. There may be a matter of days between the death of one Personality and the birth of the new, or there may be a span of several hundred years. Earth time has no value to the Soul; only the quality of the desired experience is taken into consideration. At death the Personality returns to the reservoir of knowledge in the Casual Body to enrich and expand the Soul's understanding and growth.

The Trinity of Self: Spirit (Monad), Soul, and Personality

Although there are seven clear-cut energy fields that make up the Earth Human at its present stage of development, there are only three major divisions of ego-command or ruling-force: the *Spirit* (Original Image—Monad, or Divine Spark—Identity); the *Soul* (first-in-command—the director of its destiny); and the *Personality* (the field general, so to speak—recorder of experiences).

There have been many interpretations and pictorial references to these three parts of our Beingness, some of them drawn from human imagination, some claimed as inspiration through mediumship and/or clairvoyance. I have found only one which seems to have some possibility of scientific verification.

The Summit University in Montana distributes a full color poster entitled "Your Divine Self," which depicts their artist's rendition of what the total entity of a human being looks like from the clairvoyant view.[25] This poster is reproduced (in black-and-white) as Figure 18.

At the center of their doctrines is the belief that our destiny is to ascend by purifying our aims and desires, and by putting on, or entering into (ascending into) the Christ Consciousness, as Jesus did. The following is taken from the legend on the poster:

"The three figures on the poster correspond to the Trinity of Father (upper figure), Son (middle figure), and Holy Spirit (lower figure), which the evolving Soul is intended to become and for whom the body is the temple. The lower figure is the non-permanent aspect of Being which is made permanent through the ritual of the ascension. The ascension is the process whereby the lower figure, having balanced his karma and fulfilled his divine plan, merges first with the Christ consciousness and then with the living Presence of the I AM THAT I AM. Once the ascension has taken place, the Soul, the corruptible aspect of Being, becomes the incorruptible one, a permanent atom in the body of God."

The top figure, according to the legend, is called "The Divine Monad, the I AM Presence, the I AM THAT I AM, God individualized." It is surrounded by multicolored spheres of light that "comprise the causal body that contains within it man's treasure laid up in heaven—perfect works, perfect thoughts and feelings, perfect words—energies that have ascended from the plane of action in time and space as the result of man's correct exercise of free will."

The middle figure is "the mediator between God and man, variously called the Higher Mental Body, the Real Self, the Christ Consciousness, or the Christ Self." As to the "Christ Self" concept, we might refer to John 14:6—"No man cometh unto the Father, but by me"—and also that which Paul called "the Christ in you, the hope of Glory" (Col. 1:27). This would seem to indicate that Paul recognized this Higher Self of our Being as a projection of the Godhead which holds our destiny in its Force-field.

The lower figure represents "mankind evolving in the planes of matter," and is shown surrounded by a field of violet flame, which represents the energy used to cleanse and overcome karma and the results of incorrect use of free will.

All three figures are enclosed in a "tube of light, which is projected from the heart of the I AM Presence in answer to your call. It is a field of fiery protection sustained in Spirit and in Matter for the sealing of the identity of the overcomer."

Figure 18: Your Divine Self

One theory might be as good as another were it not for the scientific curiosity with which many "personalities" are endowed. Bill Cox of California is one such student of the energies which make up the human being and other aspects of our material plane. Bill lectured one week-end at the Parapsychology Education Center. He demonstrated the use of an instrument called an "aurometer," invented by Verne Cameron, which, following the principles of a dowsing rod, measures the perimeter of the outflow of energy around each human being.

This device measures the exact outlines of the aura. His exciting demonstration also showed the existence of "wings," emanations of energy which flow from fifteen to twenty-five feet out from the shoulder blades of each person. Around the head of each individual is a doughnut-shaped halo of energy, and through the middle of each halo is another filament of energy flowing straight up from the crown of the head as far as could be reached.

After the lectures, while we were talking over a cup of coffee, Bill told me of other experiments done by Verne Cameron. One day Verne tried to find out how high the filament of energy went upwards from someone's head. On a ladder, he found that about three feet above the individual was another human-shaped field of energy with feet, trunk, neck, and head, about one and one-half times the size of the lower physical body! And above this one, too, the filament of energy continued on beyond the length of his ladder. He had the man lie down flat on the floor and discovered the energy field remained upright above his head.

Verne followed the line of energy up about another three feet and found a second human-shaped energy field above that, where apparently it terminated! It, too, was about one and one-half times the size of the field below it.

Verne Cameron died shortly after this experiment, and Bill Cox had not, at that time, done more with it. His description, however, reminded me of the poster of "Your Divine Self," and I showed it to him. He agreed that it seemed to depict what Verne had discovered, so together we did some more experimenting. In the four or five cases that we tried that weekend, the two human-shaped energy fields were found above the head of each individual! Certainly there is room for more exploring along these lines.

The Return: Ever-Widening Awareness

At present there is a tremendous awakening in minds and hearts. Perhaps it is the Soul awakening to the need to reassume its position as the Directing Force, or perhaps the Personality itself has grown to recognize its need to achieve oneness or union with that which created it. What *is* important is that the Call does exist, no matter where we might locate the starting point.

As this awakening increases, there is a progressive interplay between the Soul and the Personality. The Soul desires and moves toward purification of the ego-drives of the Personality, while the Personality gradually gives up its own aims and desires in order to work toward cooperation with the more expanded purposes and goals of the Soul.

When this Union comes closer to completion, the primary concern of both becomes a desire that nothing be done to give injury to either oneself or others. As purification advances, it is increasingly recognized that one can injure by thought and emotions as well as by physical action. The ultimate goal is, then, to achieve true harmlessness on all planes of thought and action, so that negative karma no longer has any hold over the emerging dominion of the Soul.

The term "expansion of consciousness" says it all. The return journey back to oneness with God is ever-expanding awareness of the totality of Being. Our first step is the "I AM" point of awareness of Self, or Soul—the awareness that we are something other than the body, the emotions, the intellect—and knowing that the "I AM" aspect of ourselves is the guiding force.

Once this is achieved, the next steps become progressively easier, although none are won without effort and desire, and none are won permanently with artificial means such as hallucinogenic drugs. These only serve to disintegrate the physical body and ultimately sever the connection entirely without having built any permanent structures within the trinity of Body, Mind, and Soul.

After achieving Soul Consciousness, the next step is to win through to the Monad point of consciousness, where we see ourselves as a total unit with varying levels of awareness within ourselves, living finitely in infinity, developing into that full realization of the "God within" which is sought by all religions.

It is only from this point of perception that one can then expand in conscious awareness into past and future, beyond the astral and the physical, into realms of understanding and Beingness where few have gone before.

There no one can lead you. This journey back to the awareness of the Source of one's own beginning, and the projection of one's own ultimate God-imaged goal, is a journey taken within oneself. Others might point the way. They can inspire you with their own experiences. They may draw you along intellectual flights of fancy. But no man or woman can go with you into that realm of light and revelation.

Beware those who try to do so. The realm I am speaking of is beyond the intellect, beyond the emotions, beyond pictured fabrications of heretofore untrodden paths. Guided fantasy games, in the hands of a competent teacher, are invaluable in opening up the inner Eye and in helping you to learn more about how you are using mental and emotional energies, but they are still just that—fantasies, figments of the imagination.

No matter how unearthly they seem, or what levels of consciousness they aspire to, their sources and destinies are within the astral realm, or emotional vibrations, of planet Earth. You may *feel* free, but the fact that there is a boundary around the visionary paths you tread is in itself a limitation. *Any* visual picture in the mind must, by its very nature, be within the Mental Body.

Your Spiritual Name

If you persist with unswerving devotion to bring into full fruition that Divine Potential within you, there will come a day when you will learn your Spiritual Name. This Name is sacred and is not given to you until you are able to keep it secret, because indiscriminate revealing of it on the Earth plane can leave you vulnerable to attack from its opposite energy (non-spiritual).

I can't tell you in what manner the Name will be given to you, because each person is different, but when you hear it spoken silently within yourself you will thrill to the knowledge that this is *it*. There will rise within you an unspeakable joy and an infinite longing to someday be known by that Name in its full glory.

This sacred Name is your secret of all power. You may safely substitute it for whatever mantra you are now using in your meditations. You will feel the forces within you begin to vibrate at a finer, more powerful pace, and your inner vision will become clearer and more all-encompassing. Your expansion is both inward and outward. That which you see with the inward Eye comes quickly to pass under the outward eye, and the follies and fallacies of the external plane will touch you or concern you less and less.

Beyond this, words are of no value. Logic tells us that the very fact that we have built mental and emotional bodies means that they have a function to perform as part of the God-imaged projection of ourselves. But they are tools, only, of the ultimate Self, which will be *Spirit*-dominated, in the realms beyond both intellect and emotion.

Workshop #6
Auras and the Akashic Records

≈

Individual experiences and the reactions to them leave an indelible mark on the developing Monad/Soul. These can be read in the body of energy called the Akashic Records (also known as the Causal Body), but reading these records usually requires considerable spiritual as well as psychic development to accurately tune into this information.

Reading the Akashic Records requires the ability to look deeply into the Soul of the person being read, and this can be done only from the Soul level of the reader.

The reader, to be accurate, must have conquered all personal feelings of criticism, condemnation, or resentment toward the actions of others. The only desire must be that of wanting to help. Anything less than this will bring forth information colored by the reader's own desire for sensationalism. This is the frequent cause of psychic malpractice which produces the fraud, the charlatan, and the fake.

Developing the ability to see and read the human aura is the easiest first step in gaining attunement with the Soul of another. Self-discipline and spiritual growth, along with intensive practice, will sooner or later develop other qualities which, if the desire is also present, will ultimately allow you to see the Akashic Records of anyone, yourself included.

Exercise #1: Seeing Your Own Aura

Sit in front of a mirror. The background should be white or a light color. Relax and focus your gaze at a point approximately six inches above your head and two feet behind you in the mirror. Use peripheral vision to observe the outline of the body, especially head and shoulders. You may be more successful if you are without clothes.

Gradually you should see a thin line of light around the body. This may take several minutes. Move your head and see if this pattern of light moves with it, to see whether the field is associated with you or not. Once you have seen this, try to figure out exactly how you did it so you can repeat the process.

Another method is to use a black background and illuminate yourself with a blue light, such as from a blue light bulb.

At first, you may see a colorless or misty thin band of light around the body. Later, with practice, more layers may become visible, extending outward. Colors should become clearer. Once you can see this emanation, you can begin experimenting with it. Try to gain conscious control over the pattern and shift it from side to side of the hand or head. In the same way as biofeedback, psychic practitioners claim that you can gain psychic-physical control over body processes through the aura.

Exercise #2: Seeing the Auric Field from the Hands[26]

You may practice this exercise alone or with a group.

Place a black cloth without sheen on a table in a quiet, dimly lit room. (Do not use satin, sateen, brocade, or any glazed cloth which may reflect light.) Sit in a comfortable chair and spend a few moments relaxing into Alpha consciousness. Sensitize the eyes by looking into the darkest part of the room.

Place the hands palms downward against the black background. Keep your fingers together and gaze intently at them. Avoid any strain which may affect your passive state.

Carefully study the outline of your hands. You'll see a vague or hazy outline around them. Spread out your fingers and look for the emanations from each individual finger.

Now rub your hands briskly together. In the dim light, move your palms back and forth, together and apart, a few times. You may see a greenish glow emanating from the palms of your hands.

Place the fingertips of both hands together for a minute or so, then slowly draw them apart. Auric radiations can be seen issuing from the tips of the fingers and uniting the hands. The more vital and energetic the person, the stronger and more radiant will be the aura.

If there are others at the table, point your fingertips towards the fingertips of another person. The etheric rays will be seen to reach across and unite. This "melded" aura can be seen to bend as the fingers move. If one hand is raised slightly, contact will not be broken, but the aura will bend to maintain contact. (Although, in Bevy Jaegers's experiments, the auras of the fingertips seem to rush out to meet the aura of another's fingertips when a few inches apart, Kirlian photographs show that as the fingers come closer the aura retreats and draws back upon itself and does not merge. The explanation may lie in the affinity or aversion the two people have for each other.)

Exercise #3: Seeing Another's Aura[27]

Have someone stand before a plain white wall or curtain with hands on hips, elbows pointing out. Dim the lights at the beginning. Later, you will be able to see auras in broad daylight.

Fix your gaze on the region around the subject's head and shoulders. Let your eyes become slightly unfocused, looking but not staring. When you have succeeded, you will notice that the normally clear outlines of the person have become fuzzy, and the wall behind the subject has taken on a sort of distorted look. Note the formation of any mist, lights, or rays in any portion of the body. You should be able to see a definite glow around the subject.

If you attempt to look at it directly, or let your eyes sharply focus again, the glow will disappear. If this happens, begin again and try to keep your eyes unfocused.

Some people can see this glow while wearing eyeglasses, others must remove them before they succeed in developing auric vision. If you wear eyeglasses, try it both ways. Some can see the aura with both eyes, some with only one eye. Try standing sideways to the subject and view him or her out of the corners of your eyes. Then have the subject turn sideways to you, and note any differences in the width or colors of the glow.

At first you may see only the glow, or a fuzzy, wavering haze like heat waves arising from hot pavement in the summertime. If there is interest, persistence, and desire, colors will begin to manifest themselves after a few practice sessions. Ms. Jaegers says that staring at a square of yellow paper prior to the experiment will sensitize the eyes to blues commonly seen in normal auric fields. Like all other psychic abilities, practice is essential to become proficient in seeing (and reading) the aura.

Exercise #4: To Develop Color Awareness

This exercise may help to make colors more visible in the auras you see.

Place some slips of brightly colored paper in different envelopes. Sit or recline in a comfortable position. Put yourself in Alpha consciousness, deeply relaxed. Breathe slowly and deeply. Hold the breath for a few seconds, then empty the lungs entirely.

As you breathe, visualize a ball of light in bright scintillating red. With the second breath, change the color of the light to orange, then with each breath change to the next color of the rainbow— yellow, green, blue, indigo, and violet. Make the colors as bright and scintillating as possible.

After a few minutes of color concentration, hold one of the envelopes in your hand and try to visualize the color within. Mark the colors as you see them on your record sheet and check your accuracy later. Try holding the envelope to the middle of your forehead and at your solar plexus to see which place gives you the most distinct colors and the most accuracy.

Or try visualizing one color only, say red. Holding the visualization of red, try to find the envelope containing the red slip. Do this with each of the colors.

Exercise #5: Inner Auric Vision

This exercise uses clairvoyant vision rather than optical vision.

Have the subject stand or sit in front of a plain white wall or curtain. Remove paintings, posters, or other nearby objects that may distract you. The subject should either be naked or cover all clothes with a white sheet, so that no other color impinges upon your mind. Dim the lights.

Fix your gaze on the region around the head and shoulders. Concentrate, but do not strain. Keep your attention focused for two or three minutes, then close your eyes and picture a dark void. Wait a few seconds and you will see a color gradually emerging in your thoughts. It could appear as a bright fluorescent glow, followed by a second hazier color, or it could be just the sensing of a color, "felt" rather than seen. If you are successful, these will be colors presently existing in the subject's aura.

Verification Test

Colors in the aura change according to one's mood or temperament. Ask the subject to think of four recent experiences which provoked strong, unrelated emotions, such as a happy moment, an intense argument, a frightening experience, or an exciting journey.

Direct the subject to concentrate intently on the first memory without giving you any clues as to its nature, and to clearly feel the emotion experienced at the time.

Use either optical vision or clairvoyant vision to ascertain what colors and hues are evident at this moment. Write down your observations so that you can validate the experiment. Repeat the process while your partner focuses on the second recollection, then the third and fourth, carefully noting your impressions of colors as the exercise progresses. The meaning of the colors perceived should correspond to the feelings your friend chose to recall during each stage of the exercise.

Color Interpretations

In each individual aura there is usually a basic color with shadings, spurts, and blobs of other colors. Not all authors agree what the colors mean, and two clairvoyants viewing the same subject may see different colors in the aura. I have listed below a condensed version of the most common interpretations of the colors. Through practice, learn to draw your own conclusions about the meanings of the colors you see.

In general, bright clear tones are optimistic, spiritual, with high vibrations. The darker or muddier the tone, the more pessimistic and negative it becomes.

REDS are the physical phase of mentality, indicating the state of health, vigor, friendship, and love.

BRIGHT, CLEAR RED: An energetic personality, self-motivated, extroverted, vital optimism, courage, strength.

BRICK RED: Vanity, arrogance, conceit, domineering qualities, possibly strife.

DARK RED: Emotion, desire, sexual arousal. Found in blobs, flecks, spots, and spurts.

SCARLET: Intense anger or rage, rooted in egotism, hate, or malice. May be prone to insanity.

BLOOD RED: Person who can and probably will commit murder, or has done so in past lives.

PALE RED: One who tries to overcome baser nature, but finds it hard to do so.

CLEAR ROSE: Unassuming, easily hurt, generous, warm-hearted, the mother instinct.

SOFT ROSE: A sensitive, tranquil, and optimistic nature.

DEEP ROSE: Wine-colored tones imply happy love affairs; but muddy rose warns of emotional disturbances.

BRIGHT PINK: The color of universal love. Quiet, refined, modest, loves beauty and artistic surroundings.

CLEAR, SOFT PINK: Intense and lasting devotion. Affection strengthened by sorrow or tragedy. Wishful thinking about the past.

MEDIUM PINK: The color of human love. The true friend. Affection, simplicity, sympathy, emotional involvement, warmth, compassion, comradeship, and sociability.

HOT PINK: Selfish love, extremely demanding and uncaring.

CORAL: Unsureness about decisions and/or unhappiness in one's surroundings.

PALE PINK: Weakness or confusion, lack of strength or aggression, sometimes indicates a slightly psychotic personality.

ORANGES are the union of mind and body (red and yellow), a sign of sound wisdom and justice.

BRIGHT ORANGE: A gregarious, energetic, fun-loving disposition, well-balanced. Can also imply aggressiveness.

GOLDEN or YELLOW/ORANGE: Wisdom and energy, increased mental stability, self-control, open-hearted goodwill, a happy, generous friendly person, quick-witted and humorous.

BRICK ORANGE: Tension, stubborn persistence, arguments.

BROWNISH ORANGE: Lack of ambition, laziness, or repression.

CLEAR GOLD: Friendship, sincerity, tolerance, loyalty, trustworthiness, high spirituality.

DULL GOLD: Boredom, stagnation, lack of motivation, apathy.

YELLOWS are the intellectual phase of Being.

GOLDEN YELLOW: Health of body and mind, optimism, mental concentration.

CLEAR BRIGHT YELLOW: The teacher. Mental stability, deep thought or intellectual activity, education, learning.

LEMON YELLOW: Enthusiasm, idealism, imagination; artistic, creative pursuits; leaning towards scientific ideas and invention.

VERY PALE LEMON YELLOW: May indicate sickness in the body.

MUDDY YELLOW: Literally "yellow," cowardice, fear, weakness of will or a feeling of inferiority.

YELLOW/GREEN (CHARTREUSE): Possessive, tenacious, jealous, lacks confidence in own judgments, deceit, and distrust. A tendency to hold onto what is believed to be "valuable."

GREENS mark the lover of nature, and are indicative of sympathy, altruism, charity, healing. Slow to age. People with a green aura commonly appear five to ten years younger than their actual age.

CLEAR, BRIGHT GREEN: Harmonious, practical, a fresh, interested disposition. Healers, a great love of people and nature. Faith, peace.

EMERALD GREEN: Sympathy, kindness, helpful, mercy, loving service, cooperation.

LIME GREEN: Deep love, trust, warmth, sensitivity, great joy, anticipation.

OLIVE GREEN: Emotion, sympathy, or compassion. Often moody.

DULL GREEN: Intense rage, kindled by a jealous, possessive temperament.

SLATE GREEN: Jealousy and deceit. Unhealthy state of mind.

MOSS GREEN: Brooding, moods, often depression. One who can perform a job mechanically while keeping the true Self separate. Surface activities, uncommitted to life, inner aloneness.

DARK, MUDDY GREEN: Envy, hate, or malicious feelings. Moods, depressive behavior.

BLUE/GREEN (TURQUOISE): Very aware of self, ideals, goals. A powerful intellect, soul-searching, happiness, optimism, peace of mind, healing love. Development of psychic and spiritual qualities, and extrasensory perception.

BLUES are the religious or devotional phase of Being.

DEEP ROYAL BLUE: Intuitive response, contemplation, or investigation. Honesty, integrity, loyalty, deep sincerity, wisdom, inspiration, spirituality, saintliness. Unselfishly dedicated to some work or spiritual activity, social causes, science, or art. Said by some to be the natural color of the Soul.

AZURE: Clear, bright sky-blue tones can pertain to fascination with mystery, secrecy. Also to strange psychic or occult adventures.

MEDIUM BLUE: The peacemaker, soothing, healing love. Tranquil, calm, spiritual, dependable, strength of character.

LIGHT BLUE: Spiritual progress, idealism, creative or artistic imagination, sensitivity; a feeling of Divine guidance.

INDIGO: Seeking purpose, or for a cause or religious experience. Scientist, analytical; builds slowly, but securely.

DULL BLUE: Chronic depression, lack of hope or self-esteem; can also reflect self-pity.

DARK MUDDY BLUE: Superstition, unimaginative belief; blind faith or trust. Impressionability, fear.

VIOLETS are the union of Spirit and body (blue and red).

VIOLET: Very high spirituality. One who is searching for the deeper meanings of life and existence. Psychic. The color of Truth, and the teachers of Truth.

ORCHID: Holy, spiritual, idealism, sublimity, compassionate love.

LAVENDER: Spiritual, sensitive, approaching a spiritual goal. The color of humility and worship.

DEEP PURPLE: Royalty, majesty of nature, a calm, unruffled aspect, a true concern for struggling humanity; ability to deal with worldly matters from a spiritual perspective. The leader on the path of Truth. Rare.

BLUE PURPLE: Represents accomplishments through God's Power.

RED PURPLE: Indicates power of body, human will, and individual effort, a lower vibration than blue purple.

BROWNS denote focus on external values.

CLEAR BROWN: Ambition, industry, organization. Painstaking perseverance, growth, effort, and the wish to accomplish.

DULL BROWN: Greed, the tendency to exploit others to one's own ends.

RED BROWN: Signifies an illness or disturbed condition of the body at the place where the color is. Vengeful, callous person.

BEIGE: Optimism, but with overtones of impracticality; possible instability or emotional insecurity.

GREYS indicate a loss or diminishing of the life force.

GREY: Negativism, anxiety, perhaps ill-health, disease. Grief, sorrow, loss.

BLUE GREY: Selfishness; deceit, hypocrisy, conflict, mental problems.

BLUE WHITE: The basic aura color seen around inanimate objects, trees, bushes, etc.

BLACK: The negative pole of Being, negation of Spirit. Rage, anger, hate, extremes of illness, despondency, the more savage types of mental disease, the process of death and dissolution. Impending death. Fear of, or the working of, Black Magic.

WHITES: Pure Spirit, the positive pole of Being. The more dazzling the white, the higher the vibration. Also considered the symbol of the wisdom of Divine Power and thus the most healing of all vibrations; the perfect degree of spiritual attainment and development.

PEARL WHITE: Kind, gentle, and forgiving.

OYSTER WHITE: A soul trying hard to unfold in spite of tests and lessons being experienced.

CRYSTAL WHITE: A soul who has acquired complete self-mastery. Extremely rare.

SILVER: The process of spiritual growth. If seen as a silvery mist over other colors, it will add a much higher vibration to that color.

Exercise #6: Color Healing

The emanations and colors seen around the physical body are actually the visible part of the etheric body. Spiritual healers feel that illness begins first in the etheric body and is later manifested in weakened areas of the physical body, so that if healing processes are activated in the etheric body they will correspondingly manifest in the physical.

The theory is that the colors represent states of mental, emotional, and spiritual well-being, and imbalance in any of these will outpicture in the physical body as various forms of illness and disease. One who can read the aura colors can therefore diagnose the corresponding mental, emotional, or spiritual state and recommend the correct color for healing the unbalanced nature.

Unusual successes have been reported by persons who have experimented both with colored lights and with visualized colors directed towards healing. Along with the lights and color, one can "comb the aura" to cleanse out negative thought-forms which are clinging to the auric vibrations and to speed up the dissemination of color through the etheric envelope.

To comb the aura, make sure your own vital energy is free of negativity by first visualizing purifying White Light coursing down through your body from crown to toe, sweeping before it all forms of negative thought and emotion, leaving only the desire to heal as an unselfish motivating force within your own nature. When this is done, visualize your Being filled with blue light for spiritual aspiration, and then filled with green light for healing.

Using the hands in a clearing, sweeping motion, begin at the top of the person's head, and sweep or comb down through the aura close to the body, but not touching. Sweep front, back, and both sides, visualizing a cleansing effect taking place, and snapping the hands and fingers in a flipping motion after each sweep to clear away clinging thought-forms.

In conjunction with the aura sweep, use colored lights or color visualization to rejuvenate and heal.

Exercise #7: Tea Talk

Inanimate objects also give off emanations of some kind. The higher the level of consciousness, the stronger the emanation. Try this experiment with ordinary kitchen condiments for a classroom exercise.

Choose a number of similar and odorless ingredients, such as baking powder, baking soda, flour, instant tea, parsley flakes, pepper, salt, sugar, etc. Your kitchen shelf will yield all kinds of possibilities.

Have someone place each ingredient in an airtight envelope, taping up any holes so that the contents can't spill out. The envelopes should be numbered on the back to correspond to a master list of the ingredients.

Hold the envelope in your hand. Try with your extended senses to determine which ingredient is in which envelope, by sensing or "feeling" the emanations from it. Write down your results and compare against the master list.

Looking at the master list, compare each envelope again, this time analyzing your sensations and impressions as you handle the envelope. In this way you will cultivate the inner sense pattern of combining external knowledge with internal knowledge about the contents of each envelope.

After a period of absorption (several days or weeks), try the exercise again, not looking at the number on the back until you are ready to write down your results, so as not to be influenced by your memory of the numbers.

MEDITATION PRACTICE: THE RAINBOW MEDITATION

Meditation is not an escape from life, but a means to enhance life. We are not trying to escape from the material to the spiritual, but to spiritualize the material. Do the following meditation series whenever you feel out of harmony with your environment and those around you.

Rainbow Meditation

Sit in a comfortable chair, with your spine straight. Cleanse with the purifying White Light. Go deeply into Alpha consciousness.

Imagine at your feet a bright, glowing ball of violet color. See it as the pulsating, vibrant violet energy of high spirituality, representing one who is searching for the deeper meanings of life and existence. Violet is also the color for the cleansing of Karma.

Let this ball expand and rise until it fills and permeates every atom of your body, drawing the color energy upward until it comes out through the top of your head. Then see it explode with a flashing cascade of violet fire and flow down over you like an energizing fountain.

Repeat the procedure with the rich deep tones of indigo, which represents deep thought and contemplation on spiritual matters.

Follow this with the same procedure using: blue, representing spiritual devotion and aspiration; green, for healing and oneness with God and nature; yellow, reflecting great joy and anticipation; orange, representing wisdom, justice, and goodwill to all; and bright, clear, scintillating red, which stands for vital, optimistic zest for life.

Try to visualize clear, bright colors, but let your mind be free to bring in whatever association it wishes as you draw each ball of color up through your body to explode in a shimmering cascade of color and energy down over your whole Being.

For the balance of your meditation time, allow your mind to dwell on the mystical meaning of the Biblical rainbow covenant after the flood (Gen. 9:8–17) and/or the "Rainbow Bridge" from lower to higher spirituality so often mentioned in occult literature.

Finish with an infilling of the protective White Light, while slowly returning to Beta consciousness.

Do this exercise for three days. Then reverse the procedure for three days, going from red to violet. The first exercise will seem to draw your attention downward and inward; the second will draw your attention upward towards higher spirituality and attunement.

WEEK 7

≈

Self-Awareness
through Dreams, Sleep,
and Auto-Suggestion

There are many realities, and we each create our own. What is real for one person is not necessarily real for another.

Physically speaking, one's reality is the external world, one's place of work and residence. Psychologically speaking, one's reality is one's attitude toward relationships, such as with our spouse, children, coworkers, lover, authority figures, God, etc. Metaphysically speaking, one's reality is the extent of one's ability to mentally stand aside from these, recognize and understand each in its proper perspective, and control or direct the energies that create any or all of them.

Only to the extent that we can develop this last ability can we control our own destinies. Interpreting and understanding our dreams is one way of achieving perspective on the realities we have created for ourselves.

Sleep studies show that the inner consciousness never sleeps, that on one or more levels beyond the conscious waking awareness there is continuous activity. The two densest energy fields—the physical and etheric bodies—need time for rest and rejuvenation, but if there is a similar need within the other five bodies, it has not yet been discovered by either exoteric or esoteric science.

Some of this sleeptime activity is made known to us through dreams and in "visions from the borderland"—that semi-conscious, catatonic state in which the wakeful mind seems to be fully conscious of what is being experienced, while there is either no awareness of the body, or the body seems to lie in a paralyzed state, unable to move.

Many people believe they do not dream, but sleep studies show that dreaming is necessary to mental and emotional health, and that dream deprivation results in neurotic, even psychotic states. Not remembering dreams is largely conditioning. We were told by our parents, teachers, or other authority figures that dreams were unimportant and should be forgotten as soon as possible. Therefore, we've trained ourselves to forget, and some of us do it very well.

At the moment of sleep, the Soul Consciousness in the astral body with its four components—the Causal, Mental, Emotional, and Spiritual Bodies—disengages itself from the heavier physical vehicles and, by so doing, withdraws the energy that keeps the physical and etheric bodies alert and active. Sometimes it hovers over the physical body, and sometimes it travels into other spaces and dimensions.

You can test this by running your hand through the space about one foot above the face of a sleeping person. Most times the person will stir slightly, indicating that something other than the physical body has been disturbed.

During sleep, when the finer bodies are absent, the autonomic nervous system of the body takes over and keeps it functioning on a physical level, but communication still exists between the various energy fields. Dreams, a by-product of your individualization, create the symbols whereby one energy field communicates with another.

There also seems to be some sort of alarm system which draws full consciousness back into physical awareness when either the body has had enough rest, there is a danger or a need to awaken, or the "biological clock" has been set to awaken at a certain time.

Dreams seem to fall into four major categories: externally stimulated, precognitive, out-of-body experiences, and subconscious prompting.

Externally Stimulated Dreams

Some dreams are caused by external stimuli—something that is happening in the environment, or even in your own physical body. If you dream you are sleeping on an iceberg, for example, and you waken to find that your partner has taken all the covers, this would be an externally caused dream.

If you eat something that disagrees with you, and you dream that some thug is sticking a knife in your stomach, this would also be classified as an externally caused dream. Fire sirens and other outside noises are sometimes incorporated into the fabric of the dream. This kind of dream would be centered in the physical body, probably in the brain area, and in making an interpretation these factors should be taken into consideration.

Precognitive Dreams

Some dreams seem to foretell the future. Forthcoming events often cast their shadows ahead of them and are picked up in dreams of an omniscient nature. Some psychologists, such as Jung and Freud, felt that the inner consciousness may project a number of possible outcomes of any given situation ahead of time—a trial run, so to speak, of activities under consideration—then, when a choice is made and the activity comes to pass, we get the familiar feeling of *deja vu*, the feeling that this has all happened before, and that we are reliving an event out of the past. This feeling of *deja vu* may be the actual carrying out of a precognitive dream.

Precognitive dreams can be of a warning nature. We know that prophecy is a perceived result of a present course of action, and that we have the possibility of changing these perceived results by changing the present course of action. In this way, the warnings delivered by precognitive dreams can be blessings, if remembered.

Some people can dream precognitively on a wider level, tapping into the consciousness of a group or nation. The fulfillment of a prophecy for a group or nation can be averted only by a collective action, conscious or unconscious, of the people in that group.

As we read in the Hebrew scriptures, Jonah was sent to Nineveh to tell the people that, unless they changed their ways, great disasters would befall them. The people listened to him and did change their ways, and the prophecies did not come to pass. Jonah, not understanding this, beat upon his breast in a very human fashion, and said, "Father what have you done to me? Let me die for shame!" He had done what he had been told to do in spite of great personal stress, and then felt he had lost face because his prophecies had failed. (Book of Jonah, OT).

In the same manner, Edgar Cayce's prophecies may be mitigated or even averted by the collective activity of the people who will be affected. There are a number of New Age groups located in California, for example, who are working very hard to elevate the consciousness of people in that area. If they succeed, Cayce's prophecies of destruction and major land disasters may be averted or diminished.

Consider the collapse of the Cypress overpass on Highway I-880 in Oakland, California during the 1989 earthquake. More than a mile long, that section of freeway was usually bumper to bumper at 5 P.M., the hour the earthquake struck. Early radio and television forecasts estimated that 700 to 800 people would be found dead under the massive structure. When all of the victims had been removed, the actual number of fatalities was only forty-two. Why? Because the collective consciousness of the residents of the San Francisco Bay area had provided another place for the majority of people to be—Candlestick Park stadium, at the World Series championship baseball game. Although millions of dollars in material damage was done by this earthquake of 7.1 magnitude, the number of earthquake fatalities for the entire Bay area was only sixty-four, fewer than the average daily death toll without an earthquake! I do not believe this was coincidence, but the result of the efforts of hundreds of New Age people working to create the awareness of a higher consciousness within themselves and others. I genuinely feel the future can be changed, despite prophecies or precognitive dreams.

Precognitive dreams—dreams of a warning nature, or giving direction for certain activities—are products of the mental body.

Out-of-Body Experiences

Some dreams may not be dreams at all, but remembrance of out-of-body experiences, the witnessing of events or thought-form activity taking place on other levels, or even spirit contacts. If you dream of conversing with your dead grandfather, or any other relative or friend, you may actually have made contact with the spirit of that person. This may be especially true if viable information is received. Classification of this type of dream must rely on how much symbolism is apparent in the images. The clarity and vividness of the actions and figures in the dream would be most important in making that judgment.

If the astral body travels to another space or dimension, or even other places on this planet, and memories of contact with the thought-forms found there are brought forth into waking life, this should not be considered a dream but an actual experience. Such activities would be focused in the astral body, of course.

I remember one of my own astral travel dreams most vividly because of its incongruity. I was in the air looking down upon a number of houses which were sinking into the ground. I saw people running, and although I knew they were shocked and wildly distraught, there was no emotional response within me at all. I was simply a detached observer of the scene taking place below.

I'm sure I would have passed the dream off as some fantasy being worked out within me if a friend had not called early the next morning to tell me about a news report of a town in Canada sinking into the ground during the night, a town built over an old mining area whose tunnels had collapsed. Needless to say, I was astonished to realize that during sleep I had witnessed an historic event which had happened thousands of miles away.

Dreams that are activities of the causal body may be dreams that reveal messages from the Soul to the Personality, reminders that certain things are expected, certain experiences to be desired. Dreams of past lives may come through this faculty, especially if the dreamer is involved with overwhelming karmic problems and there is prayerful or psychological searching to understand what is being worked through on the Earth plane. Dreams of past embodiments usually reveal some problem or condition in the present, and this type of dream may serve to aid us in achieving our soul's purpose in this lifetime.

Polarization between mind, body, and Soul is an important task of the causal body, so that mental and physical rejuvenation takes place when dreams are centered here. Sexual dreams are also part of this balancing activity. When dreams are continually interrupted, it is the causal body chakra that is disturbed and that brings about neurotic or psychotic states of mind.

Dreams can reveal many things to a dreamer, such as unresolved conflicts and repressed desires. Conflict dreams come about if there are unresolved conflicts in our personal lives. The "fight or flight" syndrome can be released in dreams. Today's culture has many frightening things in it, things which we often cannot see or touch. In more primitive times we could prepare ourselves to do battle with very real dangers, or even to flee, if that seemed the better course. In today's society we can do neither, but much of this repressed discord can be discharged through conflict dreams. Most of these are emotionally charged dreams and are centered in the emotional body.

Sometimes we have the feeling that we have been taught by higher Beings, or that we've been going to school while we sleep, but we cannot bring back to conscious awareness that which we learned. These dreams may be centered in the spiritual body, in which case, we won't remember them until the focus of our conscious awareness has been established at least within the Soul level of consciousness.

Within the spiritual body would be dreams of contact with other Beings on a Soul or spiritual level. From these dreams, also, would come higher spiritual understanding and awareness, stored in the Soul level and brought into waking consciousness when needed in the form of inspiration, intuition, etc.

The Most Common Dream

By far the most common of our dreams are subconscious meanderings, composed of symbolism and seemingly unrelated dream activities. These dreams center in the etheric body—that field of energy surrounding and interpenetrating the physical body. These are the dreams most frequently remembered, and they are clothed most deeply in symbolic language. I call them "state of Being" dreams because interpretation reveals that they depict present states of mind and explore present possibilities.

Dream symbols are the language of the inner consciousness, programmed by emotion and environment. Consider the artificiality of spoken language. Words which we Americans use as symbols for communication have no meaning to someone born in Russia or Japan or Spain, for instance. The symbols for communication used by those people in turn have no meaning for us, unless special effort is made to learn their language.

Therefore, the symbols for written and oral communication that are used by the Personality in this lifetime have very little relevance for the Soul Self, which has seen many languages come and go. The symbols used by the inner consciousness for communication may be the product of all the information now stored through our collective experiences as a Soul on this planet.

Much symbolism in dreams is a type of shorthand which can picture many different levels of consciousness in one brief flash. Individuals have their own dream symbolism which relates especially to their own group of experiences.

People who constantly work with their dreams often discover that their symbolism becomes more precise, and the clarity of their dream material increases as more conscious attention is focused on it. This might be because the conscious mind has been trained for many years to disregard dream material, so symbolism may be used as the only means of bypassing the conscious mind barrier to inner communication. As this barrier is released, communication from the inner consciousness becomes more easily understood.

Here are two exceptionally clear dreams which show this symbolic clarity and the propensity of the mind to follow directions and bring about a desired result.

One day, about mid-morning, I was driving by Mt. Shasta in northern California when I was suddenly taken with extreme lethargy and found myself so sleepy I was forced to pull off the road at a scenic point under some trees. I reminded myself that I desired to be in Washington before that day was over, and that I really didn't have time for a snooze, so I directed my inner mind to wake me in half an hour.

Exactly thirty minutes later by my watch, a man appeared and tapped on my car window. He was dressed vividly in a green suit and red vest and was tall enough that he had to stoop to look in when he tapped on the window. His appearance startled me, and my eyes flew open to discover that the presence had only been an exceptionally vivid dream, for there was no man in a green suit anywhere near my car.

However, the extreme lethargy was still with me, and try as I may I could not pull myself upright to take the wheel again. I went back to sleep, directing my mind to give me fifteen minutes more. This time I dreamed I was traveling up the road and I saw signs formed like large bees advertising a honey farm ahead. The words read, "See our bees make honey." Shortly I came to a small roadside stand and on the apex of the roof was a sign which read, "¼ mile."

At the end of this dream, I woke to discover I had been given exactly fifteen minutes sleep, and interpreted the dream to mean that my body needed the energy of honey to recuperate. With great effort I pulled myself erect and eased the car out onto the road again. Exactly a quarter of a mile up the road I came to a little country grocery, where I went in and bought a small jar of honey. I ate several spoonsful and in just minutes I was feeling my old self again.

In this case, the symbolism was very precise and the interpretation very clear in response to an urgent physical need and my own demands upon myself to meet a deadline.

Dream Interpretation Is Personal

When interpreting dreams one must learn to decode one's own dream symbols. Some symbols come from the collective unconscious and have universal significance, but for the most part each individual must apply his or her own meanings. Many of the verbal clichés we use can be found in similar pictures in our dreams. A bridge might denote bridging something. A shade tree could mean a shady deal.

Carefully think out symbols and dream distortions. The unfathomable aspects of the total realm of Creation beyond our known and limited awareness can only be presented to us through symbols that fit our own consciousness. Christians have visions of the compassionate Christ; Buddhists see the serene and benevolent Buddha; the American Indian walked and talked with the gods of forest and stream; the Spiritualists envision living realities of masters and inner guides who teach and direct them personally.

We should note that the completely devoted Christian would never have a mystical experience with any master other than the Christ, or the agnostic envision and speak to a Deva or forest nymph. The intellectual, sense-oriented scientist could not experience personal revelations from a discarnate inner guide.

All of these are limited by the philosophy of the reality consensus they have personally adopted. The exception might be when the Soul has an urgent need to break through to the Personality with a new, more expanded concept of universal reality. Then symbols outside of one's accepted reality may be seen in dreams. The mystical experience is personally significant to each individual, and much of it depends upon what one has trained oneself to expect. Most dream symbols used by the various energy fields reflect our present interpretations of life.

The best way to learn to interpret your dreams is to write them down every time you have a dream, as was suggested in an earlier lesson. The process of writing them down activates the intuitive faculty, and after awhile you'll begin to see a pattern emerge, or you'll receive intuitive insights as to the meaning of individual symbols. A clear, blue lake in your dream may mean tranquillity and peace, but for another who has had a harrowing experience of nearly drowning in a lake it could be a symbol of danger.

If you are one who never remembers dreams, you can direct yourself when you go to bed at night to begin to remember dreams. Place a paper and pen by your bedside as proof that you are sincere, and when you wake up, write down whatever bits you remember, even if they are only tiny fragments. In this way you will retrain your mind to remember dreams.

As soon as you awake, before any other thought enters your mind, ask your subconscious, "What did that dream mean?" You'll find that the interpretation will be given almost immediately, because the conscious mind is still close enough to the subconscious to pick up the meaning. It must be done immediately, however, before any other thought has a chance to intervene.

Learning to interpret your own dream symbols can be a fascinating study. One way is to break down each symbol individually, and analyze your emotional reaction in the dream to each symbol. Look for double meanings, a play on words. Puns are often used in a sort of dream shorthand. An airplane may mean you are finally getting off the ground, or a can of soup may mean you're "in the soup," you are afraid of being "canned" (fired from your job), or of being "thrown in the can " (jail), or that some aspect of your present life situation makes you feel imprisoned or jailed.

Or one can interpret each symbol as part of the dreamer's own Personality. Using a gestalt technique, sit in a chair, and pretend that the dream character is sitting in a chair facing you. Ask it questions. Then move over to the other chair and assume the role of the dream images, giving each of them a voice and letting them speak for themselves. Interesting insights into your own character and personality can be opened up in this way.

Nine Basic Rules

Anne Faraday, Ph.D., in *The Dream Game,*[28] gives nine basic rules for interpreting dreams, which I have condensed here.

1. First, the dream should be considered literally. That is, look for signs of objective truth such as warnings or reminders about a current situation in your life, something that may have been missed by the conscious mind but picked up by the subconscious.

2. If the dream makes no sense literally, then search for metaphorical statements about your spiritual or emotional relation to life.

3. Dreams are triggered by something that is important to our physical, emotional, mental, or spiritual well-being, something that lies on our heart or mind at the moment. The primary objective is to relate the dream to something that has happened in the past day or two, or to a preoccupation with some question of vital importance to you.

    Even when dreams reveal deep, long-standing problems, or touch on higher transcendental issues, they show how that situation is affecting us at the *present* moment in time. If a dream takes us back to childhood or some childhood event or person, it is because these past events are somehow relevant to a present concern, and the dream's meaning will be found in this reference to the present.

4. The emotional tone of the dream usually gives us a clue as to what this particular life situation is. For instance, if the feeling of the dream is miserable, then it denotes some miserable or troubled situation currently reflected in one's life.

5. Although there are some universal symbols, each dream theme* can mean quite different things to different dreamers according to their current life situations.

6. The same dream theme may recur from time to time in your dreams, yet be interpreted differently according to your current situation.

7. The main purpose of dreams is to reveal something hidden, repressed, or overlooked by the conscious mind. So if the dream seems to be dealing with something you already know about, look for some deeper meaning.

8. A dream is correctly interpreted when it makes sense to you in terms of your present response to life and moves you to make constructive changes in your life's pattern.

9. A dream is incorrectly interpreted if it leaves you unmoved or disappointed. Dreams come to reveal and to expand, not to lessen our concept of ourselves.

≈ ≈ ≈

Reincarnation dreams, prophetic dreams, and *recap dreams*, are seldom touched upon by psychologically oriented writers. When the present psychological implications and literal aspects of the dream symbols have been explored, and something still seems to be missing, then look for the possibility that scenes from a past life may have been shown to you to enlighten a present perplexing situation. This is a *reincarnation dream*.

A *prophetic dream* is often not recognized as a prophecy until after it comes to pass. Some prophetic dreamers tell me that these dreams are more vivid in detail, but most people find it difficult to tell the difference. Perhaps this is an area that needs more attention so that we can learn its subtleties.

Another, rarer dream not usually recognized is the *recap dream*, in which one seems to relive scenes from a period of months or even years of one's immediate past. In this dream the Soul may be bringing to an end a certain set of circumstances, tying up all the loose ends, cataloging them, and filing them away in its memory banks in preparation for a new series of experiences—a kind of death and rebirth process. There might even be an analogy to the reports of one's life flashing before one's eyes at the moment of death, except this is not a death but a series of events brought to a desired conclusion.

There is still another type of dream that I have not found mentioned in any dream book, and this kind may be the prerogative of writers. My dream life often gives me creative little story plots worked out simply for my amusement that do not seem to have any other subconscious function. At these times, I always seem to be reading the story and enjoying the interplay of words, as well as watching the action take place. As a writer, these give me great pleasure and titillate my imagination, but do not fall into any of the categories listed here.

Nightmares

Frightening dreams, or nightmares, must be handled in a different way. Since one's dream life reflects present concerns, a nightmarish dream reflects some aspect of life over which we feel we have no control. As emerging masters of our own destinies we must train our inner minds to stand up to whatever terrors are manufactured by the various energy fields of our own Beingness.

The affirmation "You have no power over me" is excellent in dealing with externally created situations, and will work equally well with internal conflicts. In real life I have found that any situation I feared always dissolved when I faced it squarely.

In my younger days in sales work, I felt I did not have the background or the gumption to sell to people who lived in "the big house on the hill." Never having experienced wealth or power, I was scared to death to speak to them.

After many sales pep talks, I finally gathered up my courage and knocked on the door of the largest house in town. To my amazement, the lady of the house was as sweet as could be, and later, when I met her husband, I found him charming, intelligent, and sympathetic. From then on I became more and more daring in facing squarely any situation that frightened me. Invariably, the imagined outcome never materialized, but faded away like the chimerical image it was.

This attitude of being in control of one's projections in waking life can be carried over into one's dream life. Instruct your subconscious mind before you sleep that frightening dream images have no power to harm or annoy you. Some dream image symbolizing this courageous part of your Personality will often emerge in the dream and "stand up" to the threatening image, resolving your conflict for you.

A disturbing dream reflecting inner conflicts can often be resolved at the time of dreaming. Just as you awaken, with the dream images still fresh in your mind and your mind still at the Alpha level of semi-sleep, go back over the dream images; this time make the dream come out as you want it to. Reconstruct the dream images and make them friendly instead of frightening.

As an example, suppose you dream that a ferocious animal or some kind of monster is creating a terrifying situation for you. In the dream, you are very frightened and wake sweaty and trembling. Before the mind has a chance to waken fully from the Alpha state, go back over the dream images, and this time go up to the dream symbol that appears to be your enemy and demand that it be friends with you. Make it shake your hand, or give some other evidence of friendship. When this is done, insist that your former enemy give you a token of its good will, a gift of some sort.

When the imaged gift is received, you'll know that on deep, symbolic levels an old conflict has been destroyed, and you not only are master of that particular situation but something good has come from it—and you have the "gift" to prove it! Later, an interpretation of the "gift" symbol should be very enlightening.

This deliberate interaction with your dreams can bring about "lucid dreaming," a state in which you are aware that you are dreaming, and this opens up possibilities only now being explored by psychologists and dream scientists. In the lucid dream, one has the capacity to change the dream scene deliberately. It is my theory that the lucid dream, more often than not, may be an astral travel dream wherein one is conscious of actually manipulating the emotional matter of the astral plane and creating any kind of experience one desires.

One session cannot do justice to the vast, still largely unexplored field of dreams and dreaming. A look around your bookstore shelf will reveal many exceptionally good books on dream interpretation which are more than merely "dream dictionaries." If you are intrigued by the rich area of introspection that dream interpretation opens up, I suggest you form a dream encounter group with others of like mind. It could be a very rewarding endeavor.

Sleep Programming—Mastering Your Inner Life

In Week 1 we learned that the brain can function on four major levels of activity: Beta—the waking consciousness; Alpha—meditation, sleep, and dreams; Theta—the Subconscious area; and Delta —deep sleep, coma, and some cases of mediumship.

We've become familiar with the Alpha level during our periods of meditation and most of you can now enter the Alpha state at will, to bring forth vital information, guidance, and direction. Sometimes you can even enter the Theta state, bridging the gap into subconsciously stored memories.

Probably the most important thing to remember is that as we drift off to sleep each night, the brain slows down, first into the semi-consciousness of Alpha, and then into the Theta level of unaware sleep. As sleep begins and Alpha becomes more pronounced, it is important to be mindful that this is the creative level of the brain, and everything that is programmed into Alpha is manifested outwardly in external activities and events.

Therefore, it is an absolute *must* that we lay aside all fears, worries, and cares before entering the sleep state, as we would before entering meditation. If we go to sleep mulling over negative situations and fearful thoughts (squirrel-caging), we are simply regrooving, reprogramming these same fearful activities and thoughts for the following days, picturing negative fantasies for future manifestation.

Let entering into sleep be an act of peaceful relaxation. Use a warm bath, soft music, whatever is needed to aid in putting aside the cares of the day. The activities of your sleep time are just as important as the activities of your waking time in developing extended sense perception for wisdom and guidance. If you want to be in control of your Life Path, you must resolve to be master of your intellectual and emotional content twenty-four hours a day.

It is at this time that the most effective programming for directing your life can take place. This is when the other energies that are part of your spiritual makeup can function without the restriction of the attention-claiming focus of the senses.

At this time you can allow the Soul Self to solve problems, create new opportunities, harmonize relationships, and do many other things while the lower consciousness is being rejuvenated and refreshed. When you waken in the morning, be ready to step into new, more meaningful activities which have already been prepared for you while you slept.

Problem Solving While You Sleep

No one is without problems, burdens, and worries that bear down until there seems to be no way out. Program your sleep time to solve the problem for you, or to offer guidance as to the best course of action to pursue.

Just before drifting off to sleep, state the problem as succinctly, unemotionally, and briefly as possible. Then say to your Soul Self, "I want an answer to this problem." Then forget about it; allow your mind to dwell on pleasant things—a loved one, a soul-inspiring thought, or a beautiful scene.

The answer may come in a dream whose symbols are exceptionally clear and precise. You may wake in the morning with the thought in your mind of exactly how you will handle the situation, or during the next forty-eight hours you will be led to someone who has the answer for you. Inventions, ingenious solutions, and new ideas will, without fail, come in response to your call if you use this technique.

If the problem is exceptionally severe or longstanding, or if it has been reinforced by prolonged, intense, and painfully agitated fear thoughts, then it may take more than one night of reprogramming to move Substance sufficiently to find the answer. However, if you refuse to go to sleep thinking about it, but instead keep affirming that the proper guidance will be given to you to handle the difficulty, you should very shortly begin to see a break in the circumstances. Something will happen to show you that things are making a change.

When that something occurs, whether it be a great event or a small one, or simply a new idea, be bold. Follow it up with dynamic action. Pursue whatever course of action opens up to you.

There is an old adage, "God helps those who help themselves." God provides the ideas, the means, the avenues through which our good can come, but our part in the Divine Plan is the *doing*. If we do not follow through with action when the possibility of good is presented to us, then the opportunity is lost and we remain stagnant in a negative situation. Few things are handed to us on a silver platter. "Looking for the solution" means we expectantly prepare to take action in whatever direction is revealed to us.

You'll soon learn to respect this source of guidance and recognize the value of it.

General Protection

Don't forget to surround yourself with the White Light before you go to sleep. Keeping yourself protected by the Circle of Light at all times should be an automatic response by now, something that you do every morning and every night, and before and after each meditation, for the rest of your life. Reinforce it any time a near-accident or discharge of negative energy from someone near you comes to your attention.

In addition, you can sleep-program your subconscious mind to alert you if at any time you are moving into a dangerous situation. As you drift into the Alpha consciousness of sleep, state firmly in your own words something like, "I want to be made aware of anything that I should know, any warning I should have, if I should be kept from going someplace, or doing something that would be detrimental to me; and I want to be protected from moving into any dangerous or negative situation that may arise from my own or another's thought creations."

This type of programming can be a constant direction to the inner mind. Not only when drifting off to sleep, but at frequent intervals during the day, ask for protection from negative influences. You will see some uncanny responses of the subconscious mind—when you didn't have that near-accident; when you didn't step off the curb just before a car sped around the corner; when you didn't go on the plane, train, or bus trip that ended in disaster.

Every time you become aware of this protection, be sure to say "Thank you!" to your inner guidance. An attitude of appreciation will strengthen this response mechanism, until you can truly say with David, "a thousand shall fall at thy side, and ten thousand at thy right hand; but it shall not come nigh thee" (Psalms 91:7).

To Harmonize Relationships

Problems with others can be harmonized just as we drop off to sleep. At the Alpha level of consciousness we do not have the energy to hate. It is so much easier then to allow love to flow from your emotional center to the emotional center of whomever you have a disagreement with, whether it be boss, mate, partner, child, parent, friend, or enemy.

Say to yourself as you drift off to sleep, "I find it very easy to be generous, happy, kind, loving, open-hearted, understanding, virtuous." Imagine yourself responding with each of these qualities in life's situations around people with whom you, in the past, have not been generous, kind, or loving. The peaceful Alpha level makes it easy to do, and the inner programming quickly brings that which is visualized into manifestation in outer levels.

Consciously directing love energies to another person is a very powerful action at this level. It will go a long way toward turning an enemy into a friend, a disruptive associate or relative into a considerate person, and will set up a protective barrier against dangerous acts from other people. If there are no vengeful, resentful, or hate-filled thoughts emanating from your powerful emotional center, there can be no avenue through which retaliation in kind can come back to you.

Perhaps a dream will also enable you to see how you relate to someone else, in such a manner that you can understand the relationship and initiate action yourself to smooth out the situation.

For Self-Understanding

Over the entrance to the ancient Oracle at Delphi was the message, "Man, know thyself." All systematic and intelligent endeavors to know spiritual truth must begin with self-analysis. Only when we know ourselves can we come to know God. Modern psychologists are also discovering that most of our mental and emotional problems stem from ignorance about our inner responses to life, as well as lack of information about how to discipline those responses.

If there is lack of forgiveness in our hearts, at the Alpha level it is very easy to forgive. You have already made yourself peaceful, and it does not take any energy to be happy. Happiness is the natural state of humankind and is inherently rejuvenating. It takes a lot of energy to be *unhappy!*

The physical energy output is very low in Alpha, and it is very easy to program the inner mind with such thoughts as, "I can forgive, I do forgive. I can love. I *am* Love. I forgive So-and-So for whatever he or she did to me. At this point it doesn't even matter at all." This is one of the easiest ways in the world to rid yourself of anger, guilt, resentment, a desire for retaliation or vengeance, or any other fearful or negative thought-forms.

The desire to know about and to understand whatever faults or shortcomings we have, and the means to overcome them, are available through sleep programming. Ask your deepening consciousness as you drift off to sleep to make known to you whatever you need to know about yourself, and keep affirming that you *are* the opposite of whatever problem you are working with.

New Goals and New Opportunities

Vitalize your goals at the Alpha level just before sleep overtakes you. See yourself achieving that which you want to achieve. Visualize yourself as being very successful and properly rewarded for the effort and energies you have expended. Also ask to be given the right kind of guidance, so that which you achieve is beneficial for all concerned.

If you have no goals at the moment ask your superconscious to supply you with a goal that is worthy of your talents and energy output, one in which you will receive the recognition, success, and rewards that are due you.

When ideas come to you in dreams or inspiration, be sure to follow through. If the idea is yours and there is energy and enthusiasm for it, know that the ability is also there to achieve that which you visualize. You will not be misguided if you *listen* with humility.

If life seems to be stagnant at the moment, ask your inner consciousness to create new opportunities for you. This is a time when one does not need to be specific, because the subconscious and/or superconscious can bring new opportunities and adventures into your life that are exciting beyond your wildest fantasies, opening doors into areas of experience that you never before remotely dreamed of. It will bring you into contact with new and interesting people, and maybe even set you globe-trotting around the world.

Dreams reflecting repressed or suppressed desires will often be the fruit of such a request, and in the days to come you will be given opportunities to fulfill those desires if you continue to program your sleep time to bring them about.

When you ask for new opportunities, be prepared to flow freely with whatever experiences come your way, not allowing mental or emotional restrictions or preconditioned inhibitions to keep you from fully savoring all that can be enjoyed from these new experiences. When desires are suddenly fulfilled we often say, "What a lucky break! This came right out of the blue!" It didn't really. It came about because you prepared yourself on subliminal levels, and your inner consciousness brought it to pass.

Spiritual Unfoldment

All of us reach plateaus where we seem to be stalled in our spiritual growth, where nothing seems to be happening and nothing new is being created in our environment for learning or applying what we know. This is a time of Soul evaluation, a time when the Soul itself has retreated into meditation and is digesting, as it were, the things that have previously been learned.

During these times of seeming stagnation, your sleep time can be used to reinforce present channels to the Soul Self. At the Alpha level, just as you drop off to sleep, ask that you be taught new Truths from the Spiritual plane. Don't seek teachers from the astral realm. Those who claim jurisdiction there are still struggling with problems similar to your own. Ask for teachers from the highest level that you have the ability to contact.

You need not know what that level is. The request will bring its own answers. If the level is higher than your subconscious acceptance can take you in personal belief, you may not remember the teachers or the teachings. However, rest assured that all you learn in this manner will be stored in the superconsciousness and be released in future times of need.

Later, the wisdom you received will be brought to your attention through earth plane teachers, books, and sometimes even in ordinary conversation. Whenever spiritual or psychological truths are given to you, there will be something inside of you that says, "I think I always knew that. I just never put it into words before." Then you will know the circle is complete. Teachings and the opportunity to apply them are both available to you.

Physical Healing

Physical wholeness and spiritual unfoldment should go hand in hand, but they don't always appear to. Frequently an individual who is intensely dedicated to following the spiritual path will go through a very trying time of physical deterioration. St. John of the Cross and many other mystical writers tell of personal experiences of illness, paralysis, crippling diseases, etc.

I think many of us make a common mistake of expending so much mental energy on developing spiritual awareness that we are inclined to ignore the body and its physical processes, which results in disease or disabilities caused by neglect.

Physical problems can also be caused by the acceleration of the return of karmic indebtedness that the Soul wishes cleared away. This results in the overflowing or out-picturing of long-buried effects brought into manifestation NOW, so that these, too, may pass away and no longer be a part of the Soul pattern. In this case one could consider such a physical out-picturing a cleansing and healing process of the Soul. When healing of the body takes place, healing of the Soul also progresses.

Whether caused by neglect, karma, or negative thinking, physical illness of any sort may be healed through sleep programming. Instantaneous or miraculous healings have always been a source of amazement, and they can happen to you. However, by far the most common source of healing is the normal body processes of rejuvenation, which can be speeded up through Alpha programming just before sleep.

Think of the body as a machine and the subconscious as the mechanic that keeps it in repair. Visualize the body as energetic, vigorous, and well. Consciously draw life energies into the body from the healing stream of Divine Consciousness. Forgiveness of yourself and others will speed the healing process. Recognize that being well, whole, and healthy is the natural state, and that the perfect image originally sent forth from God holds a blueprint in which it is impossible to be ill or debilitated. Try to mentally tap this original blueprint, and superimpose it over the present conglomerate of atoms in your physical body that reflects the lesser image. Know that in the long run your Soul must produce a perfect body, so the sooner all levels of consciousness cooperate, the sooner that day will arrive.

Then, as in all sleep programming, follow up with action whatever insights and intuitions are given to you. You may receive guidance through a dream, as with my dream of bees and honey; you may find yourself suddenly interested in holistic health methods, with new books, ideas, and teachers flowing freely and abundantly through your life; or you may suddenly receive an opportunity to be treated by a specialist in the field in which you need help.

Remember that, although miraculous healing can and may take place, doctors are also God's channels of healing. With very few exceptions, doctors are people who have tuned their energies into the Universal Healing Stream of Consciousness, and they consciously or unconsciously use this energy to effect wholeness in their patients.

Go Slowly

It is not wise to try to do all of the things mentioned here in one sleep programming session. This will only scatter your energies. To intensify your efforts, work on only one thing at a time for two or three nights, if it takes that long, then let it rest and go on to something else while you wait for the time lag to catch up with your visualization. If necessary, the process can be repeated at another time.

The visualizations can be intensified in a very positive fashion by remembering to energize all present experiences with the emotions of love, joy, and gratitude. Doing so releases other negative attitudes such as fear and anxiety about the outcome, and helps you to realize that whatever activity comes into your sphere will come as a servant to you, bringing with it deeper understandings for personal enlightenment and spiritual growth.

This point of view will also shorten the duration of inharmonious situations and events, because you will not fight the problem but will automatically search for the good, the lesson to be learned, the individual to be helped. By so doing you cause the "need" for the experience to be fulfilled, which then allows it to pass out of the focus of your awareness, leaving you free to pursue other activities and learning experiences.

Your Biological Alarm Clock

By this time you are aware that there is a automatic timing device that alerts you when certain things must be done. In meditation, for example, you have probably discovered that if you set yourself to meditate for twenty minutes, then no matter how deeply you go into inner consciousness or how unaware you may become of your physical body and physical surroundings, in exactly twenty minutes your eyes will open, and you will find yourself wide awake. In fact, long before you have enough confidence in yourself to give up the alarm clock, you will find yourself waking just a minute before the alarm goes off.

My own subconscious became a tyrant about getting me out of bed. I had a bad habit of waking at the time requested, only to fall back to sleep again. Soon I found myself dreaming very realistically that someone was knocking on my bedroom door, the front doorbell was buzzing, or the telephone was ringing. I would pull myself drowsily out of bed to answer the door or phone, only to find there was no one there.

Looking at the clock, I'd discover it was time to get up, and realize that my subconscious had gone to great lengths to drag me from my cozy bed. The man in the green coat who tapped on my car window was the same kind of product, concocted by my subconscious to awaken me in response to my demand that I only sleep a specified time.

To the Advanced Student

For the student whose "I AM" point of focus has risen to a spot outside or above the head, the following technique will create unlimited opportunities for powerful and dynamic action.

Instead of sleep programming (although you may do that, too, if you wish), use this meditation technique for wish and want fulfillment. Place yourself in a meditative posture—body quiet, spine straight. Center your consciousness in the "I AM" point of focus above your head. From that point, radiate your thoughts outward seeking the mind(s) of the person(s) who can be benefited by helping you fulfill your desire. This is communication Soul to Soul, and will create fantastically speedy results in obtaining that which you need or desire.

Remember to seek the cooperation of persons who can also be benefited by fulfilling your desires. Such requests should never be one-sided or you will find yourself owing a karmic debt to the person who aided you, a debt which *must* be repaid in kind, equally or to your disadvantage.

It is not necessary that you know *how* that person will be benefited. Your *intent* when requesting aid is the only criterion for judgment. Perhaps that person owes a karmic debt, and his or her assistance will discharge that debt, in which case you might never know how the interchange has been mutually beneficial. The Divine Accountant takes charge of this, and our only responsibility is to cleanse and purify our motivations.

Workshop #7
Dreams and Out-of-Body Techniques

≈

#1: Dream Workshop

Each participant in the group should bring one or more dreams
for evaluation. Even if there is a leader, participants should do
most of the interpreting for each other, giving them training and
experience in interpreting dreams. Everyone should be encouraged
to contribute his or her own ideas about what any of the dreams
mean, realizing at all times that no idea has any value unless it
hits a chord of recognition and enlightenment for the dreamer.

Exercise #2: Auto-Suggestions for Self-improvement

Prepare the following on a thirty-minute cassette tape in your
own voice, repeating it slowly over and over until the tape is
full. Play it back into your subconscious mind while in an Alpha
state—either meditation or in drowsy sleep. Your own voice will
add emphasis to the subliminal commands.

Repeat these words slowly, leaving enough time after each
sentence break for the listener to repeat the words silently.

I am an autonomous human being—totally sufficient unto
myself.

I can give Love freely. I can receive Love freely.

My relationship with others is harmonious—because I understand myself.

I accept myself for what I am—without undue criticism or
self-punishment.

I can also accept others just as they are—without the need to either criticize or punish.

I know I can make contact with my inner mind—to receive personal guidance.

Knowing this, I am free—free to follow my own inner wisdom and to allow others to do the same.

I am free of guilt feelings—and of any form of self-condemnation.

I am now free of fear—and of any emotion born of fear.

I am now free of jealousy—envy—anger—hostility—and worry.

This new freedom bolsters my integrity—and my self-confidence—and makes me eager to express my highest and fullest Self.

I have no desire to harm another, or to wish bad luck for any other person.

My own relationship with God and others is now free of inharmonious conflicts.

It is so because I wish it so, and my inner mind grants my every wish.

At this point you may add any admonition of your own that you wish, making certain that the commands are in a positive vein. State what you want to accomplish; ask for guidance, teaching, and leadership from your Soul Self for whatever personal psychological or spiritual goal you have. Write it down first, so that it is written exactly as you want to see it come to pass. Then read it slowly onto the tape. Play it two or three times a week, or whenever you feel you are not progressing as rapidly as you'd like in any of the areas mentioned on the tape.

Exercise #3: Out-of-Body Techniques

The following are two techniques for obtaining voluntary control of out-of-body experiences. Different methods appeal to different people, so choose the one that feels good to you and stick with it. Don't change techniques in midstream. It may take from three to thirty days to accomplish what you set out to do, but don't get discouraged. Stay with it and you will surely be successful.

Exercise #3-A

Lie comfortably in bed, preferably on your back. Achieve Alpha consciousness. Begin with the ends of your toes, and in your imagination draw your consciousness up the legs and through the torso, and from the ends of your fingers up the arms, until all of your consciousness seems to be centered in your head.

You may become acutely aware of noises inside your head. You may hear a rushing noise, or a roaring, or even a thudding. This is the sound of your circulatory system, the blood rushing through your veins, and your heart beating.

When all of your consciousness is centered in your head, lift it out through the crown of your head, or through the forehead. Imagine you are floating a few feet above your head. Gradually raise your consciousness until you float near the ceiling. Try to turn and look back at your body lying on the bed.

The first sight of your body on the bed may hit you with a jolt. Be prepared for this, and try to hold your emotions steady. Most people discover that their body looks much older and more tired than they imagine, or it may even look dead. This can cause an emotional reaction that will abort your attempt to achieve out-of-body experience. You will slam back into the body again, and won't be able to accomplish any more at that time.

Continue to repeat these steps at least once a day until you can hold your gaze steady without reaction to the sight of yourself lying there on the bed. Then you are ready to try to move out of the room. You will be surprised to discover that you can move through doors and walls using only your Will or desire. The first several times, do not try to leave the house or the yard. When you have been successful three or four times in moving through the house, then you will be emotionally steady enough for more extended tours.

Exercise #3-B

Prepare three 8" x 8' sheets of plain white paper. On the first sheet draw a 6" x 6' square. Color this square blue with crayon, water color, oils, or any kind of paint. Use your best talent for this.

On the second sheet, draw a triangle with 6" sides. Color the triangle yellow in the same manner, taking pains so that it is neat and very carefully done.

On the third sheet, draw a circle with a 6" diameter. In the same manner color the circle red. The amount of time and effort spent on these diagrams is an important link to your emotional system. Meditate on the meaning of the colors, and the reasons why they should or should not be placed in this particular order. Your Soul Self may create a reason for a different sequence.

Place the blue square on the wall facing the foot of your bed, where you can see it easily. Place the yellow triangle in an adjoining room, where it can be seen as soon as you enter the room. Place the red circle in the next adjoining room so that it, too, can be seen as soon as you open the door.

After you go to bed, place yourself in the deepest Alpha state you can achieve without falling asleep. Carefully get out of bed, disturbing the Alpha state as little as possible, and go to stand in front of the blue square. Stare fixedly at the square for three or four minutes.

Then move slowly, maintaining the Alpha state, through the door, and stand in front of the yellow triangle. Stare at the triangle in the same manner for three or four minutes, then repeat the process with the red circle.

Do this for three nights, concentrating on your desire to achieve voluntary out-of-body control. On the fourth night, do not leave the bed, but think about doing it. Visualize yourself standing in front of each of the diagrams in turn, holding the visualization for several minutes at each station.

Keep repeating this last step once each night until suddenly you discover you *are* standing in front of the diagram while your body remains on the bed. Hold the emotional level steady, allowing neither elation nor surprise to distract you from your project. Continue what you are doing until you have completed all three diagrams.

When you have willfully accomplished this feat at least three times, you can then consider yourself under control enough to attempt further exploration.

MEDITATION PRACTICE: MEDITATION ON THE INNER WAY

The effect of meditation is to train and discipline the mind, but its goal is to achieve oneness with the Soul Self, or union with God, and its ultimate aim is Illumination.

The mental world also has its crystallized thought-forms, dogmas, and ideologies, built by minds throughout the ages. For the first few days of this meditation exercise, your thoughts concerning the "I" may interminably rehash previous thought-forms of what "I" should mean. But as you steadily reject the old concepts and look for the laws, principles, and energies behind the seed thought, you will reach new levels of insight and understanding, until you go beyond intellectualizing and find the plane where you are able to touch the prototypes of the thought energies of the New Age.

A powerful book to read at this time is *The Mystical I*, by Joel S. Goldsmith.[29]

Meditation on the Inner Way

Sit with your spine straight. Cleanse yourself with the White Light.

After reaching a deep reflective state, substitute the pronoun "I" for whatever mantra you have been using. You will find the inner perceptions turning upward, instead of inward or down.

Reflect on the concept of "I," as expressing the total Being which has both sensory *and* spiritual awareness.

Think of your thoughts as leaves quietly floating along a stream. Allow the ideas associated with the concept of "I" to just flow. Don't grasp hold of any of them. Don't allow the conscious mind to build on any particular association. Just see and acknowledge the relationship, then let it go. Come back to the original concept and repeat. With each new association that rises, let it go, and come back to the original concept.

When finished, infill with the protective White Light, while slowly returning to Beta consciousness.

WEEK 8

≈

Transmutation and
Psychic Self-Defense

We live in a social atmosphere where "one-upmanship" means being able to outdo one's neighbor in hard luck stories. Each teller of tales has had the toughest run of bad luck; the closest escapes from death through disease, surgeries, accidents; the worst possible experiences in raising children; the most inconsiderate neighbors or relatives; and is being persecuted, maligned, and taken advantage of by innumerable unscrupulous people, etc., etc.

We are surrounded by a veritable swarm of negative thought-forms that buzz around us, carrying their dread messages of despair, doom, failure, persecution, and other malefic gifts. No wonder our psyches are overburdened in the effort to maintain poise and a positive approach to life.

The more attuned we become with the whole inner Beingness of ourselves, the more sensitive we are to the negative impact of the minds and emotions of others. When thought-forms alien to those we strive to create and maintain bombard us from without, we may even find ourselves enmeshed in a personal war against their perpetrators.

At times it may seem we are actually being psychically "attacked" by villainous entities, or the "dark forces" as some occultists call them. Understanding what is happening helps us discover the best way to deal with this. With a little detective work we can find a way to transmute the energy from negative to positive, rather than merely "protecting" ourselves from psychic attack, which is an unproductive, closed-in attitude, like living behind barred doors instead of joyously romping in the open air.

So let's explore some of the sources of this barrage of psychic energy which can create such upheavals in our lives, and discuss ways to transmute, or change, the thought-forms behind it.

Source #1: National and Global Karma

Our present experiences include our national and global karma as well as our personal karma. This type of group karma is represented by unavoidable or unchangeable things such as birth defects, pollution-caused defects or illnesses, social or economic disadvantages, war deaths or injuries, being born into a racial or ethnic minority, etc. "Overcoming" this type of karma entails not only working with one's own emotional reaction to these things, but also participating in groups which are actively researching or otherwise trying to make changes.

There are no accidents in birth time. We can enter the arena of action only when earth energies merge with our own. Astrology does not make us what we are; it provides a map indicating where we are in the ongoing evolution of the planet. If the characteristics chosen by your Soul for the Personality of this lifetime correspond to the characteristics of Virgo, then it is as impossible for you to be born in Capricorn as it is for a whale to live on dry land. You will be born in Virgo at the time and place where the vibrations of the earth and the vibrations of your Soul are exactly the same.

The cycle of the zodiac not only influences our lifetime but also the evolution of the planet. We understand that the earth and the planets move around the sun, but we may not be aware that our sun and its galaxy also have an elliptical path. Its orbit is much larger than the earth's, taking approximately 25,000 years to make one complete circle through its own zodiac signs, transiting each constellation in approximately 2,160 years. Each 2,000 year period is called an age,[30] with about 160 years allotted to a cusp period when two ages share their influences—usually a time of great turmoil.

Each age creates its own type of vibrations, symbolized by the various zodiacal signs. Each produces its own demands upon human consciousness, the response to which determines not only our evolutionary growth but also the karma created by our misuse or abuse of the energies we impact with, both individually and collectively.

There have always been spiritual leaders, and these typically arise at the beginning of each new age. Their purpose is to guide the minds of humanity into correct usage of the incoming energies. Evolution depends upon the conscious mastery of all the forces of the universe, and slowly, age upon age, we strive and attain, live and learn, grow and evolve. The struggle of each succeeding age has left its mark upon history, and we can find the testimony to this in spiritual literature and in the symbols of the times. Ancient worshipers left their mark in statuary and other art that has survived the ages.

Every time we change from one astrological age to another, our religious symbols change. For instance the Sphinx—the head of a man on the body of a lion—was created in the Age of Leo. The lion, considered the most noble of all beasts, was thought to be the highest evolution of the animal kingdom. Crowned with the head of a man dressed in priestly headgear, the statue symbolizes the rise of humanity from the animal nature, the evolutionary emergence of the human kingdom out of the animal kingdom. The astrological symbol of Leo is the sun, and sun worship was the dominant religion of that age.

History does not tell us who the spiritual leader was during the Age of Leo. Our recorded knowledge of the avatars of each age begins with the Age of Taurus, when Krishna gave birth to Hinduism. Taurus's astrological symbol is the bull, so the cow became the sacred animal of India during this time, and in Egypt the golden calf became the symbol for religious veneration.

The astrological phrase that characterizes the sign of Taurus is "I Have," which implies a sense of possession, a material orientation toward life, an identification with form and objects, represented by idols and icons. The Age of Taurus stimulated Personality satisfaction in the underdeveloped person. In the spiritually evolving individual, desire is transmuted into high aspiration, expressing spiritual will and purpose. Thus did this phase of soul growth influence all people born during that time, as it still does today in individuals born under the sign of Taurus.

In Hebrew history, we note that Abraham's father was an idol maker, very appropriate for the age in which he lived. But Abraham was subject to the new Age of Aries, when a new dispensation began. He was the progenitor of the chosen people from whom the Messiah was to be born as the leader of the next New Age, 2,000 years later; the only recorded unbroken genealogy from one New Age to the next.

Aries is a fire sign, and the symbolic sign of Aries is the sheep or ram. The religious rituals used then involved sacrificing rams on an altar of fire. The traditions of the Hebrews are alive with stories involving sheep and shepherds, such as the shepherd boy, David, who became king of the Israelites, the use of the ram's horn, and the use of sheep's blood for Passover.

A clearer understanding of the new energies infiltrating the earth was needed by the people, so Moses took leadership and brought forth the ten commandments, which were designed to outline the new spiritual identity that humankind was now evolving. When Moses came down from the mountain and found his followers again worshipping the golden calf, he wasn't angry because they had reverted to a pagan religion. He was angry because they still clung to the fixed, earth energies of Taurus and seemed unable or unwilling to go on with the new fiery energies of Aries.

The astrological orientation of Aries consciousness is characterized by the phrase, "I Am," first given to Moses from the burning bush, "I Am That I Am," the supreme evolution of Godhood. No longer were idols to hold spiritual value in the eyes of awakening humanity, which was coming to grips with its own spiritual identity and relationship to the concept of "one God."

For 2,000 years the magnificent influence of Aries worked its magic on those who could respond to it, so it is not surprising that it was in the later stages of Aries that Buddha revolutionized the Hindu tradition in preparation for the Age of Pisces.

The new Age of Pisces was heralded by Jesus who proclaimed that His disciples should become "fishers of men," and established the fish as the symbol of the early Christians. The fact that he was called "The Lamb of God" indicates the strong influence still being felt by the Age of Aries, but Jesus, like Moses before him, "came not to destroy the law, but to fulfill it (complete it)," (Matt. 5:17) and proclaimed a new dispensation upon the land.

Pisces is a water sign. Jesus was baptized in water, calmed the water, walked on water, and changed water into wine. Even today people use the Greek word and symbol for fish, *ichthys*, as a symbol for Jesus.

The astrological impulse of the Age of Pisces is "I Believe." At no time in recorded history have so many people been exhorted to "believe"—in Jesus and His works, and in what that believing could do for them. In fact, the words believe, believed, believest, believeth, and believing occur 271 times in the New Testament, compared to only 45 times in the Old Testament.

During the Piscean Age, emotional religious fervor and fanaticism ran rampant, producing the early Christian martyrs, the Crusades, the Spanish Inquisition, and all forms of emotional, devotional, and blind action, the result of the Piscean quality taken to its extreme. Religion ruled the minds of humanity and emotional belief was used both as a weapon and a crutch.

In spiritually evolving persons, who could respond in a positive fashion to the catalyzing energies of Pisces, we find the Christ principle awakening and the Christ within us being born, as Jesus meant when he said, "All these things I do, can ye do also." This brings about the release of the Soul from captivity to matter, and the emergence of the qualities of love, devotion, and reverence for God, life, and our fellow creatures. Under the water sign of Pisces we conquered the seas, and explored and colonized new worlds, the ultimate in faith and daring to believe.

Now, 2,000 years later, we find ourselves at the threshold of the new Age of Aquarius, an air sign. In 1903 the Wright brothers took to the air and the new age was officially on its way. Humankind's destiny in this age is to conquer air and space and to become master of Soul and mind.

The Christ, speaking of His return, said, "And then shall appear the sign of the son of man in the heavens" (Matt. 24:30). Aquarius is the only symbol of the zodiac that is all man. The others are either animal, part man and part animal, woman, or man and woman, as in Gemini. Who is to be the new spiritual leader, the

Christ returning, of the Age of Aquarius? Or are we to be our own spiritual leader, our own guru, as we respond to the new astrological characteristics of "I Know," exploring both inner and outer worlds and accepting as also true within our own Being all that the Christ Consciousness stands for?

There is even now evidence of a plethora of spiritual leaders upon the planet, most of them coming from etheric realms through the channelings of mediums. I predict there will be many, many more of the same ilk, the true ones urging us to accept our own divinity and stand on our own spiritual feet.

Uranus, one of the rulers of the sign of Aquarius, is known as the awakener and liberator. "Expect the unexpected" is the keynote of Uranus, and strong earthquakes are frequently felt when Uranus makes important transits. It is often shattering in its journey, as it represents freedom, change, and originality. We have already seen drastic Uranian effects in the form of two world wars, the splitting of the atom, and the drug scene, which have destroyed many old established patterns of thought and behavior forever.

What has all this to do with "Transmutation and Psychic Self-Defense?" Review history as it has been outlined here. At the beginning and ending of each age is a time of great turmoil. Humans respond very slowly to new ideas and new energies. There are always those who do not wish to see changes taking place, who cling to the old as being safe, tried, and true, refusing to let go no matter how strong the pull of the new age. Conservative, fundamentalist, reactionary, traditional—this form of consciousness fought the changes of Moses and brought about the death of Jesus, and it is the same attitude that will resist the advance of Aquarius. Unless we would be part of that reactionary turmoil, we must learn how to ignore it or avoid it.

In all ages there is much misuse of energies, and nations and individuals must account for the chaos and conflict occasioned by their own lack of spiritual and psychological development. As the Piscean Age draws to a close, humanity's unresolved karma will intensify fear thoughts in those around us. The chaotic out-picturing on the planet will also intensify. During this time our primary need is to learn how to keep ourselves from taking on inharmonious elements not of our own making and how to determine when a situation has been triggered by our own values (or lack of them). This, too is a step in personal mastery.

Source #2: Return of Our Own Thought-Forms

The most common causes of negative manifestations are reflections of our own past thoughts that have not yet been cleared from our consciousness.

People who bring us the return of these thoughts, words, or deeds are part of past visualizations, now appearing in our lives because of the time-lag between thought and manifestation. They are illusions—end-products only. As such, they should have no power to tempt us into retaliation or like-minded conduct. We know that if we respond in kind, with similar thoughts, words, or deeds, we are only keeping the chain of cause and effect going, creating new causes exactly like the old for future effects exactly like the present.

As we work with the purifying powers of the White Light, we gradually close off the avenues through our solar plexus center which are the only access these unwanted thought-forms have of getting through to us. That is why it is so important to get the emotional center under control, and why we have spent so much time on that aspect of our spiritual growth.

The only way to the higher spiritual consciousness is through the mental nature, and the mental nature can be developed to its fullest only when there is little or no energy being given to the products of the emotional center—when we are equally indifferent to (detached from) pleasure and pain, praise or criticism, rewards or the lack of them.

Sending out forgiving thoughts and love energies, or simply ignoring people who reflect the negativity of the past, will set up new causes until, finally, we either become completely unaware of offending thoughts from those around us, or those around us are changed so that they no longer send out negative thought-forms. This may mean a change taking place within persons we already know, or a complete change in environment and type of people we deal with, like a move to a new home or a new job.

Jesus gave us this same admonition in the beautiful Sermon on the Mount: "Return good for evil, pray for those that spite you," etc. (Matt. 5:44). He knew and taught that the directing of our own thought energies was more important than any energy directed our way from someone else.

Source #3: The Demands of Karmic Indebtedness

The spiritual path is difficult to travel when loaded down with an ages-long burden of unresolved karma. A common first effect of a sincere and determined program of meditation and spiritual awakening is a seeming increase in the difficulties and problems in our daily life. Meditation has a cleansing effect upon the immediate environment. It acts upon our motivation to be a more spiritually aware person, and, in so doing, draws one's attention to flaws of character and Personality that need adjusting. This reflects upon activities within our daily routine.

Unresolved karma sometimes shows up as the "reversed effect syndrome" we've talked about—the apparent manifestation of exactly the opposite of what we asked for—and there can be times when these negative manifestations really do seem to be the out-picturings of psychic attacks upon us. It helps to know that, instead, we are only the victim of our own past programming.

The first rule in adjusting these energies is to check out our motivations, purposes, and intent, both past and present. The best way to transmute the energy of a reversed effect, or any other manifestation that can be laid at the door of karma, is to call upon the Law of Grace. Ask for forgiveness for past and present shortcomings, and for guidance on how to deal with them. As you *listen* for inner direction, a person or situation may come up in your memory. Bestow forgiveness upon that person or situation and you will immediately transmute the energies from the past that may be influencing the present, changing them into more harmonious effects.

Don't become discouraged when difficulties arise. Sooner or later one must meet and discharge all one's karmic indebtedness, either in facing squarely the results of past action or in facing squarely the internal tendencies which create present and future action. Wisdom and growth come when one meets karmic debts with love, determination, and true aspiration. During these times the virtues of courage, endurance, compassion, and tolerance are strengthened and tempered. They will be of greater usefulness on a higher level of activity when the future brings the corresponding opportunities for action.

Both the Law of Reversed Effect and the Law of Karma have been covered thoroughly in previous weeks, so little more need be said about them here, except to point them out as possible causes when looking for the source of inharmonious situations and relationships.

Source #4: The Life Force of Prior Creations

Everything that is created has life energy, including those things which we personally create, such as lifestyles, emotional ties from and to associates, our obligations to family, community, and nation. All of these things are reflections of how we feel about life, for we tend to draw around us people with similar ideals and modes of living.

Also, we reflect that same life energy in the minds of those who make up our friends, family, and associates, and when we deliberately change our approach to life and our responses to life situations, the old ways are threatened. The life force of the old lifestyle seeks to preserve itself from extinction by attacking and/or clinging to its source of life—you, its creator.

I see this take place invariably in my ESP courses. A good ten percent of the students will drop out in the first four or five classes. Old responsibilities and commitments suddenly *demand* their attention, and so fill their time and energies that there is no room for the ESP class. Families, committees, clubs, all the things that meant so much and took so much emotional energy are now fighting for their existence—the emotional tie through which they drew their sustenance. Whenever one starts something new, one finds opposition from the old will develop almost at once.

Students who stick it out through the succeeding classes are the ones who re-evaluate priorities and give a different status to the things and people in their environment. They don't give up their families they place them in a new perspective and help them to adjust to the new relationship. They may or may not give up clubs, committees, jobs, or whatever, but they reassign their energies so that these things fill a different allotment. Some people and things drop away entirely since they have no value any more.

While this is going on there frequently is chaos in your life, and you are often hard put to stand your ground emotionally. If you stick to your newfound values, you soon find there develop different kinds of emotional and mental ties, and the new life-style settles into a routine of its own.

Source #5: The Power of Loved Ones

One of the most difficult negative forces to deal with is the antagonism within one's circle of family and friends. Your changes in values and life-orientation create changes in the images of what *they* think you should be. You no longer fit the mold that their thought-forms conceive for you, and the change is very threatening to them.

You may be accused of becoming a fanatic, insane, even evil or devil-possessed, because your spiritual values no longer correspond to their spiritual values. A deeply religious person within your circle may even attempt to "save your soul" by long and intensive prayers to God on your behalf, which in extreme cases can become a real psychic attack.

Most religious prayers for salvation consist in asking God for enlightenment, which is exactly what we are striving to attain, so the two prayers, while differing in intent, may work together, and we will be aided rather than harmed.

Others, more fanatical, seek our destruction as a means of destroying the "devil" within us, forgetting that doing so throws out the good with the bad. I'll discuss how to cancel out this kind of negative energy later.

For the most part, family and friends have your well-being at heart, but they don't understand your new values. The best way to handle this is just to cool it! No matter how enthusiastic you are about the wonderful new way to live that you've discovered, don't talk about it, except where seeds can be sown that have a chance of growing. The obvious contrast between the old, ineffectual you, and the vibrant, loving, powerful new you will soon be all the sermon that is needed. The new, harmonious approach to the relationship will either dissolve it or change it, and that is all that is required of you.

Let it be. No one can stop you from thinking, from reading, from finding fifteen minutes a day to meditate. Just be yourself, and let the family situation resolve itself.

Some New Age people break up their marital relationships, declaring, "If he (or she) cannot accommodate to my new way of thinking, then I'm just going to live my own life." This attitude does not consider the retribution placed upon both souls.

When you accepted the responsibilities of marriage and family, presumably the two of you were on the same or a similar level of spiritual growth, or you had a karmic indebtedness to each other. Now you are inclined to think that you've outgrown your partner, and you find the responsibility onerous.

So you've grown a little bit! The odds are that if you were on a close level at the time of your marriage, this person isn't so far behind you. With prayer and good example, he or she has an excellent chance of being lifted up, of learning comfortably what you have learned so excitedly. Every soul is growing at its own pace, and it will come along from wherever it is, however it can.

If there is truly an end to a karmic situation between you, then the end of the marriage will come about amicably. You will part friends. You will not tear out the fabric of the inner Beingness of either party with the severing. The only thing you will feel is a deep sense of relief. Forgiveness will come easy, and there will be no hard feelings, heartbreak, or remorse.

When any of these unhappy emotions are externalized around a marital breakup, you may be sure that your relationship has not ended. One or the other of you must at some time in the future make it up to the other. Better not to create that kind of cause. Weigh the situation with spiritual maturity, and make only the choice that is for the greater good of all concerned.

Source #6: Gossipy People

Rarely do we find people who with malicious forethought set about to do us harm. But people often send out negative thought-forms maliciously without being aware of what it is they are doing. Any hate-form, any sharp critical assault for the purpose of "putting another down," is a malicious attack, but seldom is it a deliberate use of thought-with-intent, such as we have attained in the spiritual exercises of this class.

This is a way of Being that many people have been conditioned to accept as normal. Usually it's careless—a way of making the gossip feel better than the one being put down, a way of patting oneself on the back for being smarter, saner, more moral, or what have you.

For the most part, this type of psychic output is the easiest of all to handle. Gossip can get through to your emotional center most easily when there is an avenue of guilt or fear on which to ride. If you fear what others think of you, then you will attract that which you fear to hear.

I have never been a very good liar. In fact, I always get caught when I attempt to lie. As a consequence, an early determination in life was to never do anything in secret that I would not care to face in public. This required some heavy and extreme rationalizations, but out of it came a deep ethical sense, knowing I could not harm others without harming myself, and that the only good for me was also the good of all humankind.

The result was not only a clear conscience but a total disdain for gossip and gossipy people. I learned to keep my distance from those who dared to probe into what I considered my personal life, answering no questions, offering no explanations, making no apologies, but leaving them to think what they liked, because the only one who had to know the truth was me. Nothing else mattered as long as I was satisfied with myself. Any dissatisfaction was my own to work with, not anyone else's.

I also learned to dare to be different, unconventional, and even in some cases, radical, without destroying the composure of others. This response, surprisingly, brought about a complete change in the way people think about me. True, they still talk about me, perhaps more than before, but the malicious content is exceptionally low and without power to damage.

Rarely should one do anything other than ignore gossip. Anything else will only fan the flames, drawing attention to that which you don't want to focus upon. Being essentially negative in character, gossip has very little life-force and quickly dies and falls away of its own weight.

The White Light shield of protection is an exceptionally good barrier against the emotional impact of malicious gossip. The shield not only keeps it from coming to your attention, which is the only way it can hurt, but also tends to soften the thoughts people hold in regard to you, doing double duty in bringing back only those things which you send out.

Source #7: Deliberate Mischief

For reasons as varied as the minds which practice it, there are some who with deliberate and conscious intent set about to do others harm. This can truly be termed a psychic attack, whether the assault comes about directly, through a physical attack by the perpetrator, or is more subtly located on the psychological or spiritual levels. This energy is directed at you with deliberate malice and intent to harm. Fortunately, the percentage of these deliberate attacks is very small in comparison to all other sources of negative manifestation in our lives.

Always, the first place to look for the source of any inharmony is within ourselves, in keeping with the rule to not blame others for our troubles, but to seek to purify our own motives and objectives. If, after much prayer and probing, we determine that the source of trouble is truly outside of oneself, then we need to know how to deal with that.

The expert, called an Adept in metaphysical circles, uses both negative and positive energy with equal facility, while remaining detached from both. It is within this detachment that one finds both the source of the trouble and the means with which to deal with it.

How A Psychic Attack Led to A Profitable Lecture Tour

It is helpful to remember that *all* negative manifestations, whether self-inflicted or induced by others, can enter our lives only through pathways we spin ourselves. This knowledge is the key to turning the tables—turning the energy around and making it manifest in a positive form instead of a negative form. We are not helpless chips on the stream of consciousness. We are captains of our own destiny. This means that we can learn how to use negative energy as a positive force for good, the greatest kind of transmutation.

One of my former students was led through fear into a fundamentalist religious group which convinced her that metaphysical teachings were weapons of the devil. Because she loved me and had become convinced I was deluded, she called one day, sincerely concerned for the "state of my soul." We talked for some time while she tried to convince me to give up my work in the school, and I tried to explain that I had explored thoroughly and fully all that the "old-time religion" had to offer me, and that I felt the new thinking had opened up more expansive and productive avenues for my spiritual growth.

I ended by telling her that it was all right if she felt she needed more time in the path she was pursuing, that if it was right for her, then that was where she should be. She ended by saying that if I persisted in my "wicked ways," I would be attacked.

When I hung up the phone I sent her a silent blessing and put the incident completely out of mind. The school had prospered for a number of years. I felt that as long as I remained tuned to the Will of God for me and the school, no one from the outside world could get inside my shield if I held no fear of them and gave no strength to any threats.

Gradually, over the next three or four months, prosperity in the school began to slacken. Attendance and income both dropped off. As is my habit when things go wrong, I turned inward to meditation to find the answer, and to reaffirm my position that my whole intent was to do the Will of God for me. If God wanted me to quit what I was doing and turn to something else, I would be most happy to do so. All I asked was that a definite sign be given me as to which way I should go.

I began to think about my aged parents in the Pacific Northwest whom I had not seen in several years, and began to feel guilty because I had left their physical care in the hands of a brother and sister-in-law who felt I wasn't contributing my proper share to their support.

As the days wore on and blank walls sprung up in every direction I turned, the anguish in my heart deepened. One day, in meditation, I had totally released all responsibility for maintaining the status quo and offered myself anew to be used in any way God so desired. Suddenly into my mind came B.'s voice: "But you *will* be attacked!"

Instantly, I saw the whole picture. Her group had been praying with great intensity that I, as the devil's representative, be destroyed, so that their town might be free of what I taught. Their prayers were as sincere as mine, although misguided, for they thought they, too, were doing God's Will. That was the thread by which they got through to me—that, and the fact that a teacher and a student have a strong tie linking them together. B. was the *link*, and their desire to do God's Will was the avenue of approach.

A psychic attack always hits where one's weakness lies, and my weakness was the hidden guilt I felt about not being able to spend more time and money on my parents.

Now I knew what to do about it. I immediately set up a mental image of a brick wall through which the group's prayer-forms could no longer penetrate, and I asked that their very considerable energies be directed into some useful activity that would be a blessing for them as well as the town they loved.

Then, knowing I had inadvertently taken their negative energies into myself and environmental manifestations, I asked that I find a way to use those energies in a positive fashion. A couple of days later, while arranging my class schedules for the following months, I saw that all classes came to an end in May. I did not need to start instruction again until September, giving me three summer months to plan a lecture tour that I had been wanting to make for several years.

I immediately set about doing just that, and within a month I had twelve weeks of lectures lined up which took me into the Northwest, where I was able to spend several weeks with my parents. The lectures were profitable enough that I was even able to give extra money for their support. This was my first lecture tour, and it was destined to become a regular activity in my life.

You can see that all the elements were there; the prayers of the opposing forces were meshed into the highest good possible. They wanted me out of town, both of us wanted to do the "Will of God," and I wanted to help my parents and to visit with them. I used the energy directed my way to go on the lecture tour, which increased my knowledge of what other groups around the United

States were doing, and when I came home, the Center prospered as never before with the new energy and information I brought back. What is more, I never again heard from or about B. and her group.

But please note two things. I wasted no energy on recriminations, vengeance, fear, or anger. The first step was to use a process of mental imaging to block off further energy from the recognized source, and the second was to transmute existing energy into a positive force for action.

Transmuting the Negative Energy of Others into Positive Energy for You

The first step in transmuting negative energy into positive is to look for the good that can come out of every situation. Look for ways in which it can be turned into something beneficial.

Consider your own past and I am sure you will find that out of every seeming tragedy have come blessings for spiritual growth and fulfillment. It is harder to do this while still enmeshed in the situation, but train your mind to think in terms of looking for the good and you will find the path out of any trouble much more quickly.

Once a thing, a form, has been established in or by mind, it moves freely through time and space into manifestation. Time and space cannot break or delay its progress, but an act of Will can. Dion Fortune said, "What one man's mind can create, another can destroy." This, of course, works two ways. One can use positive force to destroy a negative image, or one can use negative force to destroy a positive image. Since, in this lecture, we are dealing with negative thought-forms which seek to harm us, let us consider the former.

Some authors recommend that you reverse the attack—that is, send the negative energy back to its point of origin, which brings the malicious energy down upon the individual who initiated it. This is very effective, but it seems to me that to do so requires the same kind of malicious intent as that which started it in the first place.

Such desire for vengeance can only create more of the same kind of energy in one's life, which perpetuates the vicious cycle.

What is more, there is always the chance that you may be wrong in your judgment of the originator, in which case a perfectly innocent person could be harmed.

There is a story told about the Kahunas, the ancient priests of the Hawaiian Islands. When one Kahuna was angry with or afraid of another Kahuna, he would fashion a thought-form whose sole purpose was to kill his enemy. The thought-form would go forth to do what it was designed to do, and would hover around its target until it had created from the enemy's own thought-energies a situation that would bring about his death.

However, if the "magic" of the offending Kahuna was greater, or if his protective device was strong enough, he would be able to ward off all the evil brought on by the killer thought-form, whether or not he consciously knew about the attempts on his life.

The thought-form, whose only function was to kill, would then have no choice but to return and wreak its purpose upon its creator, for it could not be dissolved until it had done what it had been created to do. We do have the power, of course, to recall our negative thought-forms and dispel or destroy them, but the moral of the story is the whiplash effect of desiring harm to any other person, whether that person is an active enemy or not.

Another method of getting rid of negative energy is to expel it. The technique is to take a deep breath, drawing all the negative energy into yourself, and then, with body tense, using all the energy of your physical, emotional, mental, and spiritual nature, expel the breath with a sharp explosive sound, using your visualization to send the negativity into space, the deep sea, or the north pole. The danger here is that, no matter where you send untransformed negativity, there are life forms which can be adversely affected by it.

There is one place on the planet which has as its purpose the transmutation of energy, and that is the ground. Every element of the earth forces is used in transforming one type of energy into another. All animals and insects within the ground spend their lives keeping the soil aerated, changing rocks and decayed matter into more soil, and bringing forth new life from seeds and roots.

It is possible, and perhaps even permissible, to occasionally send negative energy into the ground for transformation. One must be sure, though, that a request for transmutation accompanies the transmission. This is not the most ideal way to handle the problem, because it is also possible to make the ground sterile if too much negative energy is thrown into it.

The transforming of negative energy into a positive force through *intelligent action* is still the best way to deal with an overload. It is also the most creative way, and helps to build one's mental and spiritual resources. You will also be doing your part in helping to transmute some of the tremendous layers of karma that overshadow our planet.

Thought-Forms as Protective Devices

Persons with highly advanced psychic powers can see images and thought-forms on the astral plane. If one has reached this level of development, then an actual banishing ritual may be performed which will effectively destroy any thought-form sent by an enemy. It is called the Banishing Ritual of the Pentagram.

The pentagram is the five-pointed star shape which encloses a human figure with the head in the upper point and the four limbs in the four other points. The drawing, usually accredited to Agrippa, is enclosed in a circle representing the Cosmos. It symbolizes the human Soul rising in Spirit from the lower unaware nature.

This magic pentagram, or star of the microcosm, is also the five-pointed star of occult masonry, the supreme symbol of White Magic, and has been used by many magical societies as a protective device. (Reversed, with the single point downward, it is the hieroglyphic sign of the goat of Black Magic, and the sign of Satan, representing antagonism and fatality, the elevation of conflict and aggression above peace.)

Its positive use, with the single point on top, can banish any form of terror or fearful manifestation. If the threatening thought-form or image is visible before you, face it squarely and quickly perform the banishing ritual. If it is unseen, but the origin is known, face in the direction of the source.

To use the pentagram as a protective device, you need only imagine the outline of the star. Then, with forefinger outstretched, point your right arm and hand towards your left foot. Bring the finger upward until it is in front of the center of your brow, at the same time imagining a glowing trail of blue-gold energy being left behind in the path you are tracing. Next, point your finger towards the right toe. This creates an inverted V almost the height of your body. Then come back to a point level with your left shoulder, then straight across to your right shoulder, then back to your point of commencement. This creates on the astral plane a powerful mental image of an ancient symbol of protection. If needed, you may repeat on the East, North, West, and South sides of you.

Secret society practitioners emphasize that you should make a fairly large, well-proportioned figure, with all lines equal in length, completing the final diagonal line exactly where the initial ascending line began. When finished, you should be able to perceive by the mind's eye, with the eyes closed, the pentagram(s) flaming quite vividly in front of and around you.

Of course, to be able to use this ritual quickly in times of danger, one must practice it many times, and use it constantly as a form of protection. Some people find the physical performance of a magical act an aid to the imagination. The results are the same as for those who can imagine and use the protective White Light without needing a physical counterpart to assure them that it is real and in place.

There are also other types of thought-forms one can use as protective devices, which require only a little imagination and intense desire energy.

For several years, I supplemented my income by renting out five bedrooms of a large house I lived in. When one lives so closely with others, one has some strange experiences with their emotional projections. I could relate several that required expert neutralization of negative force, but one stands out as extraordinary.

Two young men—I'll call them Bob and Tony—rented a large upstairs room. They were personable, charming, and sociable, often spending time with me and helping with household chores. During this time, several items were stolen. On the morning that I discovered a missing window air conditioner, Bob was most consoling, helping me nail all the windows and reinforce locks on the doors.

As usual, I went into meditation to discover the cause of the trouble. I traced it to someone upstairs, but couldn't pinpoint the source. The tenants used the back stairway to and from their rooms, and it was difficult to keep them from leaving the back door unlocked. I felt that one of their visitors might be the guilty party.

Deep in the Alpha state, I fashioned a menacing thought-form to guard the back steps. Its only purpose was to frighten, not to harm, and my desire was that whomever was responsible for the thefts would simply be scared off and not come back.

The next day while Bob was gone, and in my absence, a terribly brutal and menacing man came upstairs, kicked in the door to Bob and Tony's apartment, and demanded some money he claimed Bob owed him. Tony was home and reported that the man threatened to kill Bob if he didn't pay up, and acted as though he were capable of carrying out his threat. Bob came home a few hours later, packed his bags, and not only left town but left the state, going back to his folks in California.

My first thought as I surveyed the wreckage of the room, was that the protective thought-form had failed, but as I found out more about Bob's activities (I learned he had been selling drugs, and the man was a supplier), I discovered the thought-form had worked in an immediate and most effective way, bringing to Bob the only thing that was menacing and frightening enough to scare him away. That same day someone called anonymously, telling me Bob had been my thief and where to find the air conditioner.

A Technique to Destroy Unwelcome Thought-Forms

One rule I tried to enforce in that house was no drinking, as well as no drugs. People who use drugs or alcohol are erratic and unpredictable in their thinking and actions, and can create situations that are embarrassing and even dangerous to others in the house.

In spite of care in the selection of tenants, I rented a room to a man who was an alcoholic. He paid thirty days rent, then promptly went on an alcoholic binge. By law I couldn't evict him until his rent ran out, at which time I refused to renew. I cleaned the room, and the next man who rented it also turned out to be alcoholic, and spent his thirty days in an alcoholic stupor.

This was a new experience for me, since one of the questions I always asked was, "Do you drink?" and each man had answered, straight-faced, "No."

At the end of the month, I ousted my unwelcome tenant, cleaned the room, and rented it again. To my amazement and consternation, the same situation was repeated! I then realized that a thought-form created by my alcoholic tenants was alive in that room, drawing to itself minds that would sustain it and continue to give it life.

When this tenant, too, was gone, I used the following technique to destroy the ugly thought-forms in that room. Place a large amount of salt (a pound will do) in a glass oven dish. Pour alcohol over the salt, and set it aflame. Move the burning alcohol around the room, making sure that the glow from the flame gets into all dark places, behind pictures and drapes, under the bed, in closets, etc.

This sounds like pure superstition, and I've never been able to find any logical explanation of why it works, but it does. I suspect it may be part of an ancient alchemical formula created into a thought-form so strong that it is still effective.

With the room cleansed of old thought-forms created by my unwelcome guests, I filled it with a White Light visualization, and the next roomer was a beautiful young lady interested in metaphysics. She further cleansed the room by painting the walls a bright canary yellow, and the atmosphere was so completely different there was no comparison.

I also found this technique helpful in cleansing the leaden atmosphere of an attic room where a group of young men had practiced all kinds of spells and magic and left some strange and uncomfortable energy forms behind.

Create the Opposite Effect

Another effective way to deal with antagonisms is to mentally create the opposite thought-form of whatever negative energy is being directed your way. If you feel ill and beset by unknown energies, visualize bouncing, vibrant health. If sources of income dry up, visualize new sources being opened up for you. Focus your attention on the creation of a harmonious environment, and of clear-headed, intellectual activity.

Most of all, use the Substance of the creative level freely and with knowledge of what *you* want, rather than allowing the negative thought-forms of others to gain a foothold in your mental and emotional bodies. Give no thought energy to any temporarily manifesting negative situation. Ignore it. Know that first of all the White Light is purifying. It uplifts and cleanses as well as protects. As you direct your thought energy into the goal of what it is you *do* want, the *end-product* of existing inharmony *must* dissolve for lack of sustenance.

Focus your aspirations on bringing forth the Divine Plan of your Beingness and on obtaining Higher assistance in your life. This will serve to create within you your own transformer of negative energies, which becomes stronger the more it is used.

The "Dark Forces"

Patanjali described, as we have discussed, five afflictions that beset human spiritual progress: ignorance, self-conceit, attachments, hatred, and false pride. To these, I would add one more: fear. Its insidious tendrils push into every aspect of life. There is probably no human being who doesn't experience fear in some degree, from minor anxieties to full-blown phobias. I do not refer to normal caution that should be exercised against possible physical hazards, but to that soul-crippling emotional paralysis that hides behind and is the cause of every action that prevents the full enjoyment of or full participation in the experiences that are offered to us.

Throughout the Piscean Age, the Christian's greatest fear, instilled by early church theologians, was fear of the Devil—fear of a nebulous Something that can eat away one's salvation unless one keeps a constant guard against people, places, situations, and events.

Among developing psychics, this fear of the Devil translates into fear of the "dark forces." Both the Devil and the dark forces are intangible, unseen enemies that are impossible to grapple with in open combat, so fear of the unseen becomes transferred to something that can be seen, human beings themselves. From this the most dangerous fear of all evolves, fear of one's fellow humans. The goal of the metaphysician, as well as the rest of society, is to transcend the social ills of prejudice, injustice, caste, and class systems—laws that restrict and condemn—and other judgmental and segregating actions that arise out of fear of one's contemporaries.

Among metaphysical students, I have frequently seen one major distressing factor that has set students against each other, caused members of a class to withdraw, and even created tensions among teachers, workers, and leaders. That fear is that some particular person or another may be in league with the "dark forces." Almost invariably this fear has proven groundless, but still the damage was done and the individuals themselves restricted from fully participating in activities that could have been most beneficial.

Our desire is to become master of our own life and environment, and fear prohibits our achieving that desire. It doesn't matter whether the fear is justified or not. We do not need to allow it to restrict our activities.

The first thing to remember is that your personal environment can always be free of negativity, no matter what others around you may be doing. You are always protected from the encroachment of any negative energy by the strength of your White Light shield. Secondly, as a knowledgeable spiritual entity, you have an obligation to help lift the negative karma of the planet by transmuting it into positive energy whenever you can.

Developing psychics are constantly trying to interpret the vibrations they feel from people and places. If you are in a room where the fear thoughts of others are strong, or around people whose higher chakras have not yet been opened, you may mistakenly interpret the vibrations you feel as evil or negative. Or you may actually be in a room where the dark forces have been evoked. It doesn't matter. The easiest method to eradicate fear thoughts—your own and others—is White Light cleansing.

In your mind, see the whole room (the whole building, if necessary) filled with White Light, or the Christ Presence. Start at one end and finish at the other. All negative vibrations will instantly disappear, and you will have fulfilled your obligation to your environment as well.

One of the most outstanding things I've witnessed was a simple prayer performed by a metaphysical minister, Dr. E. A. Winkler, president of St. John's University, Louisiana. He wanted to use a certain room to do some psychic counseling in, but we both felt that the energies in that room were not as clean as they should be. I started to perform the White Light cleansing ritual, when suddenly it felt as if the whole room was full of light. "Wow!" I said, "that was fast! What did you do?"

He looked at me and grinned. "I just asked God to make this room suitable for His work," he replied.

Don't run from negative energies. Transmute them. In that way you prove you are the master, not the pawn of the energies around you.

No one is evil. Everyone on planet Earth is working with negative energies. No one is exempt. Our purpose as Light Beings is to transmute these negative energies. Our job, and ultimately our exaltation, is to bring all material energies into the Light. To do so we must first experience them, before we can understand enough to transmute them. To serve God and our fellow beings, we must learn to recognize the turmoils brought on by this mighty task, and through this recognition discover the compassion within ourselves. The lack of recognition (the Forgotten Path) is only one more negative energy to be transmuted.

An Invisibility Experience

While we are considering the power of thought-forms and the effect they can have on our environment and our lives, I'd like to share an experience I once had that was created by a thought-form of invisibility.

On the day before my birthday in August, I left Omaha, Nebraska, about 8:00 P.M., enroute to Oklahoma City. My schedule was tight, and I planned to drive until I reached the Kansas state line before sleeping. I knew it would be a long, hard push, so while the speedometer needle crept over the speed limit, I kept affirming to myself that I was invisible to the highway patrol, that I would be kept clear of traffic entanglements, and that the way was smooth before me and without difficulties or obstacles.

I crossed the state line exactly at midnight. I don't know if there is any occult significance to the fact that midnight before my birthday meant that a new day, a new year, as well as a new state all came together simultaneously.

A few miles into Kansas, I found an all-night café and, as a break, went in to get something to eat. I sat on the end stool at the counter near the cash register. Next to me was an empty stool, and on the next stool a man sat drinking coffee. The café was fairly busy, with three waitresses coming and going. A waitress refilled the coffee cup of the man next to me, and several people paid their bill at the cash register while I waited to be served.

I had probably been there six or seven minutes when I noticed that all three waitresses were standing together talking as though they had nothing to do. I turned to the man next to me and, partly in amusement and partly in chagrin, said, "What's the matter? Am I invisible, that they can't see me sitting here?" The man kept staring straight ahead and drinking coffee as though he, too, was totally unaware that I was there!

I'd like to report that I followed through with some kind of verification that I truly was invisible, but the truth is that I was so shaken that I got down from the stool and left the café. I relate this experience to you only as another example of the truly remarkable phenomena that the mind can bring forth. And, too, perhaps that was my punishment for using occult powers to break the law!

Workshop #8
Techniques for Spiritual and Psychic Healing

≈

The body has a will to be well. Nature is its own healing force. The natural condition of each cell is perfect health. The consciousness of a liver cell, for instance, has as its purpose to be a perfect liver cell, bringing forth the fullness of what it was designed to be.

The consciousness of the individual, however, overrides the consciousness of these tiny lives, and they are forced to reflect the disturbing, restricting qualities which stem from the conflicts of the subconscious.

Psychic healing serves to mitigate these negative forces, to cleanse or eliminate their influence. In a cancer clinic in Texas, Dr. Carl Simonton, pioneering in the effect of the mind on the body, took terminal cancer patients, taught them to meditate, and during meditation to use whatever imaging faculties they could draw out of their own consciousness to destroy the cancer cells. One cancer victim pretended the cells were mice and the healing forces of his own body were cats which ate up the cancer cells. One person imagined that the white blood cells were warriors which attacked and destroyed the cancer cells.

Every day, three times a day, the patients used this imaging meditation for five minutes at a time. More than thirty percent of these terminal cancer victims actually reversed the dying process, revived their will to live, and created with their own minds an automatic remission of cancer! This technique is now being tried in other medical centers across the United States with outstanding results. There is much evidence that we can consciously influence the flow of life forces within us.

The following are energy transformers which I have personally tried and found effective.

Exercise #1: To Lift Fatigue

This is an excellent cleansing technique for sweeping away the clinging clouds of negative thought-forms with which we are bombarded each day. Try it at the end of the day, or at a rest break during a particularly hectic time. It is as refreshing as a shower.

Rub the palms of your hands together briskly several times. Place the fingertips of both hands near but not touching the middle of the forehead. Pull your hands downward over the face and neck, not touching the skin, but moving through the aura. Draw the hands outward and snap your wrists and fingers as though shaking off water or some clinging substance. Repeat three times.

Next, place the fingertips near the middle of the forehead as before. This time, draw your hands over the top and back of the head, and the back and the sides of neck, not touching hair or skin, but moving with a combing motion through the aura. Repeat the snapping motion. Repeat the full motion three times. This is excellent for tension headaches as well as fatigue.

Exercise #2: To Relax Eye Tension

Rub the hands together briskly several times. Place your palms gently over your eyes for fifteen minutes. *Do not* press or rub. Allow the healing energy from the palms of the hands to rest and heal the eyes.

Exercise #3: To Prevent Bruises

There are many unknown energies which come out from the fingertips. This exercise is unfailing. You need only try it for yourself to see that it always works.

If you have tender skin and bruise easily, as many women do, try this. At the moment of impact against a sharp object, or whatever might cause bruises on your flesh, *immediately* place the tip of the middle finger of either hand against the bumped spot.

Rub lightly until impact hurt is gone, and then forget it. *You will not bruise!*

Exercise #4: Levitation

I have no explanation for why the following procedure works, but it does. It is a fantastic party stunt, but it has practical applications, too. Four women used this levitation method to move a grand piano. Five people used it to move a fallen tree from a lawn after a windstorm.

Choose five people, men or women. Seat one person in an ordinary chair, preferably one without arms. Place the other four around the chair, two at the back and two in front. Let each of the four clasp their two hands together, fingers interlaced, with the two forefingers pointed outwards and touching.

Have the two people at the back place their two extended and touching forefingers under the armpits of the seated person. The two people in front place their two forefingers under the bend of each knee. Try to lift the person off the chair.

Of course, it won't work. But now let the four people inhale vigorously in unison three times, on the inhale raising their fingers, still together, up in the air. After the fourth inhalation, intone the words, "He's (She's) light."

The four people then place their right hands lightly on top of the seated person's head, alternating around the circle, one hand on top of the other, followed in the same manner by their left hands, until there is a stack of hands on top of the seated person's head.

Then they inhale in unison again three times. On the third exhalation, they remove hands one at a time in reverse order. As soon as all hands are down, all four people quickly place their two forefingers in the previous position under armpits and knees and lift in unison. The person, no matter how heavy, will rise lightly off the chair with no exertion from the lifters!

Exercise #5: Talk To Your Body

The body will obey verbal commands. If you are afflicted with foot or leg cramps at night, as many people are, tell the foot or leg to *stop cramping!* Speak out loud and make it a real command, with emphasis and authority, and the cramping will ease immediately. (Then check with your doctor about the calcium content in your body. Cramps usually mean you need additional calcium.)

Assume that your body belongs to you, not you to your body, and treat it as a valuable possession which needs proper diet, exercise, and good care, but which must also do its duty as a fit vehicle for the activities in your life. Take the attitude that your time is much too valuable and filled with too many exciting things to do to waste time being ill or disabled.

Exercise #6: To Find and Erase Negative Areas

The following exercise will help to eliminate conditioned memory responses which may be subconsciously poisoning your body. The visualization of the changed outcome will create a different response in the subconscious body.

Lie comfortably on a bed or couch. Cleanse with the White Light. Relax your body and put your mind into the Alpha state.

Pretend this is the last day of your life. Go back in memory over your life and see what you would change or do differently. Then, in your mind's eye, imagine that you really are doing it differently. See the changed result that occurs when the situation is handled in the better way. Work with one subconscious memory each day.

When finished, fill your body with the color red. Turn your attention inward; become one with your body. Think of each of these negative emotions in turn: anger, envy, hate, jealousy. Note where they make the most impact in your body.

Imagine a brilliant White Light at the area of impact, and in your mind's eye cleanse the area completely, sweeping away any places of darkness in the body. Do this daily until there is no further response to the thought of any of these emotions.

Now fill your body with the color blue. Become one with your body and note where these positive thoughts make an impact: love, gratitude, peace, joy.

End this exercise with a blessing for your body, and a sincere thank you for its efforts on your behalf.

Exercise #7: To Increase Vitality

Sit erect but not tense, or stand easily with weight evenly balanced between both feet. The posture should be comfortable, but one which will hold the spine straight, with the chest, neck, and head in a straight line.

Relax for a moment, and try to empty the mind of the cares and vexing trivia of the day. Then exhale all the air from the lungs, drawing in the abdominal muscles to force out the residual air that our customary shallow breathing allows to remain in the lungs.

Refill the lungs, drawing in the air very slowly, as you count up to seven. Pause for a count of one, then again exhale slowly to the count of seven.

During the intake of air, mentally repeat the mantra "OM," and imagine that the breath flowing into your body carries with it a stream of Cosmic Life Force (called *prana* in the Vedic scripture), as indeed it does.

Repeat this cycle of 7:1:7 breaths at least twelve times to clear the nasal passages.

As you inhale and exhale, think of this vital current as circulating through the psychic channels of your etheric body and into the physical form, energizing every cell of your body. As you hold the breath, realize that you are storing this vitality and energy within you.

This exercise takes about three minutes to do, but a quite noticeable stimulation will be apparent within fifteen to twenty minutes, with a general increase in overall energy which will persist for several hours.

MEDITATION PRACTICE: GO WITH THE FLOW!

There is a flow of eternal Life Energy that permeates all things, visible and invisible, and all activities, human or otherwise. By tuning into this energy flow during meditation and being aware of remaining within its force field during waking hours, we can energize and enhance all inner intuitive awarenesses. We can also maintain health and balance and keep proper personal control over the manifestations of Substance in our lives. The pulsating living energy of this meditation will awaken that mental and spiritual awareness that is too often bred out of human beings from birth onward.

Go With the Flow!

Lie on the floor or on the bed with your head to the north, so that you are in line with the polar energies of the earth. As your body and brain slow down to Alpha awareness, feel the pulsing of the Life Force in your body. Submerge yourself into it. Get into that pulsating, vital, living core of yourself and just float away. Feel as if you are being swept off headfirst, still in a prone position, and drifting with a sea of energy. Mentally soar off into the stratosphere, with the earth becoming smaller and smaller as it recedes from your vision. Go with the flow, gently moving along in a spiral motion, and be completely immersed in the universal rhythms, feeling yourself a part of the Divinity.

After a time, return gradually to waking awareness. Fill your body with the White Light of protection, recognizing this light as the Oneness with All that Is, a Light that will transform your life in many important ways.

Consciously remain in the force field of this flow of eternal Life Energy during waking hours, and you will find that the communication with your Soul Self will be enhanced. If you must choose between two courses of action, your intuition will be sharpened and one of them will seem more right. Follow that course as if it, too, were a part of the Cosmic force, and fear will disappear. So, too, will any nagging doubts. The still, small voice within is always right. Frequent, even daily, re-energizing with this meditation will enhance that inner intuition, so that you need never again rely upon the often fallible judgment of others as to what is right for *you*.

WEEK 9

≈

Soul Consciousness—
Mysticism Understood

By now you've made great strides toward Soul Consciousness. Some of you have even had one or more mystical experiences of your own. Certainly you have a clearer idea of yourself as an unique spiritual entity, an individual with his or her own personal path to Oneness with whatever you conceive as God, or Absolute. You know you have a long way to go, that this is just the beginning, but you also know that you have made giant changes in your life and that further changes are not only possible but already in the making.

You won't stop here. In fact, it's spiritually impossible to stop here. You've opened up vistas of dreams and potentials within yourself that will not let you relax in your spiritual progress. You may reach a plateau in which you seem for awhile to stop studying and striving and just let life happen to you, but that is part of the normal process. This leveling off is a time when the Soul is contemplating what it has learned. It withdraws, in a manner of speaking, within its own rhythmic cycle for meditation and rest, and leaves its external self to a time of relaxation, without challenges or awkward situations to think its way through.

Some people even seem to return for awhile to the old, more familiar concepts of religion, like the young person who longs to return to the relative safety of childhood and mother's knee, where decisions are made by others and one can, for a time, abdicate responsibility for spiritual labor and growth. But even there one cannot help comparing the old concepts with the new, and through this one receives new insights into the true meanings behind old dogmas.

It matters not what you do or how long it takes you to do it. Time is irrelevant to the Soul. The passing parade of experiences is transient and illusory, and all experiences sooner or later come to an end. Only the NOW moment is eternal, never beginning, never ending, and it is in this space that the Soul expends its energy—receiving information, correlating it, and making its judgments and evaluations.

The Soul is only concerned with the progress of any set of consecutive circumstances, no matter how long it takes in temporal time. In its journey through eternity, it searches through various experiences to create perfect understanding of harmony and inharmony, the resonance of creation. No experiences are denied it so that correct evaluation may be made. For the Soul, also, incorrect judgments and perceptions lead to the need for more of the same kind of circumstances in order to permit the transmutation of lower vibrations into higher vibrations.

It is in this respect that the relationship of the Personality to the Soul is most important. When the conscious, reasoning mind of the Personality perceives an error in thinking, the information is imparted instantly to the "data bank" of the Soul, and adjustments are made.

The same thing happens when the Soul makes the perception; the warning of error is immediately transmitted to the Personality. The difference here is that the Personality, with its separate Will, may or may not act upon that perception. How many times have you known you were acting in error, yet through habit, desire, or the need to save face, you continued in the old familiar pattern?

Through regression research, I discovered a perfect example of this in my own immediate past life memories. Born the daughter of a rich Southern merchant during Civil War days, with Negro servants and every material want satisfied (the actual existence of this life has been partially verified), I married a Northern soldier and went to Iowa to live.

Life was not as I expected it to be, nor what I had been used to. I was the daughter of a socially prominent man and didn't like and, I felt, didn't deserve, the situation I found myself in—a comfortable but modest home, required to do my own cooking, laundry, child rearing, etc. I also had to help my husband in our small country store, doing menial tasks I considered far beneath my proper status.

So, like a petulant child, I became a shrewish wife who never stopped letting her husband know that she considered she had "married down," and that such a life as he could offer was beneath her dignity.

At the end of that remembering experience, as I looked back over that span of years and tried to evaluate it, I saw there had been countless opportunities when I could have said, and even many times had the desire to say, "I love you, and we can make the best of what we have and be happy."

To actually say it, however, was a different thing. Pride got in the way, and I would have had to admit I was wrong, and all the things I thought I stood for were wrong. So to save face, I continued acting in what I considered my proper stance. My self-inflicted attitude added much to my unhappiness in that lifetime and to the unhappiness of others.

The urge to act in a more spiritually rewarding manner was put forth, even pushed forth, by the guidance faculty within me many times, but the stubborn streak so often found in the Will of the Personality would not allow it to be demonstrated. As a result of that remembering experience, I gained much insight into the origin of the pride, stubbornness, and rigid thinking patterns that have plagued me throughout my present lifetime. The persistent behavior of the personal Will, in the face of the Soul's endeavor to correct the path the Personality was taking, built a pattern of thought-forms that my Personality has had to deal with in this lifetime.

The Search for a Soul

When I first entered metaphysical studies I was told that the Soul knew all things, and one had only to live in Soul Consciousness to immediately right all wrongs and eliminate all karma. This was probably a carryover from the fundamental religious dogma of the Piscean Age, that one need do nothing for one's own spiritual growth as long as one believed that Jesus died to "save us from our sins."

The contradictions and fallacies of both statements are immediately apparent if followed through logically, and raise innumerable questions that do not have adequate answers. What is "sin"? How can we be lost, if we are made of God Substance in the first place? And if the Soul is already omniscient, knowing all things, what is the need for the struggle and strife of life on this planet? If Jesus made reparation for our sins, why is there still "sin"? If we are being tested, what are we being tested for?

The first step along my own personal path at a youthful age was complete and total faith in and obedience to the assurance that Jesus had saved me from my sins. Great was my dismay to learn that no matter how hard I struggled to live a righteous life as a true follower of Christian doctrine, the apparent result was poverty, ill-health, afflictions, and emotional trauma. The "sins" I was being saved from were all too apparently still with me.

I was told I was being tested, as a father chastises his child for the sake of righteousness, and the more I had to endure, the more the Father loved me. Finally, I absolutely rebelled against that theory! I hadn't done anything to deserve the kind of chastisement I was getting, and certainly no loving father would deliberately punish a child just for his own amusement.

The soul-searching and questioning inevitably led me into metaphysics and the study of mysticism. What I found made more sense than anything else I'd ever known. Metaphysics turned the old dogmas around and gave them new, more expanded meanings.

My next goal, at that point, was to become Soul-conscious, so that I, too, might "know all the answers," as my early teachers taught me. I set out upon the path of "I AM" awareness, just as I have started you.

My early training in spiritual devotion stood me in good stead, and my life became a twenty-four hour search for spiritual insight. After nearly fifteen years of learning and application, trial and error, there finally came the day when I realized beyond a shadow of doubt that I had truly reached a level of intuitive consciousness and, indeed, had been operating from that level for some time. This is that attunement with the Superconscious Mind this book has been striving to define for you.

However, there was still more to learn. I found that the Soul itself is not omniscient. It doesn't already have all the answers.

Even the Masters in the Hierarchy try first one plan and then another when seeking to further the Divine Plan. Then came the realization that if the Soul already knew all there was to know, there would be no need for the constant infiltering of experiences from the Earth plane or, indeed, any other plane.

That should have been apparent to me from the beginning, but for some reason it wasn't. Now I had to start all over again, with a whole new set of questions, and re-examine just what the Soul was, what its goals were, and where we were going, the Soul and I, now that we knew each other as one and the same thing.

My first realization was that the experiences and the activity of the Personality nourish the Soul's need to learn how to use cosmic principles. I also saw that the Soul has access to information from sources not normally available to the conscious mind. It is when the Personality can consciously, consistently, and deliberately tap these sources for guidance in handling earth situations and, at the same time, be aware of perceptions, conclusions, and new information that originate from the Soul itself, that you may assume you have attained the same consciousness as the Soul. You are then in attunement, One with that Higher part of yourself.

Soul Consciousness is a fully aware cooperation between these two magnificent aspects of the Trinity of Self, undertaking a mutual experience, using the faculties of both to bring about a harmonious outcome. This puts the Soul in charge of the Personality's abilities, and the Personality serves as a willing contributor to the enlightenment and growth of the Soul. The benefit is mutual. With time, the purified Personality becomes the Identity, and the three merge under dominion of that highest aspect of the total Being, Spirit. The Adept then becomes a Master, at least of this plane. What awaits us beyond earth experience, I have no personal conscious knowledge of at present.

The Soul-Conscious Person

Soul Consciousness doesn't come in one gigantic burst of fiery illumination, but gradually and gently, step by step through the years. As you build your Inner Guidance faculty, you also build and expand this level of communication and illumination.

Very little is written about this step in spiritual evolution, although hundreds of books attest to its reachability, and it is the end-goal of all the mystical schools and practices. The most difficult handicap is finding adequate words to explain that which has no words. How does one describe snow to someone who lives in the tropics, or a rainbow to someone who is blind?

God as the Life Force is never static. Divinity is continually, constantly changing, experiencing, becoming—infinitely creative. Oneness with this Life Force allows the Soul-conscious person to move in thought and emotion into the complexities of a leaf, a ground slug, a pet bird or animal, and feel the Life Force flowing through these simple manifestations as God *knowing* Himself, *experiencing* Himself as that bit of Himself. Through that experiencing, God may be growing and evolving, also, in a complexity far beyond our present comprehension.

In the same manner, as a Soul-conscious person, you know yourself to be at one with and at peace with a god or an angel, a devil or a human being. There is within you a deep realization, not merely an intellectual acceptance, of the unity, the essential Oneness of all things. You accept without question and take responsibility for the knowledge that whatever you do affects others, either for good or for evil, and that what others do affects you in turn.

Even though we can become more or less in complete control of our personal environment and our personal lives, we are also part of the planetary karma, which is here because of what we have done in past lives as well as from the thoughts and actions of those who are here now. We realize and accept that we are born into the race, the country, the childhood experiences that make such great impressions upon the flexible mold of our personalities, as stepping stones toward the comprehension that we are part of one Great Beingness, incredibly diversified.

Each group of people, from three to many thousands, each town, each city, each race, each nation, has a collective consciousness of which we are a part. If we are a portion of that group, we are there because the essence that makes up our Being, our consciousness of Self, is in some way comparable to the consciousness of all the others in that group, race, or nation.

It is said that a nation deserves its leaders, no matter how good or how bad they may be, because they emerge from the group consciousness of the people they rule or serve. They appeal in some way to those who elect them or those who are born in subjection to them.

The only permanent way to make changes in government or any portion of the group we are in union with is to raise the consciousness of its members, to educate the people into a better way of thinking and doing. Then, because the group has a higher quality of consciousness, the leaders will naturally be of a higher quality, because they are of the same mold—part of the unity of the whole.

When you change yourself and elevate your own personal consciousness, you will affect the whole, because everything you do affects those with whom you come in contact, and they in turn are somehow elevated. The Soul-conscious person is very cognizant of the Law of the Whole and Its Parts, and feels this unity quite keenly. From that empathy, you develop a great compassion for everyone who struggles within it.

THE UNANSWERED QUESTION: What does one do with this realization, ethically and spiritually? How can this knowledge be put to work so that it may be of value to oneself and the Whole of which we are a part?

To answer that question is the task Soul-conscious persons set for themselves. They gradually learn to think, act, and live no longer for themselves alone, and when their concept of service expands to include all of humanity, then consciousness merges into the larger Cosmic Life.

Material Transcendence

Soul-conscious persons appreciate the sacredness of all things and know that nothing is profane. A weed, for instance, is only a plant out of place. It is still part of the divinity of the Cosmic Whole. They recognize, search for, and try to maximize the divinity within each individual whose Life Force crosses their path.

They learn to perceive the labels "good" and "bad," "negative" and "positive," and "right" and "wrong," as having no value within themselves, but only as terms we use to define certain types of experiences. It is true that harmonious experiences such as love and health are more desirable than whatever we have labeled the opposite, so we might consider that whatever moves towards harmony is good and whatever moves towards inharmony is bad. But *all* conditions have power over us only as long as they have the power to hold our attention. Whenever we choose to take that power away from them, the situation dissolves and has no more substance than a turned-off television or an empty movie screen.

Soul-conscious persons have a deep, positive awareness of all that is going on around them, but they are serene within themselves. Material possessions, while useful, are not essential to their happiness. They realize that no person, place, or thing can either give them happiness or take it away. It doesn't matter what happens to them in the external experiencing, because it isn't the person, place, or thing that makes them happy or miserable, but only their inner reaction to that experience.

Happiness and joy are natural attributes of the Soul. The more serene, calm, and peaceful one can be in dealing with life experiences, the more one can be sure that one is experiencing Soul Awareness. The "I AM" within you, the Objective Watcher, views with equanimity whatever is passing in review. The ability to experience brings joy to the Soul. It is the emotional nature that passes judgment on whether the experience is good or bad. If the emotional nature is in subjection to the spiritual nature, then all things are viewed in their proper perspective as parts of the Whole, and are considered neither good nor bad but simply experiences in transmuting negative energy into positive energy.

There is a deep inner realization that people, places, and things flow through our lives in a transitory fashion according to the needs of the NOW moment. Nothing of value is ever lost, for if any thing or experience moves out of our lives, it can and will be replaced by something of equal or probably greater value.

Soul-conscious persons set themselves to expect and to look for the good that will arise from whatever situation they find themselves in. They move with serenity and flexibility into the next experience when the chronological sequence of events changes the passing scene.

They reject the concept that the material world is the only basis for reality, recognizing that whatever is being experienced or visually perceived is created by their own psychological and spiritual needs. It can be uncreated by the power of their own Will or desire, or it will pass naturally once all inner needs from that situation have been met.

THE UNANSWERED QUESTION: How does one reconcile the obvious need for material things and material experience with the equally obvious need or desire for spiritual transcendence?

Part of this question is answered by nonreliance on or nonattachment to material things, places, or persons, but that is not the whole answer. The unity of the whole, spiritual and material, must not be contradicted by one's action or philosophy. The emotions of love, joy, and gratitude play an important part in the resolution of this question in the life of the aspirant.

In meditation, explore the concepts within these phrases: "materializing the spiritual," and "spiritualizing the material."

Transcendence of Time and Space

The Soul-conscious person can transcend at will the limitations of time and space. This is done through detachment. From the "I AM" point of awareness, detach yourself from the situation both mentally and emotionally. Look at it as though it were happening to someone else.

One can use a gestalt technique and ask questions of the situation and of oneself, such as: What is the value of this experience to me? What am I getting out of it? Should it be changed, and if so, how? Is there a better solution than the one I am applying? Ask the situation itself questions: How do you feel about what is happening? What solution would you suggest?

Wait for the answer. It may come immediately, or it may come in other ways, as we have discussed previously.

The Soul-conscious person is capable of letting go completely, emotionally and mentally, of any inharmonious situation. This means being happy and joyous *in spite of* appearances, refusing to allow the lower emotional energies to control you. Whatever the situation, it cannot place your inner happiness in jeopardy if you remain attuned to the serenity which flows through you naturally.

The Soul-conscious person is aware of the Truth behind circumstances, the reasons why certain conditions exist, both in the personal world and in the world as a whole. As such, you are the ruler of the manifestation, instead of being subject or servant to it.

The experiences and situations in your life may be likened to a clay statue that you mold with your hands. You may take great pleasure in the skill and ingenuity that you used to create this statue, but suppose the statue gets broken. Does that event, the act of breaking, happen to you? No, it only happened to the statue. You needn't let the broken statue place scars on you.

So it is with the situations you mold into your life from the God Substance given you. What happens to and within the situations only happens to the situation. It happened to your creation, not to the inner "I AM" which views these things with the detachment of the Objective Watcher. You can remake the statue, or the situation—or create a new one.

Sanction and boycott are the only tools needed to create your environment. That to which you give your attention (sanction) is fed and nourished. That from which you withdraw your attention (boycott) dies for lack of sustenance.

When using the tool of boycott, don't reject with such vehemence that that which you have rejected comes back to haunt you. Vehemence is a form of energy, and the amount of energy used in rejection is used by the situation to help it remain in your life.

Reject lightly. Give no condemnation or criticism to it. Simply withdraw your attention. Denying the existence of a thing is in effect affirming that it exists, or there would be no need to deny its existence. Boycott means simply to use that energy to create, enjoy, or give attention to something else. This practical and intelligently directed action affirms without words that the situation has, indeed, no power to hold your attention.

Thus transformation occurs and the new person emerges. This is the Soul-conscious person—living outside the limitation of time-space concepts, expressing the Life Force as love, joy, and gratitude, in selfless service to others. It is a way of life that must be lived to be fully understood, and is itself an "experience in becoming."

THE UNANSWERED QUESTION: What is immortality? Is it the purification, transformation, and ascension of the physical body as Jesus demonstrated? Is the integration of Spirit, Soul, and Personality, which results in clear conscious communication between these three, also a step toward immortality? If death is the last enemy to be overcome, does losing one's fear of death make it no longer an enemy, or is there further meaning?

The Soul-conscious person ponders deeply the significance and value of life and death as parts of the Cosmic Whole.

The Twelve Higher Psychic Powers

Having safely traveled the bewildering, joyful, provocative path of the neophyte, avoiding the pitfalls and victoriously disciplining the lower mental and emotional natures, the rewards are now at hand.

There are twelve higher psychic powers that are awakened in the Soul-conscious person. Only an Adept has them all, but their development can serve as guidelines by which to measure our intuitional faculties as we see them unfold one by one. As a practical definition, each of these can be considered an octave higher than the lesser principles most of us consider "psychic," and each of these is attained only when one's motive is to serve rather than to be served.

1. Contact With the Plane of Intuition

Intuition is the language of the Soul. As you practice *listening* for direction from the Soul Self, you begin to come into contact with what Vera Stanley Alder calls, "The Fifth Dimension."[31] This is the realm of ideas, prototypes, and concepts which carry high voltage energy and enthusiasm.

This is the realm activated by the great men and women who conceived and carried out great plans and brought forth magnificent new inventions, paintings, music, writings, and other creations that have benefited humanity. One touches into this plane of consciousness whenever one gets a tremendous new idea which brings with it all the vigor and enthusiasm needed for carrying it out, and when one knows that the end result will benefit a great number of people.

2. Sensitivity to Impressions

This includes the power of telepathy and the awareness of mind contacts from those around us, from higher teachers, a great Center or Being, or from the Soul Self. Through mental objectivity one can discern the difference between one's own thought and the thoughts of others, separate them, and discard or use them at will.

The highest use of this power enables the disciple in full waking consciousness to decipher messages coming from Higher Sources and direct them through useful forms of creative expression. In this way deeper insights into the mysteries of spiritual evolution and growth are gained and shared.

3. Perception of Reality

With the aid of this psychic power, one's perspective is from the Soul Self point of view, and one sees things as they really are. Hidden motives, distortions, twisted forms or events are penetrated and understood for their reality, not their appearance (or illusion). With this power, one's reactions and attitudes are based not upon the distorted face value of things and events but upon the Truth behind the facade, not only in personal everyday contacts but also in the ongoing evolutionary cycles of humanity.

The lesser counterpart of this psychic power can be recognized in the practice of psychometry.

4. The Recognition of the Real Need

This power is the result of combining intuition and intelligence. The heart chakra is fully opened and one understands the real, unspoken needs of others, needs that lie behind personality disturbances or apparent desires. This perception is an immediate recognition and response coming from the Soul level, which does not create any reaction or friction within one's own Personality. With this power comes a deep compassion and a quick response to fill that need intelligently and with the right action at the right time, through the right means. This power of quick response may provide a real psychological service to a fellow traveler, who may be led a step nearer his or her own inner Light or awakening.

Its lesser psychic counterpart can be recognized in sudden bursts of clairvoyance and/or claircognizance.

5. Understanding and Correct Use of Personal Power

True psychics have control over their powers, the powers do not control them. Physical, mental, and emotional energies are correctly and intuitively used for the advancement and liberation of others, in harmony with the Divine Plan for the evolvement and uplifting of humanity. Our achievement can be measured in the ways and degrees in which we use the forces of our nature and the forces under our influence. We must function from the Soul level, to actually *be* the Soul, before we can use these powers without distortions from needs and wishes of the Personality.

We can gauge the degree of correct usage by the results. Incorrect usage increases one's pain, displeasure, and the scorpion stings of environmental reaction. Correct usage, in personal or public life, leads to more unfoldment, illumination, service, and power.

The lesser correspondence is found in the practice of psychokinesis.

6. A Sense of Right Timing

There is a "season for all things," and the more evolved psychic knows intuitively when is the right time to say the right words, start a project, expand a business, a concept, or an idea, make decisions; when the right synchronization of all favorable factors allows for maximum development.

This power is activated when you intuitively are "in the right place, at the right time, doing the right thing" for the most favorable outcome. Lower psychism recognizes this as the "hunch."

7. An Overview of Human Events

All manifestations on the physical plane are but symbols reflecting attitudes, ideals, motivations, and causes behind events, happenings, movements, speech, and writing. Through this advanced psychic power one can see the motive or cause behind each of these, and recognize the direction it is taking. One can read the heart, the mind, the spirit embracing all forms of expression, and can respond accordingly.

A lesser reflection of this psychic ability is often found in astrologers, card readers, numerologists, and others who use symbology for counseling or divination.

8. Being Mentally Centered

Evolved psychics live and have their Beingness in the higher mind. They are objective observers of the passing parade and control their everyday affairs through the creative thinking, visions, and abstract ideas found on the mental plane. They do not fall into destructive emotional states, dream states of mind, physical inertia, or lower mental meanderings or illusions. Their minds are sharp, keen, and analytical, and bring inspiration and enlightenment to those with whom they interact.

This is the disciplined state of the "I AM" that is centered in the head or higher.

9. An Intense Aspiration

Aspiration is the Soul's response to the energy of the God Life which interpenetrates, uplifts, enlightens, and calls to the inner Self, pushing away and dissolving the illusion and unreality of ordinary perceptions. It is a passionate longing to be what you really are, to achieve what you have the potential to achieve. One's entire Being is oriented towards the Eternal, which helps one gradually overcome all Personality obstacles and continuously surpass oneself at all levels.

Aspiration leads to the final merging of the Trinity: Spirit, Soul, and Identity—Identity being the purified and fully evolved Personality.

10. Devotion to the Soul Self

The Soul Self is the source from which flows all creativity, love, beauty, compassion, inspiration, invention, art, and sensitivity. Advanced psychics have a great devotion to this Soul Self, not only in themselves but in others: the group, the nation, the earth, and the God Life which interpenetrates and sustains the Whole.

This is not an emotional devotion but a deep, pure sense of kinship, an active striving toward unity, one-pointedness, clear thinking; an extreme attraction towards oneness with the greater Whole. Their activities, prayers, and devotions extend to the Soul Self of the group, the planet, and the Cosmos.

The lesser psychic counterpart of this quality manifests in intensely patriotic or religious persons who devote themselves to special doctrines or creeds, often resulting in flashes of claircognizance in times of deep need to know.

11. Continuity of Consciousness

This is a state of consciousness in which one is or can at will become aware on all levels of the mind, on both the higher and lower planes. One recognizes and keeps in proper perspective all levels of consciousness within the brain, the Soul, and even into higher realms.

The beginnings of this psychic ability can be recognized in flashes of precognition or prophecy.

12. Conscious Communication with One's Teacher

This psychic power marked such great disciples and adepts as Alice Bailey, Helena P. Blavatsky, and others whose works and writings have given us a great legacy of spiritual literature. It grows from a constantly maintained awareness of the subtle promptings from one's higher mental and Soul levels, gradually expanding into fully conscious awareness of mental communication from more evolved Spiritual Beings.

This awareness and communication is consummated on the Soul level rather than in the astral realm, and is completely mental rather than emotional, although love and joy will undoubtedly be present. To differentiate between communication from the true spiritual masters of the planet and other self-proclaimed "messengers," watch for appeals and manipulations that strike the lower emotional nature, that seek to shame or frighten one into obedience, dependency, or change. The true spiritual path is one of freedom, love, joyous enlightenment, and fulfillment of the total Self. If there is a feeling of lack in any of these areas when evaluating a spiritual channeling, seek your own Higher Guidance instead.

The list does not end here. These powers and others unfold and develop as one lives a life of true meditation and sacrificial service. Disciples discipline and control their mind and energies. As they serve with love, they naturally and easily unfold into greater and greater awareness, service, and power.

As You Go Forth into the Field of Service

In this book we have been working with Self, developing intuition, striving to broaden and enhance the sources of receiving as well as of giving. This is the time for a few last thoughts.

Our bodies, our minds, and our emotional natures are tools for spiritual growth as well as physical experience. They are instruments for our use. To have complete control of any instrument is to be able to take it up, use it efficiently, and lay it down again at will. Only then can one stand back from it and say, "This is not me, but it belongs to me; I am separate from it and I control it and direct it."

I, the thinker, exist independently from the thought. It is only with the true realization of this separation that we can lay down the thought and remain conscious at the "I AM" level alone. Then we cross the bridge into the higher mind and Soul levels.

To do this, maintain a questioning attitude. Don't assume that any particular belief system or reality construct is the "right" interpretation of *your* personal experiences, especially subjective ones. Less distortion will take place if you remain open-minded and objectively curious about both inner and outer sense impressions.

Be aware; be alert for incongruities in your thinking. Watch your own progress with a critical eye; constantly evaluate and monitor your beliefs and thought structures. Look for inconsistencies in the way you relate to life, and be sure that the new ideas you form make sense inwardly. Don't be gullible, buying any philosophy that happens to be expounded by the latest guru or offered as a spiritual fad.

Seek *new* ways of relating and new verbal and nonverbal interpretations of Inner Life experiences.

Let life happen to you. Flow easily with your consciously directed psychic experiments. Don't become tense and don't strain. There has to be meaning and joyful participation in any research into the hidden areas of life. Regimentation and intensity of purpose may bring the brain into Beta activity, where the whole project will fail. Intuitive experiences most often take place when you are actively engaged in the business of living, rather than in "classroom" structured types of activity.

Be the Path. Jesus said, "I am the Way, the Truth and the Light, and no one cometh unto the Father except by me" (John 14:6). Dr. Russ Michael, in one of his many appearances at the Parapsychology Center, shocked his audience with the announcement, "I am the Way, the Truth, and the Light!" Then he went on to explain that as one grows in dedication and service, the path of spiritual attainment becomes not only the goal but the very essence of one's Being. As one daily *lives* the principles discovered along the way, one's whole life is absorbed by them, and one actually *becomes* the path one trods.

We have a natural tendency to regard any program of self-improvement as though it were a progression toward an ultimate destination, that final perfection toward which we are continually growing and evolving. We tend to represent the journey in terms of space and time, as if growth came to a stop when we reached that point of perfection. The road does not lead to a final goal. *The road itself is the goal.*

Life is eternal. It is not static, but a dynamic ongoingness. The act of experiencing is the path. The goal is the knowledge that we choose our own path and benefit from it. The end is the endless reality of eternity, the true eternal endlessness of the NOW.

Although we move along through stages of evolutionary growth, the highest and most rewarding advancement is the ability to let oneself slip into the eternal flow of life, allowing goals and achievements to be but stepping stones along the path rather than ends in themselves. Jesus became the Path. Truth and Light were the absolute essence of His Being. We, each day, can live the Truth as we know it, and in so doing increase the inflow of further Truth and spiritual understanding in an endless panorama of eternally becoming one with God.

This is a great challenge, and may require great courage. For the last 2,000 years at least, humankind has been persuaded to subscribe by faith alone to doctrines and creeds that don't always make room for the human equation or the uniqueness of the individual situation. The moral discipline may have been necessary for the development of the emotional body during the Piscean Age, but the new Aquarian Age is the age of mentality, and now individuals are required to exercise their own intellectual capacities and work their way through the leftover fallacies of Piscean emotionalism.

HERE IS A MEDITATION CONCEPT: Take a few moments and repeat the following phrase: "Allow yourself to Be!" Repeat it several times, each time putting the emphasis on a different word: ALLOW your self to Be! Allow YOUR self to Be! Allow your SELF to Be! Allow YOURSELF to Be! Allow yourself to BE! Meditate on what this exercise arouses within you.

"Freely Ye Have Received, Freely Give" (Matt. 10:8)

Guidance from Spirit is free for the asking. In return, give freely of yourself whenever and wherever you can be of service. Money, or the lack of it, will never be a real problem if you give as freely and generously of yourself and your talents as you have received and will receive.

Especially if your talents qualify you to be a psychic "reader," don't let money stand in the way of your development. Pouring out in service for humankind whatever energies are manifested in your talents will create further pressure for the opening up of larger and larger resources, and the giving enhances the receiving. You will be amply rewarded monetarily, and in more subtle ways. As long as you give freely that which is received freely, you will never lack for any necessity, tangible or intangible. You may find that the receiving of this world's goods comes in highly unorthodox ways, but that is the nature of Spirit—to be eternally and inventively creative. Expect it to be so.

The methods of Eastern mysticism usually aim for the annihilation of the ego-self. The methods used by Western mysticism aim for the intensification of awareness on all levels, which brings about a transformation of the Personality. The highest forms of Divine Union impel the Self to some sort of active rather than passive life.

In her classic book, *Mysticism*,[32] Evelyn Underhill writes:

Here, then, stands the newly awakened Self; aware, for the first time, of reality, and responding to that reality by deep movements of love and awe. She sees herself, however, not merely to be thrust into a new world, but set at the beginning of a new road. Activity is now to be her watchword, pilgrimage the business of her life. That a quest there is, and an end (revelation), is the single secret spoken. Under one symbol or another, the need of that long, slow process of transcendence, of character building, whereby she is to attain freedom, become capable of living upon high levels of reality, is present in her consciousness. Those in whom this growth is not set going are not mystics, in the exact sense in which that word is here used, however great their temporary illumination may have been.

Workshop #9
Telepathy—The Sixth Sense?

≈

Since we have demonstrated that psychic sensing may be only an extension of our present inadequately functioning five senses, this leaves us with the definition of telepathy as possibly the next separate sensing power to be developed or evolved by humankind.

Communication from mind to mind is not so difficult to accept if we remember that there is a physical counterpart within our bodies. Nerve cells and ganglia do not meet; nerve ends are separated from their companion nerve ends by distances of varying lengths. Mental and emotional messages traveling along the nerve cells must leap these distances to reach their destination.

Telepathy is this same process, leaping from mind to mind or from emotional center to emotional center. On the highest level can be found communication from Soul to Soul.

Exercise #1: In the Swing of Things!

Choose one person to be the subject and one person to be the sender or demonstrator. Let the subject stand relaxed, facing the sender with eyes closed. The sender must convey a thought-form of a physical motion to the subject, indicating a wish for the subject to lean forward, lean backward, sway to the left or to the right.

Vividly picture mentally what you want the subject to do, then silently act out the thought-form sent, while intensely sending the thought to the subject. If the subject does not respond with a corresponding movement, place your hands against the aura field and push or pull in the direction desired without touching the physical body.

The subject should begin to sway in the desired direction. The key to success for the subject is to not try to mentally analyze what is wanted, just feel and allow the body to move of its own accord.

The subject and sender should remain aware that this is a demonstration mutually agreed upon as a visual demonstration of the power of thought. The sender should not use this ability to willfully manipulate unsuspecting persons, and the subject should bear in mind that with faculties under control, one cannot be manipulated against one's own will.

Exercise #2: Find the Object

Send someone out of the room. The group decides upon an object. When the subject returns to the room, everyone concentrates on the object selected. The subject tries to visualize what the group is concentrating on. When there is a clear feeling or thought-form, he or she goes to or points to the object seen or felt in the mind.

Exercise #3: Emotional Guidance

This exercise is similar to #2, except that after the object has been selected, a guide is chosen. After returning to the room, the subject takes hold of the guide's hand and moves around the room trying to locate the object.

The guide remains passive, mentally concentrating on the selected object, but otherwise not consciously trying to influence the subject. The subject, however, tries to become attuned to subconscious or subliminal actions on the part of the guide which could lead to the selected object, such as a slight physical tenseness which occurs in the body when the guide is mentally saying, "No, no, go the other way!" or similar physiological signals.

Exercise #4: Get the Picture?

Each person participating should have several sheets of paper. The sender mentally chooses several simple diagrams or sketches with easy, basic lines, such as a round baseball, a child's toy block, an umbrella, a tree, a sailboat, etc.

The sender will draw one sketch on each sheet of paper, mentally sending the thought image to the other participants. After the drawings have been completed, check them against the original. Look for overall resemblance to the target image, as well as similarities in shape, size, form of lines, and so on. Be objective. You may check the sketches after each drawing, or wait until all have been completed.

Exercise #5: Your Nose Knows![33]

Have someone put a few drops of some familiar, strong-smelling household substances into identical small containers, preferably opaque, with an identifying number on the cap. Choose several different odors: alcohol, cinnamon, coffee, garlic, kerosene, onion, peppermint, or vinegar. Use your imagination for others. Perfumes or flavorings should have a distinctive, recognizable scent, such as rose, jasmine, strawberry, lemon, vanilla, etc. Participants should be familiar with whatever products are used. (Do not use ammonia; it inflames the sensitive tissues of the nose and may even defeat the rest of the program if the sender cannot smell!)

The sender opens the bottle and smells the substance for a short period. The participants try to relate to what the sender is smelling.

Write down your impressions. If the smell is vinegar, for example, you might record sour, acrid impression, nose tingles, etc. If vanilla, sweet, cloying odor.

Exercise #6: On Deck!

Let the sender concentrate for sixty seconds each upon the numbered cards of an ordinary playing deck. Leave out the face cards. Count as hits any correct suit, color, or number. Score one point for each correct call, i.e., two points for correct color and number, or correct suit and number. If you get as many as ten points in this exercise, you have achieved an outstanding score.

Exercise #7: Phono-Vision[34]

When talking to a friend on the phone, try to visualize what he or she is wearing. Ask your friend to corroborate your impressions.

Exercise #8: Telepathy—Space and Time

Sit by the window, or in some place where you can see a portion of a street or highway where traffic is light. Try to decide from which direction the next car will come. Check your number of correct hits in relation to the total number of cars which actually pass by.

This also exercises your prophetic faculty, since you are actually extending ahead in time.

MEDITATION PRACTICE

Sit erect, with spine straight. Cleanse yourself with the White Light.

When you have reached Alpha awareness, concentrate on the heart chakra. Let your whole Being become as one with the heart chakra.

Now expand this awareness outward from your body, making a sphere of awareness several inches larger than your body. Return to the heart chakra.

Repeat five times, making the sphere larger each time.

Move your attention to the "I AM" point of awareness. (If this point is in the heart chakra, remain there in consciousness.)

Concentrate your attention in the "I AM" point of focus. Recognize it as the point where Soul and body meet. Become now the total awareness of yourself-as-a-Soul. Expand this awareness outward several inches from your body. Return to the original point of focus. Repeat, making the sphere larger. Hold for a few minutes, then return to the originating point.

Do this for the remainder of the meditation, each time making your sphere of the "I AM" consciousness larger and larger until finally you are as large as the Universe, or as far as you can go.

Return slowly to your everyday consciousness. Fill yourself with the White Light of protection. Take a moment to be grateful for all the blessings in your life. When you leave the meditation time, put a smile on your face, and notice how easily life flows around you, in you, and through you.

APPENDIX A

≈

To the Advanced Student

The following exercise is most effective for the person whose "I AM" center is normally at the throat, or, even better, in the head or above; however, anyone may experiment with it. For the greatest success it is necessary to have mental discipline enough to be able to move the "I AM" center around to the various chakra centers at will.

Experiment with position. You may sit with your spine straight, or you may prefer to lie flat on your back with your head to the North. Overlap the hands an inch or two above the head, with both palms facing the crown chakra. The hands must remain in this position throughout the exercise. Forces in the palms are instrumental in pulling energies up through the body.

Start by so concentrating the point of "I AM" focus that you can move it into the base-of-spine center. Become completely centered there, being able to imagine the legs beneath you and the torso above you. If successful, you will immediately feel a gathering of energies that in a minute or so will suddenly erupt in a strong burst not unlike an orgasm. (For the success of this experiment, there must be no sexual activity in any form taking place.)

As soon as the energies subside, move the "I AM" attention to the solar plexus chakra and repeat the process. When you can feel the point of focus within the solar plexus, allow the strong influx of energies to gather and erupt.

Do not pause in the upward movement. Quickly move to the heart chakra and expect the surge of energies to follow. Then repeat at the throat chakra, and then move into the head chakra.

At this point you may feel that the surge of energy is too much to contain. Imagine that the crown chakra is opened and the energy pours out through the top and cascades down over your body. Whether or not you actually feel this take place, your imagination will be enough to create the desired effect of releasing the pressure.

Within moments after completing this exercise, you will feel an influx of energy and elevation of mood that can only be termed as ecstatic. Mentally and physically, you'll be at top proficiency.

Don't do this exercise more than once a day, and don't do it late in the afternoon, for the store of energy will be so great you will not be able to burn it up before bedtime, and you will get very little sleep, or maybe none at all. A good time is in the morning when you have just awakened, while the mind is still deep in the Alpha state and mental discipline is high. However, you should experiment and find your own best time. You may find you won't need to do this exercise more than two or three times a week, or only once a week.

If you are on any kind of medication, or suffering from psychological maladjustments related to grief, hate, revenge, or jealousy, approach this exercise with caution. You may experience a sense of disorientation, or a slight headache after the exercise, for the upward thrust of energies will burn through any physical or psychological blocks to achieve their purpose. The headache or other minor side effects will soon dissipate, and the discomfort will ease. If it doesn't, discontinue the exercise until you are more emotionally stable.

APPENDIX B

≈

"I AM" Centering Meditation

This is an excellent centering meditation to increase awareness and prepare the way toward enlightenment. If you wish, you can put this meditation on tape, leaving silent spaces long enough to follow the instructions and to allow you to recognize thoughts from the Soul Self.

When meditating in a group, arms and feet should be uncrossed so that energies may flow freely through the group. When meditating by yourself, you may close the circuit by closing thumbs and fingers and keeping feet and legs together. This allows your energies to remain focused within your own Being. In either case, sit with the spine straight and body relaxed. Fill your body with the White Light as a symbol not only of protection, but also of the desire for enlightenment.

AFFIRMATION

As Paul prayed: Let that Mind which was in the Christ Jesus be also in me. (Phil. 2:5)

Center yourself in the "I AM." This is the point of God in you, eternally creative, eternally becoming.

Somewhere between the heart and navel you will find a small whirling center of energy. This is the solar plexus chakra, the emotional center. Command this center to be still, then turn your attention to something wonderfully pleasant. Let yourself become now so contented, so happy that you could even smile if your body were not so relaxed.

Now in this feeling of peace and good will, turn your attention to the heart center.

AFFIRMATION

I am God expressing in me—through me—and as me . . . . God is infinitely, eternally creative, never creating anything the same way twice . . . . I am unique . . . . God, expressing Himself as me, knows Himself to be His special creation in me . . . part of the beautiful, perfect whole, but doing that which He created me alone to do . . . . I am that special, unique creation—I AM THAT WHICH I AM.

Now raise your attention to your throat center. This is the point of power through which God speaks. "In the Beginning was the Word, and the Word was with God and the Word *was* God." God was and is the word of creative power. Words of creative power are God-in-Action.

AFFIRMATION

Within the Divine image God speaks the perfect Word of Creation. I now dedicate this powerful energy center to do the Will of God and to speak only the Word of God (good). I will not use the power of this center to speak into manifestation that which I do not wish to become reality. I am expressing wisdom and right judgment in the use of this center. All words I now speak use God's word aright in all my daily activities.

Now raise your attention to the third eye center in the middle of the forehead. Someone once gave this definition of God: "God is becoming more of God."

AFFIRMATION

I am becoming more of God becoming more of me. Within my Soul is the perfect blueprint of that which God first imaged me to be. I am that perfect image coming into Being. I am NOW aware of that Divine Image—that Divine destiny which only I can fulfill.

Now turn your attention to the top of the head, the crown chakra. This is the gateway into Pure Being. If possible, move the awareness of the "I AM" outside the head into the space above the head. If this is not possible, then be content to be wherever you are, because where you are, God is. Know yourself to be one with God, one with the universe, one with all that is.

There is no longer a sense of duality—no longer a need to speak or not to speak, to create or not to create. There is neither good nor bad, right nor wrong. All that is—*is*. Just pure Being, peace, goodwill, unity. One with the whole. One with God.

AFFIRMATION

I know myself to be that which I AM—I AM THAT I AM.

(Keep silence for as long as you wish.)

Now easily, slowly, return to the place where you find the "I AM" consciousness within you, bringing back something of peace and expanded awareness into your daily activities.

AFFIRMATION

Let that Mind which was in the Christ Jesus be also in me. Amen.

APPENDIX C

≈

The Occult Meaning Behind the Lord's Prayer

The Lord's Prayer has never been fully understood, in spite of many scholarly treatises on the subject. Perhaps there are many levels of meaning in the prayer, something for everyone, so to speak.

Whatever else it was meant to be, I do not believe it was meant to be just something that is learned by rote. Doing so, of course, has kept it in the hearts and minds of the people, so that its deeper meanings have not been lost through the centuries. But those of us who meditate can find within this prayer an encoded set of instructions, a step-by-step process for effective meditation.

Jesus' instructions were precise. He said, "Pray ye in this manner...." "Manner" means "method." His words mean to use this method—or series of steps—when you pray or meditate.

OUR FATHER, WHICH ART IN HEAVEN, HALLOWED BE THY NAME

This is the beginning of your meditation, the time of devotion. "Seek ye *first* the Kingdom of Heaven...and all else will be added unto you" (Luke 12:31). Now is the time in your steps of meditation to seek the Source, the Illumination, the merging. Spend as much time as you need to feel at-one-ment with God before continuing.

THY KINGDOM COME, THY WILL BE DONE
IN EARTH AS IT IS IN HEAVEN

"I will to will the Will of God." Ask for direction; place the lower ego in submission to the Higher Ego. Essentially, you are allowing the God-in-You to take charge of your life and to direct you on your daily path.

It is important to understand (to know as well as to believe) that the God-in-You *is* the "Father Within."

Go to the Father within, as Jesus did. The Father Within is your God-Self, your Soul Self, that which created the present focus in time and space known as your Personality. In its center is the Spark of Divinity, your portion of God-Substance that is individuated as you. This recognition allows the God-Self core of your Being to expand and become more all-encompassing and self-directing in your daily activities.

GIVE US THIS DAY OUR DAILY BREAD

NOW is the time to do your occult work, to visualize, to seek attainment of your goals—*after* you have first made contact with the Father within. Of what use is it to pray to God before the communication lines are open? Meditation is a two-way street. A time of asking *and* a time of listening, but first, you have to be sure there is someone on both sides of the line.

AND FORGIVE US OUR DEBTS
AS WE FORGIVE OUR DEBTORS

Ask that you be forgiven all negative thoughts, attitudes, and deeds. Even those negative thoughts that made you think you lacked anything in the first place.

Forgiving others will also speed up the release of karma. "Love your neighbor as yourself" (Mark 12:31). If you would be forgiven, then you must first forgive others. All beings on this planet are in a state of growth, and ninety-nine percent of our growth results from errors made in our attempts to learn. Allow others their growth process, as you recognize your own.

AND LEAVE US NOT IN TEMPTATION,
BUT DELIVER US FROM EVIL

Ask that your steps be guided this day, so that you will not make errors in judgment. Ask to avoid manipulation, so that the right people will be brought to you for the experiencing of the thing you ask for, that it might be of mutual benefit for everyone who experiences it with you. Ask that you be shown how to avoid or redeem whatever particular character flaw you are presently working with.

"Leave us not in temptation" is a Unity Church interpretation of this sentence in the Lord's Prayer. Unity people do not believe that God would deliberately "lead" anyone into temptation. They take the responsibility themselves for all errors in their lives, therefore they ask God to help deliver them out of the snares they have created.

FOR THINE IS THE KINGDOM
AND THE POWER AND THE GLORY FOREVER

Once completed on the inner planes of consciousness, the work is done. The request will soon manifest on the illusory material plane. All that is required of you NOW is to live in a state of expectation. Give thanks at this point that it is already done, that the eternal power and glory from the inner Self is NOW manifesting through you.

AMEN

The meaning of the word "Amen" is "So Be It."

Footnotes

≈

1. Napoleon Hill, *Think and Grow Rich* (New York: E.P. Dutton, 1979).

2. Robert Ripley, *Believe It or Not!* (New York: Simon & Schuster, 1929).

3. "New Age Teachings." Issue 133 (February 1979). A free subscription to these channelings may be obtained by writing to: New Age Teachings, 2–4 Maple Street, Box 346, Brookfield, MA 01506. Tel.: 508-867-3754.

4. Figure 8 is adapted from Carl Hulsmann, *Awakening of Consciousness: An Interpretation of Its Process* (London: Momenta Publishing, available from Hunter House, Claremont, CA, 1982).

5. Adapted from Lee Sannella, M.D., *The Kundalini Experience: Psychosis or Transcendence?* (Lower Lake, CA: Integral Publishing, 1987).

6. Manly P. Hall, *Spiritual Centers In Man* (Los Angeles: Philosophical Research Society, 1978).

7. Sheila Ostrander & Lynn Schroeder, *Psychic Discoveries Behind the Iron Curtain* (New York: Bantam Books, 1971)

8. Bevy Jaegers, *Mark I ESP Training Manual* and *Mark I ESP Advanced Training* (Sappington, MO: Aries Productions, 1972, 1973). For a full catalogue and current pricelist of books by Ms. Jaegers write to: Aries Productions Inc., P.O. Box 29396, Sappington, MO 63126.

9. Bevy Jaegers, *Mark I ESP Training Manual.*

10. Sheila Ostrander & Lynn Schroeder, *Handbook of Psi Discoveries* (New York: Berkeley Publishing, 1974). For further information on the work of these authors contact: Superlearning Inc., 450 Seventh Ave. Suite 500, New York, NY 10123.

11. Bevy Jaegers, *Mark I ESP Training Manual* and *Mark I ESP Advanced Training.*

12. Ann Herbstreith, *Hidden Secrets Revealed by the I Am That I Am* (P.O. Box 1582, Grand Rapids, MI 49501, 1984).

13. Paul Hawkins, *The Magic of Findhorn* (New York: Harper & Row, 1975).

14. Biorhythm information taken from Bernard Gittleson, *Biorhythms: A Personal Science* (New York: Arco Publishing, 1975).

15. Dion Fortune, *The Cosmic Doctrine* (York Beach, ME: Samuel Weiser, 1976, and Thorsons Publishing Group [Aquarian Press], a division of HarperCollins, London).

16. Kingdon Brown, *Power of Psychic Awareness* (W. Nyack, NY: Parker Publishing, 1969).

17. Sybil Leek, *Diary of a Witch* (New York: New American Library, 1972).

18. Alice A. Bailey, *The Light of the Soul* (New York: Lucis Publishing, 1927).

19. Dion Fortune, *The Cosmic Doctrine*, pp. 220–21.

20. Annalee Skarin, *Ye Are Gods* (Marina del Rey, CA: DeVorss Publishing Co., 1973). These documents can be seen at the offices of the publisher.

21. Abraham H. Maslow, *Motivation and Personality* (New York: Harper & Row, 1970).

22. Korra Deaver, *Rock Crystal: The Magic Stone* (York Beach, ME: Samuel Weiser, 1985).

23. Bevy Jaegers, *The Extra-Sensitive Pendulum*, (Sappington, MO: Aries Productions, 1972). See Note 7.

24. "Point-of-Power Technique" used by permission of Dr. Russ Michael, Church of the Humanities.

25. To receive permission to reproduce the poster "Your Divine Self," (Figure 18) we have been asked to also print the following paragraphs:

    "Summit University was founded in 1971 by the messengers Mark and Elizabeth Prophet to form the main educational arm of the Great White Brotherhood's outreach to mankind in our modern era. Mark made the transition and ascended into eternity in 1973.

    "Elizabeth, known affectionately by thousands of her followers as 'Mother,' remains with us today, carrying on the service Mark originally began in 1958 with the founding of the Summit Lighthouse (now Church Universal and Triumphant). Mrs. Prophet's life is devoted to teaching at Summit University, writing and healing, and providing ongoing spiritual guidance to their growing international organization."

    Further information about their spiritual work can be obtained by writing to Summit Lighthouse, Box A, Corwin Springs, MT 59021.

26. Bevy Jaegers, *The Human Aura* (Sappington, MO: Aries Productions, 1971).

27. Bevy Jaegers, *Secrets of the Aura* (Sappington, MO: Aries Productions, 1974).

28. Excerpted from Anne Faraday, *The Dream Game* (New York: Harper & Row, 1974).

29. Joel S. Goldsmith, *The Mystical I* (New York: Harper & Row, 1971).

30. My thanks to Anthony J. Fisichella, author of *Metaphysics: The Science of Life* (St. Paul, MN: Llewellyn Publications, 1985), who filled in the gaps in my information about this outline of the ages.

31. Vera Stanley Alder, *The Fifth Dimension*, (York Beach, ME: Samuel Weiser, 1970).

32. Evelyn Underhill, *Mysticism* (New York: E.P. Dutton, 1961).

33. Bevy Jaegers, *Mark I ESP Training Manual*.

34. Bevy Jaegers, *Mark I ESP Training Manual*.